Mot

Her Life and Legacy

1886 - 1964

Barbaralie A. Stiefermann, OSF
School Sisters of St. Francis

Barbaralie Stiefermann, OSF

COPYRIGHT

DEDICATION

To all educators and students who
promote the "good, the true, and the
beautiful."

TABLE OF CONTENTS

FOREWORD

I entered the School Sisters of St. Francis after women religious had their newfound burst of freedom. Consequently, I never wore the habit or experienced the rigorous discipline of religious life before Vatican II. In reading Sister Barbaralie Stiefermann's, *Stanislaus...with feet in the world*, I discovered the spirit of the foundresses and the charism are still part of our DNA as we address the needs of our time. This compelling biography of a ten-year-old orphan child placed in the care of our foundresses twenty-one days after their arrival in the United States captivated my attention. Little Theresa Hegner eventually became Mother Stanislaus, Mother General, of our international congregation. As provincial of the U.S. Province, this remarkable woman in our history (1863-1944) became my mentor, spiritual guide, and model of leadership.

Another great woman, Mother M. Corona (1886-1964), Mother Stanislaus' successor, intrigued me because of the bits and pieces I heard from the older sisters about her. I never had the privilege of knowing Mother Corona. I firmly believed that someone needed to stitch all these spoken fragments of awe, wonder, and mystery together and provide an historical document for future generations. Mother Corona's story had to be told or a great segment of the history of the School Sisters of St. Francis would be lost and difficult to retrieve.

I asked Sister Barbaralie, who is still capable of researching and writing, to write Mother Corona's story. Because of Vatican II renewal, she no longer had to obediently say "yes" to my requests for over three years. In the final analysis, it was probably not my words that urged her to write this book. In reading her introduction to this publication, I learned of Sister Barbaralie's promise to Mother Corona seventy-one years ago. Sister Barbaralie was an aspirant at the verge of being dismissed from the Order for a daring act of misbehavior. She made this promise to Mother Corona, "Someday I will take a risk and do something great for this community."

I loudly proclaim to this reading audience that Sister Barbaralie has done "something great for this community." Read this biography and you will understand why.

Sister Carol Rigali, OSF
U.S. Provincial

INTRODUCTION

How does one attempt to write about a courageous woman who was big in stature, had a mind as expansive as the horizon, and a heart enlarged with compassion? Mother Corona Wirfs' life spanned 15 United States presidents, four wars, the Great Depression, the Catholic Worker Movement, the Nuclear Age, the Civil Rights Movement, and the Space Age. She not only lived through many historical events, but also made history. For 18 years she was the Mother General of an international congregation of women religious with nearly 4,000 members who greatly impacted the lives of many people here and abroad, especially in education and healthcare. Walter Brueggemann's statement: "What God does first and best and most is to trust people in their moment in history" is certainly true of Mother Corona.

Unfortunately, Mother Corona's personal file in the School Sisters of St. Francis' Archives was exceedingly sparse. There was little reference to her family and early history. With the use of the internet, that file has now been expanded.

The sisters with whom she lived during those early years are with Mother Corona in eternity. Sisters who were received into the congregation in the 60s and thereafter, have no knowledge of her. The sisters between these two categories only knew her as the Mother General of the School Sisters of St. Francis for 18 years and as a business woman. They never had the privilege of knowing her as a person, so the human-interest stories are minimal.

As members of the community, we must be grateful for Mother Corona's business shrewdness, organizational skills, mental acumen, and incredible memory. In my research, it was overwhelming to see and ponder the tremendous work she did with limited staff and finances, and no modern technology. Sister Deodigna Schirra, her secretary, and later, Sister Thomasine Nels, generated hundreds of typewritten letters that were mimeographed and mailed to all the missions. In fact, it is the letters that tell her story in her own words.

In addition, Mother Corona personally dealt with Rome, bishops, superintendents, pastors, sisters, architects, contractors, mission assignments, retreat schedules, fundraising, finances—the list goes on and on. As Father Steven Avella, Milwaukee Archdiocesan historian and archivist, so aptly said, "She was a one-woman Human Resources department."

In reading this biography, one must see Mother Corona through the prism of the post-war era. The *Second Vatican Council* (1962-1965), promulgated by Pope John XXIII, occurred after her death. *Perfectae Caritas* issued by Pope Paul VI in 1965, a document resulting from the Second Vatican Council dealing specifically with consecrated life, also happened after her death. Vatican II impacted the School Sisters of St. Francis under the leadership of Sister Francis Borgia Rothluebber (1966-1972).

It might be well, also, to reflect upon the words of the great German poet of the 20th century, Rainer Maria Rilke.

> Even the next era has no right to judge anything if it lacks the ability to contemplate the past without hatred or envy. But even that judgment would be one-sided, for every subsequent era is the fruit of previous periods and carries much of the past within it. It is fortunate if something of the ancestors lives on in it and continues to be loved and

protected; only then does the past become fruitful and effective.

Early Journals

In the latter part of this book, I have included several writings of Mother Corona that are worthy of publication: "Modern Comfort and Convenience in Their Relation to the Religious Spirit;" "Noisy Mannerisms;" "The Literature of the Victorian Age;" and "Metaphysics." The latter two writings must have been written while teaching at St. Philomena School in Chicago because on the title pages, she had the address of the school. This gives evidence of her attending classes probably at DePaul University, since most sisters in the Chicago area attended there, according to Sister Ellinda Leichtfeld. No records could be found. She received an A+ on these two essays. Perhaps her writings can define more clearly who Mother Corona was. It is my hope in writing this biography that sisters, associates, her family, and others will come to know the "real Corona."

I have spent countless hours digging in the archives, making telephone calls, communicating with the Chicago Archdiocese Archives, searching websites, without any success in determining where Mother Corona went to high school. Many Chicago Catholic school records were destroyed when parishes merged. I spoke to Sister Charlita Foxhoven who worked in the business office for two years during Mother Corona's administration. She concluded that Mother Corona must have gone to a commercial high school because she was so efficient in shorthand, bookkeeping, typewriting, and business.

Mother Corona did not have a college degree. The first mother general of the congregation who had formal education was Mother Clemens Rudolph, who earned a Bachelor of Science from Chicago's DePaul University in 1936. In addition, she had certification and training in commercial.

One thing is certain. We owe a debt of gratitude to Mother Corona who valued what she did not have and made sure that her sisters received an education from Alverno College and other renowned universities in this country and abroad.

And now, allow me to relate to you one of my personal interactions with Mother Corona that also offers great insight into the "real Corona." Even though I chose not to include this in my memoir, I feel compelled to do so now.

I entered the community in 1946, at age 14, as an aspirant and high school freshman. During my sophomore year, I chose to do some adventuresome, reckless, thoughtless actions that I certainly am not proud to confess publicly in writing.

Being a creative, lively, daring person in my youth, I conducted midnight tours to the chapel dome and cupola with small groups of aspirants, who were also eager to explore this new venue. After months of this great venture in the dark of night: climbing up a catwalk, walking across a narrow cement path without guardrails, and gingerly processing to the sanctuary domes, was a sense of accomplishment like no other. Had any of us tripped or fallen into the chasms below, which were the structures of the arches, we could have been seriously injured, possibly killed. And, how would a paramedic even rescue us from the depths of those convolutions?

One night, when I, the leader of the group, had reached the Holy Spirit dome, my foot slipped. Fortunately, I was able to grab a metal strut that was attached to the long chain that hung down into the sanctuary with the red lamp attached. When I pulled on that strut, the sanctuary lamp moved in circles down in the chapel. (The sanctuary lamp is no longer suspended from the ceiling.)

Unbeknown to me, Mother Corona's personal assistant, Sister Heremita Haupt, was praying in the large chapel (not the adoration chapel). She, who had a heart condition, was terrified, breathless, and panic-stricken when she saw the sanctuary light dancing in the dark. I had no idea that pulling that metal contraption would evoke such movement in the "holy of holies," but it saved me from losing my balance and possibly falling through the glass—a seventy-five-foot fall.

The next morning after Mass, we proceeded as usual to the dining room for breakfast. In the corridor, I heard all kinds of whispers from the senior sisters and Mother Corona's office personnel. This was normally a time of silence. I sensed word had gotten around. I knew there would be an investigation comparable to Robert Mueller's of the Donald Trump 2016 election and Russian interference, which is happening as I write this book. I just knew I would eventually be caught.

I went to Sister Juan Haubl, aspirant director. She went to Sister Viola Blissenbach, postulant director. Needless to say, after telling them what I had done, I felt like a criminal in an orange suit.

Up the stairs we went to Mother Corona's office. Assistant Mother Amanda Schoenenberger was standing near Mother Corona, who was seated at her desk. Terrified, I told my story. When I had finished, Mother Corona remained silent while the other three sisters vehemently took turns saying, "Send her home, send her home." Those were harsh words I did not want to hear.

Finally, in a calm, subdued tone of voice, Mother Corona said, "I want you to go to chapel and pray before the Blessed Mother for one hour. Then come back to see me."

I pleaded to Mary to intercede for me. I prayed for a miracle. It was a moment in my youth when I felt totally disarmed and that some power greater than I was in charge.

When I returned to Mother Corona's office, she was alone seated at her desk. I sat in the chair facing her. She looked at me and softly said, "Do you realize the liability on this community had something serious happened to you or the other aspirants?"

My reply was, "I didn't think of that at the time, but I am aware of it now." Mother Corona continued speaking peacefully and convincingly to me. I cried. I apologized. I pleaded with her not to send me home. Then in a prophetic tone I said, "Someday, I will take a risk and do something great for this community."

I sensed by her serene facial expression and her intense look, she was stunned that such words could be uttered by a high school sophomore, let alone, by someone who had just broken all the rules in the book.

Shifting position, she placed her two, large hands on the desk, bent forward, and calmly said, "I will put you on probation for one year."

It seems unreal that the word "probation" was delightful to hear at that moment. In the history of the community, no one ever was put on probation. Young women were sent home or went of their own accord.

I thanked Mother and assured her that I was willing to accept the consequences of my misbehavior. Ironically so, I have conducted many tours through our beautiful, historic chapel for the past 30 years. Was I predestined to give chapel tours already at an early age?

At this writing, I am 86 years old. I can't proclaim that I have done something "great" for the community; however, I feel called at this time to write about Mother Corona. If I do not do so, the iconic name "Corona" will fade into oblivion. Perhaps this is my way of returning the favor. Were it not for Mother Corona's kindness, I would not have been a School Sister of St. Francis.

CATHERINE WIRFS
MOTHER CORONA

CHAPTER ONE

FAMILY HISTORY

The year 1886 is of little importance to most people today; however, there were some noteworthy events to highlight. That year, 1886 (MDCCCLXXXVI), was a common year starting on Friday of the Gregorian calendar and a common year starting on Wednesday of the Julian calendar. As of the start of 1886, the Gregorian calendar was 10 days ahead of the Julian calendar, which remained in localized use until 1923.

Three other events happened that impacted the entire country for generations to come. 1) The Statue of Liberty was dedicated in New York Harbor. 2) The first train-load of oranges left Los Angeles via the Transcontinental Railroad. 3) A general strike began in Chicago's Haymarket Square, which escalated into the Haymarket Riot, and eventually won the eight-hour day for workers.

Unbeknown to many, 1886 had special significance for the School Sisters of St. Francis. Why? A baby was born named Catherine Wilhelmina Wirfs on June 1, 1886, in Chicago, Illinois. This child was destined someday to become a member of the School Sisters of St. Francis and its international leader.

Catherine's father, Anthony Wirfs (1859-1921), was born in Detroit, Michigan, and her mother, Ursula Grassl, in Bavaria, Germany. They were married in Cook County, Illinois on August 2, 1885.

The Baptismal Record Register of St. Paul Church on 2127 W. 22nd Place in Chicago indicates that Catherine Wilhelmina was baptized on June 27, 1886. Her godparents were her uncle and aunt, Joseph Wirfs and Wilhelmina Grassl.

St. Paul Church was established by a small German community in 1876. The cornerstone was laid in 1897. The church was built entirely by parishioners, many of whom were brick layers. This church was recently singled out in Ripley's "Believe It Or Not" as the church built without a nail. It is not far-fetched to think that Catherine Wirfs' father, Anthony, and her grandfather may have assisted in building St. Paul Church.

According to convent records, the family later belonged to St. Nicholas Parish, 113th Place and State Street, Chicago, Illinois. The School Sisters of St. Francis arrived in 1897 to take over the responsibility of educating the children in St. Nicholas Parish. They began teaching in a large room, then a part of the convent. The first teachers were Sisters Benedicta Noel, Borgia Esser, and Friedberta Fritz. Catherine Wirfs attended St. Nicholas School when John Bonifas was the teacher for a period of six years (1890-1897) before the sisters arrived. Therefore, Catherine was under the tutelage of the sisters for two years to complete her elementary education. No doubt, the sisters influenced her greatly because in 1904, at the age of 18, she entered St. Joseph Convent. A new St. Nicholas School was built in 1906. The School Sisters of St. Francis remained teaching in the school until 1972. The parish no longer existed after that.

Catherine's great-grandparents, Johann Joseph Wirfs (1783-1847) and Maria Catherine Gerhards (1789-1834), were born and remained in Germany. Her grandfather, Michael Wirfs (1827-1892), born in Prussia, immigrated to the United

States in 1846. Her grandmother, Maria Catherina Schaaf (1831-1873), also born in Prussia, immigrated to America (date unknown) and married Michael Wirfs.

Catherine's grandparents, Michael and Maria Catherine, had seven children:

1. Helena (1852-?); died before 1860 census.
2. Agatha (1855-1934); married Frederick Thome; did not have children.
3. Gertrude (1856-1936); married Andrew Lange; had eight children.
4. Anton (1859-1921); married Ursula Grassl; had three children.
5. John J. (1862-1886); unable to locate further information on him.
6. Catherine M. (1863-1963); married Adam Pohl; had at least three children.
7. Nicholas (1864-1922); did not marry; spent most of his adult life in state mental hospitals.

One wonders how Catherine related to her uncles, aunts, and first cousins. At that time, extended family was of great importance.

The name "Catherine" is prominent in four generations. In the *Twelfth Census of the United States* in 1900, Catherine is listed as Katie, which she was called in childhood. Also, the following interesting document verifies her nickname.

> January 24, 1964
>
> Metropolitan Life Insurance Co.
> New York City, New York
>
> Gentlemen:

> This is to certify that Mother M. Corona, OSF, formerly known as Catherine Wilhelmina Wirfs, to whom Policy No. 18624729 was issued on January 1, 1912 under the name of Katie Wirfs, is one and the same individual.
>
> Mother M. Corona expired on January 6, 1964, as the accompanying death certificate will testify.
>
> Yours very truly,
> SCHOOL SISTERS OF ST. FRANCIS
>
> Mother M. Clemens, OSF
> Mother General

When Catherine was four years old, she welcomed her baby brother, Joseph Henry (1890-1956), into the world. One can only imagine a little girl's delight at having a brother. He must have been a playful companion to Catherine as they grew older.

Shortly after the birth of Joseph, the family moved to St. Louis, Missouri, where their daughter Anna was born on December 13, 1892. Ursula, Catherine's mother, following labor in childbirth, contracted acute septicemia and died two days later at age 33. Death came "like a thief in the night" and snatched Ursula from her family.

Imagine the intense sorrow and grief of Anthony, who was left with three small children: Catherine, five-and-a-half years old; Joseph, two; and baby Anna. How quickly the present can become past and erase all hopes for the future. In the wake of Ursula's sudden death, "normal" ceased to exist. Anthony was not ready to say goodbye.

How sad for Catherine to lose the nurturing and love of her mother at such a tender age. How did she remember her mother? Memory is never idle, even in a child. Death at that moment must have touched the core of this child's soul. Who knows the emotions—the feelings, the fears, the struggles—that resided in Catherine in her formative years. That traumatic time in her life had to have become the blueprint that showed her, at a young age, out of her own experience, how to live, love, forget, and how to continue-on in life.

Provisions had to be made for the children. Being a responsible father, Anthony entrusted his three children to his sister Agatha in Chicago, who was married to Frederick Thome. They had no children of their own. With this transition, a change in parenting had to be difficult for Catherine. When researching *Stanislaus*, the author interviewed sisters who had lived with Sister Corona at St. Philomena Convent. They mentioned that Aunt Agatha was very strict. Perhaps that offers some explanation as to why Catherine became scrupulous and a perfectionist at a young age and even struggled with this burden as a young adult. The sisters said, "She outgrew scrupulosity in time."

Aunt Agatha must have had a big adjustment also. Having inherited three children overnight had to be challenging. She must have had a great influence on Catherine, especially in her deep faith, prayer life, and devotion to the Mother of God. Mother Corona's admonitions to the sisters regarding courtesy, refinement, etiquette, lady-like behavior, and manners probably reflect her upbringing with Aunt Agatha.

Agatha died in 1934 at age 79 and was buried in St. Mary Catholic Cemetery and Mausoleum in Evergreen Park, Illinois. A memorial card of Agatha was in Mother Corona's personal file. She undoubtedly kept this card in her *Manual of Prayers*.

What happened to Joseph? At age 28, Joseph married Kathryn Kennedy, age 25, on August 27, 1919. They had two daughters, Elizabeth and Agatha. It appears he had a close relationship with Catherine, not only in childhood, but adult life. In Joseph's obituary, he is listed as "the fond brother of Rev. Mother Corona, OSF."

The *Chicago Sunday Tribune*, October 25, 1953, featured an article on his career: "Fire Marshal Looks Back on 38-Year Career." He joined the Chicago fire department for "excitement and steady employment," and after 38 years, retired at age 63, the compulsory retirement age for firemen.

> Following his graduation from St. Nicholas Elementary School, Joseph worked as a steamfitter and served four years in the Navy from 1907-1911. He joined the fire department in 1915. Promotions came regularly: lieutenant, 1926; captain, 1937; battalion chief, 1944; 4th division fire marshal, 1948.

> Joseph had his share of 'excitement.' One of the fires in 1920 broke out in a home for the elderly operated by Little Sisters of the Poor at 31st and Prairie Avenue. Joseph and other firemen carried more than 30 persons safely from the burning building. In 1931, he carried a woman from the second floor of a burning apartment house at 51st Street and Michigan Avenue. Joseph received commendations for these two feats. He supervised the rescue of many people over the years and was awarded numerous citations. One of his firemen was awarded the Lamber Tree medal for carrying an invalid woman from the third floor.

> At his retirement, Joseph said, 'The fire department has come a long way since I joined. The equipment is better, and I think the working conditions have improved.' He went on to say, 'When I joined, the fire wagons were pulled by horses. Now everything is motorized.' Other than planning a trip to Washington, D.C., Joseph had no retirement plans.

On August 27, 1956, the *Chicago Tribune* headlines read, "Joseph Wirfs Dies; Retired Fire Marshal," age 65.

> He died August 26th at Roseland Community Hospital. His wife, Kathryn, had died in 1953. Surviving were two daughters, Mrs. Elizabeth O'Malley and Mrs. Agatha Durnell; eight grandchildren, and two sisters. His funeral Mass was held at St. Nicholas Church.

Mother Corona and Anna once more faced death—this time a beloved brother who gave back to life through his active and dedicated service as a fireman. That same capacity to feel consuming grief and pain also allowed Mother Corona to embrace life, joy, and beauty as a woman religious.

At age 26, Anna married a Chicago policeman, Edward Doyle, age 28, on April 26, 1919.

In 1960, Sister Terese Bartl, who was teaching at Immaculate Heart of Mary School in Madison, Wisconsin, wrote a letter of gratitude to Mother Corona. Included in the letter was this message:

> Your sister, Anne, stopped in to see us the other day. She was visiting Tom here at Madison. She looks well. I think it is good for her to visit her grandchildren and they love her, too. I told the little fellow that I was going to keep grandma, and he didn't like it. When they were leaving, he said, 'Come Gramma!' Tom has certainly been blessed with good children. He loves them, and they love him.

Anne's obituary reads as follows:

> *The Shawnee (KS) Journal-Herald,* Feb. 13, 1980, p. 18.
> Mrs. Anna Doyle, 87, of 819 E. 9th, died Thurs., Feb. 7, at St. Mary's Hospital. She was born in St. Louis and had lived in

this area 12 years. Mrs. Doyle was a member of St. Ann's Catholic Church, Prairie Village. She leaves two sons, Thomas F. Doyle, Prairie Village, and Joseph A. Doyle, New York City; eight grandchildren; and a great-granddaughter. Services were Sat., Feb. 9 at the church; burial in St. Mary's Catholic Cemetery, Evergreen Park, IL. Arrangements by Newcomer.

When Catherine, Joseph, and Anna, at an older age, had adjusted to living with their aunt, and time had offered healing from their mother's death, their father embarked on a new course in his life. In the *U.S. City Directories*, 1822-1995, Anthony was a resident in Bakersfield, California in 1906, and listed as having employment with AT & SF Railway. In 1913, Anthony lived in Pueblo, Colorado doing car repairs—AT & SF. In the California *Railroad Employment Records*, 1862-1950, Anthony Wirfs is listed as a laborer who began work on July 31, 1919 on the railroad, the Salt Lake Division. One wonders how comfortable were the children in having their father living a great distance from them. He was conscientious in writing letters to them and sending money to Agatha to help support his children. Was roaming the country a way of dealing with his grief at the loss of his wife?

Anthony's life ended in tragedy. On September 5, 1921, he was killed by a southbound train on the Chicago Eastern Illinois railway as he was walking the tracks. The obituary reads as follows:

Newport Hoosier State, Sept. 14, 1921. Body identified. The unknown man killed by the C & E. I, one mile north of Newport on Monday of last week, was identified as Anthony Wirfs of Chicago. Undertaker Chipps called Sister M. Corona of 1832 Kedvale Avenue, St. Philomena

School, Chicago, describing the man and telling her that letters found in his handbag were addressed to her. She, after telling the undertaker, 'It is my father,' broke down and was unable to talk further except to say, 'My brother will come at once.' The brother, Joseph H. Wirfs, who is a member of the city fire department of Chicago, came Wednesday and easily identified the body as that of his father and made arrangements for its shipment to Chicago for burial at once. Anthony Wirfs was a molder and car repairer and had been roving over the country ever since the death of his wife 30 years ago. The son, who is a fine appearing young man, told the writer that there was no occasion for his father traveling over the country; that he could have had a home with his son or either of his two daughters.

The sudden death of a father is a great loss in life, but the greatest loss may have been what died inside Sister Corona as she continued to live. The most painful goodbyes are the ones left unsaid.

URSULA GRASSEL WIRFS
MOTHER CORONA'S MOTHER

CHAPTER TWO

MISSION LIFE

Catherine Wilhelmina Wirfs was received into the School Sisters of St. Francis on December 6, 1904, at the age of 18. She was given the religious name Sister Mary Corona (crown), a name well-suited to her personality, character, and who she was yet to become. Fifty-three other young women were received that year, eleven of whom came from Europe. The parents of these sisters lived in Germany, Prussia, Poland, Austria, Luxembourg, Canada, and the United States.

Receptions were held in St. Joseph Hall, which was then the original chapel. Already in 1904, it became apparent that the congregation needed a larger chapel. Due to the size of the 1904 class and the candidates' different dates of entry, the ceremonies were held on the following days:

March 19 – 1 candidate	June 21 – 23 candidates
April 12 – 3 candidates	November 22 – 2 candidates
April 24 – 1 candidate	December 6 – 24 candidates

Even though receptions were held on different days, that did not minimize the excitement and class spirit of the 1904s. However, the novices had little time to bond because they were destined to follow the Gospel message, "Go forth and teach." At that time in the community, novices were "sent forth" without further education and teaching experience. Because of their family backgrounds, most of these women were responsible, mature adults at a young age.

In 1900, the church in the United States supported 3,500 parochial schools, usually under the control of the local parish. By 1920, the number of elementary schools reached 6,551, enrolling 1,759,673 pupils taught by 41,581 teachers. Secondary education, likewise, boomed. In 1900, there were only about 100 Catholic high schools, but by 1920, more than 1,500 were in operation. For more than two generations, enrollment continued to climb.

The Association of Catholic Colleges and Universities was founded in 1899. In 1904, Catholic educators formed an organization to coordinate their efforts on a national scale: The Catholic Educational Association, which later changed its name to the National Catholic Educational Association.

What happened on a national scale greatly impacted the schools staffed by School Sisters of St. Francis and the constant demand for more sisters that plagued Mothers Alfons, Stanislaus, and Corona during their times of leadership.

After reception, Mother Alfons Schmid sent Sister Corona to St. Matthias Parish School, 2310 W. Ainslie Street, Chicago, Illinois. St. Matthias Parish became the reality of the sincere faith and hopes of the early German settlers in Bowmanville. The area could best described as vast prairies and woodlands surrounding the farming villages of Bowmanville and Niles Center. The parish went from vacant land to a church, school, rectory, and an active parish community. The parish school first opened its doors in the fall of 1888 to 17 students. By the end of the year, 50 pupils were enrolled. Nic Alles was their teacher.

In 1893, two School Sisters of St. Francis, Angelina Logelin and Wilfrida Biebrick, took over the operation of the school. Three other sisters joined them in 1896. When Sister Corona was sent in 1905, there were four other sisters with her. There are no records or oral histories of her first-year teaching. How quickly she must have learned to be a good teacher, instilling Christian values in her students. No doubt, she was mentored by an older sister, which was customary at that time.

When St. Matthias Parish was founded in 1887, it was the only parish for miles around, but by 1904, a year before Sister Corona arrived, there were eight other parishes in the area. This was indicative of the growing pains and expansion of Chicago. The electric streetcar and elevated train meant that the population of Chicago, which was now more than one million, was crowding out farming and crossroad villages like Bowmanville.

The population of St. Matthias steadily increased so that within a few years, the parish school was staffed by 19 sisters. The sisters remained at the school until 2005. Due to mergers, it is now called St. Matthias Transfiguration School, which has a large Filipino population. Sister Corona witnessed the rapid growth at St. Matthias Parish within her one-year teaching there. Then, Mother Alfons chose to transfer her to another large Chicago parish, St. Philomena. It was there that her abilities in leadership blossomed.

A petition for a missionary parish for the German Catholic community of Hermosa was issued in 1888, and in 1889, the first church building was erected. The first resident pastor, Father Peter Faber (1894-1897), established St. Philomena as an independent parish. The following year, 1895, the rectory was built. That same year, three School Sisters of St. Francis began teaching on the lower floor of the church building with only two classrooms. There they welcomed 90 children whom they divided into four grades in each room. In 1901, when the permanent school building was erected, four classrooms became available for the increased number of children. For a long time thereafter, each succeeding year witnessed an increased attendance, taxing the pastor's ingenuity to find available space for schoolrooms.

During this great influx of students, Sister Corona arrived on the scene in 1906. At this time, nine sisters staffed the school. Sister Corona had not yet made her canonical novitiate as required by church law, so she taught at St. Philomena for only two years and returned to Milwaukee in 1908-1909. At that time, there was no official novice director, so it is difficult to comprehend what that year was like for Sister Corona. The novitiate is a year of discerning one's vocation; a time for prayer, meditation, and reflection to deepen one's spiritual life.

In 1909, she was sent back to St. Philomena to continue the work she had begun. In 1911, Sister Corona incorporated a Commercial High School course into the curriculum. Occupations open to women at that time were exceedingly limited: homemaking and raising children, teaching, care of the sick, midwifery, and helping with the family business. It was wise on the part of Mother Corona to prepare young women especially for many aspects of business-related careers and provide an ethical basis within a Catholic setting. In retrospect, this curriculum was the forerunner of college preparatory education.

A great asset to the commercial department happened when Sister Clemens Rudolph, who was trained to teach business courses, joined the faculty in 1915 and remained at

St. Philomena until 1927. She and Sister Corona operated as a legendary team and the school's enrollment boomed even more than previously.

During this time of success and happiness, Sister Corona was faced with the tragic and sudden death of her father just days after school had begun, September 5, 1921. Despite the immense sadness, life and progress at St. Philomena continued.

By 1923, the school had 16 rooms of grade-school pupils with three rooms in the commercial department. When the latest addition to the school building was completed in 1929, a kindergarten was added. By the time Sister Corona left St. Philomena in 1925, 27 sisters staffed the school. When Father J.P. Schiffer learned of her appointment to the motherhouse, he hesitated to let her go. According to Sister Mina Schaub, who also was transferred that year from St. Philomena, he said, "If it's not for something higher and better, I won't let her go." For something higher and better, she was to eventually become the Mother General of the congregation.

The first graduating class of 1918 in Commercial Course by Sister Corona, held a reunion in 1958 and invited Mother Corona and Mother Clemens, her assistant. The following displays the students' love and affection for their teachers.

WELCOME REV. FATHER SIEGER, REV. MOTHER CORONA, AND MOTHER CLEMENS

Our hearts are filled with delight, upon this Re-Union Day! We have the privilege today to honor our Reverend Teachers.

Forty years ago, a class of enthusiastic boys and girls, then twenty-one in number, were graduated by Reverend Mother

---

Corona, for a Course in Business, in which Mother Clemens was our foundation, upon which the superstructure was built.

An oak tree grows from an acorn; so we who had busily engaged as a class for two productive years, completed our work together. Then we parted, and each went a separate way to seek his fortune, as it is said in fairy tales.

We have kept smiling through High School...are we smiling through our trials and through good fortune alike? We are happy to be together today to greet our Reverend Mother and her Assistant; to greet old friends, and to talk about old times. Someone has said that the most fascinating words are: 'Do you remember?'

Stories were shared, quotes of Mother Corona's insistence on perfection were played back to her in a humorous way, and a spoof on their two teachers evoked much laughter, especially from Father Sieger, who probably for the first time saw these women from a different perspective. Perhaps some of these former students were the ones who came to visit Mother Corona in Milwaukee and sought counsel in how to run their businesses. It was not uncommon to see Mother Corona in the art parlor advising businessmen from Chicago.

Not only was she good in business, she had many other talents. The sisters who lived with Sister Corona at St. Philomena Convent often spent their evening recreations listening to her elocution. These sisters were mesmerized by her art of public speaking. Unfortunately, there are no recordings of those evenings and the responses of the sisters.

Her life was not all work. She was also a pro in Chinese checkers. She met her match when she came to the motherhouse and played checkers with Sister Valencia Van Driel, the director of the printing department. Both of them, powerful women in every way, "played for blood and money" according to the sisters at the motherhouse at that time.

* * * * * * * * * * * * * *

During Mother Corona's time as Mother General, she was still held in high esteem by the people and pastors of St. Philomena long after she had left the parish. It worked to her advantage to have served the parish for many years and to have exhibited strong leadership.

The following letter had to be difficult to write to Father Gehrig because of Mother Corona's emotional ties to St. Philomena Parish, but her strong sense of fairness and justice prevailed.

> April 9, 1953
>
> Reverend and dear Father Gehrig:
>
> This is a letter which I hoped would never have to be written. We all know that the increased number of children pouring into our city schools has given rise to many problems which cause headaches and heartaches to the Reverend Pastors, to the parents of the children, and not least, to the superiors of teaching communities. The teaching personnel has been stretched to the breaking point. Every available Sister, including those needed for supervisory and administrative work, has been assigned to classroom duty. We have resorted to every means within our reach and have made extraordinary efforts to keep our schools staffed with Sisters, but the time has come when, regardless of our preferences, lay teachers must of necessity become a part of the teaching staff.
>
> During the past few years, we have found it necessary in some cases to request the employment of lay teachers, especially when new classrooms were opened, or substitutes were needed. The Reverend Pastors as a whole were kind and

understanding and we have had no appreciable difficulty. For this we are truly grateful. Of late, however, an element of unrest has manifested itself due, perhaps, to the fact that some of our schools have been obliged to engage lay teachers while others have not. This situation was brought about by circumstances. We are fully aware that a completely Sister-staffed school is more satisfactory to all concerned, but to continue placing added burdens on some in order to relieve others serves only to increase our difficulties. At the present time, thirteen Sisters are absent from their classrooms on account of illness, with no Sister substitutes available. During the current school year, God saw fit to call to Himself four of our teachers whom we have not been able to replace. Each year brings its quota of elderly Sisters who must be relieved of the strain of classroom duty. The fact remains that new parochial schools must be opened if the Church is to flourish and grow. With practically all religious orders lacking teaching personnel, this will not be possible unless we all work together and share the Sisters.

We have reached the end of our resources and in fairness and justice to all, we must do as other communities have been doing—namely, distribute the teachers on a ratio basis. Every school having six grade teachers is asked to engage one lay teacher; schools having twelve grade teachers will engage two lay teachers. Out of every six elementary school teachers, one is to be a lay teacher, but for the coming year we will make allowances for schools that would be obliged to engage more than two lay teachers in the elementary grades. Furthermore, the Sisters teaching Kindergarten will be withdrawn at the close of the current school year.

The Sisters thus released will not be many since more than half of our schools are small schools located in rural areas. Neither will the class leaving our college to enter the teaching field be large because Sister students have been withdrawn at intervals to meet the demand for additional teachers. These Sisters must continue their studies by means of extension courses often carried in addition to the duty of teaching large classes, and by attendance at summer school. All Sisters in the teaching field are expected to meet the high standard of present-day teacher education, and if we wish to safeguard their health, we must give them an opportunity to complete their courses before they are appointed to teach.

God has blessed us again with promising vocations, but the number is relatively small. It may be of interest to note that more than half of the members of our reception classes are girls who received their high school education here as aspirants and postulants. Were it not for our preparatory school or aspirancy as we call it, our reception classes would be small, indeed.

A point which requires clarification is the opinion that the work of our Sisters in the nursing field is a contributing factor to the shortage of teachers, but that is not the case. Each postulant has the privilege of expressing her preference for a certain line of work. Only from among those who indicate a desire to care for the sick are future nurses selected.

In closing, permit me to express our sincere gratitude for your kindness and consideration toward our Congregation and particularly toward the Sisters who are working in your parish. We shall continue to cooperate with you, Reverend Father, and assure you that our interest in the welfare of your school is as vital and keen as ever.

Sincerely yours in Christ,

Mother M. Corona, OSF

An open letter regarding the Commercial High School was published in the October 11, 1959 parish bulletin. Father Harold Sieger still respected and heeded the wise advice of Mother Corona 50 years later.

October 11, 1959

My dear parishioners:

The parish of St. Philomena has had a Commercial High School for approximately 50 years. Mother Corona and Mother Clemens were among the early teachers. Other sisters have been engaged in this assignment, including Sister Mariella [O'Brien], who now teaches the first-year pupils. And, of course, the incomparable Sister Hermenegild [Dombrowska], who is in her 39th year among us, is still demonstrating her 'sparkling' teaching technique, featuring her own home-made psychology.

Many priests have served as instructor of religion, confessor and advisor, including the popular Fr. Kupinski, who now serves in these capacities.

Shorthand, Typewriting, Bookkeeping, Mathematics, English and Spelling have been the subjects offered. The basis for all was the Religion Class intended to develop proper Christian morals and character formation.

The school has had an excellent record, and the success of the graduates in the business world has attested to the high caliber of the faculty's teaching abilities. Despite this excellent record, a decision has been reached to discontinue our Commercial High School. I need hardly say that the decision was made reluctantly and with regrets. The reasons listed below demonstrate that our decision was founded upon sound judgment.

Here are the reasons:

1. Mother Corona is encouraging the discontinuance of all Commercial schools in which the School Sisters of St. Francis teach because:

   a) Of the shortage of sisters.
   b) She feels that the type of course (special emphasis on business qualifications) is not adequate for girls who intend to continue their full course in other High Schools.

c) She feels girls should not limit themselves to this 2-year course.

2. Next year our grammar school will need an extra classroom and the following year two extra classrooms, because more and more grades are demanding three classrooms instead of two.

3. Two thirds of the students are from other parishes, and therefore, are not our responsibilities.

4. We have been told that next year there will be a sufficient number of Catholic High Schools for girls in our neighborhood to absorb these students.

The School will close according to these specifications:

a) No new pupils will be registered.
b) Those who are in second year now will graduate in 1960 according to schedule.
c) Those who are in first year now will complete their two-year course and graduate in 1961 according to schedule.

And what will happen to Sister Hermenegild?

Mother Corona has promised that she will exert every effort that Sister Hermenegild continue in some capacity in our parish. Sister Hermenegild will have completed 40 years of teaching in our Commercial and a splendid time to 'bow out.' This is not a good reason for closing our Commercial, but I cannot think of a better coincidence.

Confident you will understand the wisdom of our decision, I remain,

Devotedly yours in Christ,

Father Sieger

Sisters had to seek permission to drive during Mother Corona's administration. As time went on, she became more lenient in her permissions.

August 27th, 1958

Dear Mother Corona,

It was kind of you to grant permission for our sisters to have exclusive use of the station-wagon. The reaction of our sisters was even more enthusiastic than I anticipated.

This gift from our people will make them more aware of the great debt they owe the School Sisters of St. Francis who do such Christlike work among us.

I have spent much money in the short time I have been here and will spend much more before the year is completed, but I feel this purchase has given me the greatest satisfaction. And, Mother, feel free to suggest any other way we can be helpful in assisting the sisters here or the Order for your continued progress.

Grateful too for favoring us with the sisters we did not expect, I am, Dear Mother,

Sincerely in Christ,

Reverend Harold H. Sieger

Requests for money were not uncommon for Mother Corona. In Franciscan humility and poverty, she implored the help of many to carry on the mission of the congregation.

June 20, 1959

Dear Mother Corona:

I have already disclosed my desire to respond to your appeal for financial help at this time when the need is an urgent one. Sister Amanda has relayed our first response. Shortly I shall send $500.00, contributions for our Novena of Masses and prayers for the fathers of our parishioners. And now rather than wait, I am sending enclosed a check for $2,000.00, the amount of the proceeds we will probably receive one of the nights of the carnival designated for this purpose. If the occasion presents itself, I will use other opportunities to help ease your financial burdens. Actually, these donations fall far short of the debt we owe the School Sisters of St. Francis for their devotion to duty while serving the people of our parish.

It pleased me very much to hear Archbishop Meyer had increased the salaries of your teaching sisters.

I feel confident that the relationship between your community and our parish will be hereby strengthened and become even more affable.

With no effort at flattery may I remark, Mother Corona, that the School Sisters of St. Francis have enjoyed much of their measure of success, because of your excellent leadership and inspiration.

I remain,
Sincerely in Christ,

Rev. Harold H. Sieger

Mother Corona was always grateful for any financial assistance large or small. This letter is a sample of the many "thank yous" that came from her heart.

July 3, 1959

Reverend and dear Father Sieger:

Our 'Thank You!' is a feeble sign of the gratitude we feel toward you and the good people of St. Philomena's for the continued interest you manifest and the kindness you show toward our cause. Truly, you are co-apostles, for it is all for the honor and glory of God and the salvation of immortal souls. May God bless and reward you, Reverend Father, your kind Assistant Priests who have helped to promote this good work, and your faithful parishioners. It was, indeed, thoughtful of you to advance the income of 'our' Spring Festival Day.

And the extra donation from the Father's Day Fund! What shall I say! I sent stipends for ten Holy Masses to Archbishop Aloisius J. Muench, Apostolic Nuncio to Germany (a Milwaukee boy) who helps support many poor priests who have little or no means of income, and stipends for ten Holy Masses to other needy priests, for the fathers of St. Philomena families, living or dead. One hundred dollars will be used to enhance our St. Joseph Shrine in the Convent Garden, and the remainder for the support of our postulants.

Many a prayer will be said at the Shrine for the fathers of St. Philomena's now and in time to come. A Holy Hour will be offered for the fathers in the Convent Chapel from 7:00 to 8:00 p.m. on Friday, July 10. May God hear our prayers for these good fathers and for all who prompted this worthwhile movement!

Sincerely in Our Lord,

Mother M. Corona, OSF

During Mother Corona's administration, she strongly communicated with pastors who were building new convents that the sisters must have private rooms. For too many years, the sisters were huddled two and three in a bedroom. She insisted that the demands in teaching were becoming more stressful, and for psychological and health reasons, the sisters needed private space. Most pastors complied with her wishes.

A new convent at St. Philomena was dedicated in 1945.

This is a day on which, by means of the solemn blessing, we formally dedicate our new convent building to the uses for which it was intended. It is now fifty years since the good School Sisters of St. Francis first came to the Parish to take charge of our school. It is the Golden Jubilee of their labors here. And it seems eminently fitting that at this time there should be presented to them, as the concrete evidence of the gratitude of our people, this new home in which they are henceforth to live among us. We have tried to make it a becoming expression of the thankfulness of St. Philomena's parishioners. In doing this we have had the enthusiastic cooperation of all the members of the Parish. In very truth, the new convent is the thank offering of a grateful people to the Sisters.

Later, when Father Sieger became pastor, he honored Mother Corona's wishes and made more improvements in the convent.

♦ Sun deck—sun and fresh air, which most sisters sorely need.

♦ An elevator—it is getting more difficult to attract young ladies into the sisterhood—let's keep them as long as we can. I am not referring to comfort, but heart strain from climbing.

♦ Every effort will be made to direct our planning toward practical details rather than excessive comforts. In fact, the entire project is intended to develop the sisters spiritually and physically so that they may be even better fitted to educate our youth. Confident that you will be in accord with this purpose, I remain,

Devotedly yours in Christ,
Father Sieger

When St. Philomena Parish was founded in 1888 as a German National Parish, it expressed the culture and unique Catholic heritage of a single ethnic group. Over the years, St. Philomena welcomed other groups—Austrians, Hungarians, Poles, Italians, Irish, and Latin Americans. Each in their own way enriched the culture of the parish. Yearly celebrations reflected a wonderful variety. The feasts of St. Nicholas, Epiphany, St. Patrick, St. Joseph, and Our Lady of Guadalupe were among the many celebrated. In honoring all traditions, they united all their people in cultural exchange and oneness of Faith. The year 2018 shows another ethnic shift. The parish is 90% Hispanic.

Fluent in Spanish, Sister Mary Ray, who taught for 12 years at St. Philomena, was the last sister to leave the parish in 1999. Thus, the School Sisters of St. Francis ministered to the students and parishioners for 106 years.

To Mother Corona's final breath, the people at St. Philomena remained loyal supporters of the woman they deemed "A Gallant Lady."

ST. PHILOMENA SCHOOL – 1901
WHERE SISTER CORONA WAS
TEACHER/PRINCIPAL FROM 1906–1925, WITH THE
EXCEPTION OF 1908–1909, HER NOVITIATE YEAR

FEAST OF THE   January 12, 1964
HOLY FAMILY

OUR LIFE
in st.philomena parish

A GALLANT LADY

MOTHER M. CORONA

Builder, administrator, spiritual guide, advisor, and Major
Superior from 1942 to 1960, died January 6th, 1964. Priests,
sisters, and laity of St. Philomena Parish are deeply saddened by
her passing.

Mother Corona was inflamed with an intense desire to serve
with an understanding heart, that led thousands of sisters to the
pattern and mind of Christ.

God grant her a life of eternity with Himself, to Whom she
espoused her life of dedication.

CHAPTER THREE

MOTHER ASSISTANT

Mother Alfons must have been impressed with Sister Corona's performance at St. Philomena and decided the parish prospered enough under her leadership. "She needs to come to the motherhouse and help us." In 1925, Sister Corona returned to Milwaukee. This is a hidden time of her life. There is no job description in the records for the years 1925-1930. Sister Corona was elected Third Councilor on June 6, 1928, to replace deceased Sister Praxeda Hansen. This was the time in which Mother Alfons' health was diminishing. More and more, her assistant, Mother Stanislaus Hegner, was assuming responsibility for the congregation. What better person to assist in the office than Sister Corona, who no doubt did a lot of work behind the scenes.

Mother Alfons died April 5, 1929. Sister Stanislaus automatically became Vicaress General until election and seemed so much part of the community's founding that her leadership tempered the loss of Mother Alfons.

The time for election approached. In a letter dated December 27, 1929, she made an official announcement.

December 27, 1929

My dear Sisters,

    Herewith, I wish to announce to you that the election will be held January 2. Venerable Mother Catharina [Moehring],

---

Sister M. Berchmanns [Schmidt], and Sister M. Callista [Messmer], the three delegates from Germany, are here, and, as delegates for America, Sister M. Charity [Reiter] and Sister M. Anthony [Lynch] have been elected by the members of the General Chapter. The election will be held according to the revised Rule which we received from Rome several weeks ago. The manner of holding the elections has not been changed. When you receive your copy of the revised Rule, you will find that the elections are to be conducted in exactly the same way as heretofore. Therefore, we shall hold strictly to the requirements of the newly-revised Rule which is signed by the authorities in Rome.

At present, I am having the Rule translated into English, and, when this is finished, it will be translated into German. It will then be printed without delay, and each Sister will receive her copy. A few minor points have been changed, but we can easily keep all our Rule contains, and, with God's help, we will do so. Immediately after the election you will be notified of the outcome.

Asking your prayers, and wishing you God's blessing for the coming year, I am

Your loving

Sister M. Stanislaus, OSF

On January 7, 1930, Sister Stanislaus informed the sisters of the election results:

Mother General	Mother Stanislaus [Hegner]
First Councilor and Assistant General	Sister Corona [Wirfs]
Second Councilor	Sister Seraphica [Loewel]
Third Councilor	Sister Loretto [Thill]
Fourth Councilor	Sister Charity [Reiter]
General Secretary	Sister Immaculate [Geller]
General Procurator	Sister Fidelis [Westhauser]

After the election, the members of the chapter (body of delegates who elect the mother general and councilors) went to chapel as prescribed by the Rule; Right Reverend Monsignor Bernard G. Traudt, vicar general and chancellor of the Archdiocese of Milwaukee, made the announcements to the assembled community. In his address which followed, he spoke highly of the congregation.

> I heartily congratulate you on your choice of Venerable Mother Stanislaus as Superior General of your Community. To succeed Venerable Mother Alfons in the important office of guiding the Community is not an easy task. Venerable Mother Alfons was a woman whose name will stand out, not only in the history of the Community, but in the history of this archdiocese and in the history of the whole Northwest. She will ever be remembered as one of the greatest religious of our time. It was my privilege to have been personally acquainted with Mother Alfons for many years, and I have always considered her an ideal religious and model nun.

> I have watched this Community grow from its very infancy into one of the largest religious bodies in the United States. But more important than its numerical strength, is the great work that the Sisters of this Community are doing for the education and religious instruction of our American youth. Many people, even some priests, do not appreciate the work that religious accomplish. It is a regrettable fact to me to have heard certain priests remark that Sisters are only a necessary evil. It is indeed a pity that those who should really be the ones to uphold the Sisterhoods and work hand-in-hand with them, do at times undervalue the great work they are doing. However, despite all such harmful criticism, the good accomplished by the Sisters of this Community is inestimable.

> In Mother Stanislaus you have found a worthy successor to the saintly Mother Alfons...

> *Stanislaus,* Barbaralie Stiefermann, OSF

When Mother Stanislaus assumed her new responsibility in 1929, the School Sisters of St. Francis staffed 142 missions in the United States, in addition to Sacred Heart Sanitarium, St. Mary's Hill Hospital, the Motherhouse, St. Joseph Convent in Campbellsport, and St. Anthony Farm in Greenfield, Wisconsin. The 1930 Quinquennial Report sent to Rome indicates membership in the congregation as 1,486 professed sisters and 254 novices.

One of Sister Stanislaus's first duties in office—assigning sisters for retreats, summer schools, and missions for the next school year—was no small task. In a letter to the sisters, May 10, 1929, she says, "As good religious, go where you are sent, and you will have God's blessing. I do not intend to make many changes. I dislike them as much as you do, but some have been requested."

After her election, the first letter Mother Stanislaus wrote to the sisters sets the tone of her administration. The four-page missive manifests diversity of interests and concerns. She begins on a note of gratitude and within the same paragraph, the community knows there will be "no standing still," especially with Mother Corona as her assistant.

> First of all, I wish to thank the Sisters, each and every one, for their wonderful spirit of loyalty and goodwill so beautifully manifested at the time of the election. To know that you are with and for me, will enable me to continue the good work of our good Mothers Alexia and Alfons with more courage and enthusiasm. Our beloved foundresses have worked up our Community to a very high standard. With the grace of God, we will continue the good work and ever uphold the standard so nobly set. But we shall not stand still, for not to move forward means to go back, and we know it would be the earnest wish of

> our good Mothers, were they here to tell us so, that we should make progress spiritually and materially. (February 12, 1930)

Almost immediately, she shifts to concerns for the poor. The United States' stock market crash in October 1929 began to affect the American people; however, her compassion for the poor embraced the whole world.

> Besides taking our own financial needs into consideration, we must not forget that there are so very, very many poor who are waiting for our help—poor people in the greatest misery—here in America as well as in Europe and other missionary countries. You have no idea of the number of letters I receive from those in need. My heart goes out to them, and I wish we could do more to alleviate their misery. Therefore, dear Sisters, save whatever you can; be careful of your clothing; do not discard anything which can be worn; you know how expensive our habit material is. Take good care of everything given you for your use. Remember you have the vow of poverty and will one day be obliged to render a strict account to God as to how you fulfill this obligation. (February 12, 1930)

In August 1930, Mother Stanislaus, Sister Jutta Hollenbeck, and Spiritual Director Father Adolph J. Klink left for New York to visit the sisters in the European Province. This was to be Mother Stanislaus' first trip back since her days at San Remo. Her love of travel, which she said, "stretches the horizons of one's mind," prompted her to see more than the sisters in Europe. After an absence of more than three months, they were happy to return home. She never once worried about what was happening back home because Mother Corona had full command of all the daily activities.

After the travelers' homecoming celebrations, many activities awaited them. "Life is passing; time is fleeting; and there is still so much to be done," Mother Stanislaus wrote in her Christmas letter of December 15, 1930.

The day after the trio had left for Europe, Bishop Samuel Alphonsus Stritch was transferred from Toledo, Ohio, to Milwaukee and raised to the dignity of an archbishop. Mother Corona made arrangements with the new archbishop to come to the motherhouse after Mother Stanislaus returned from Europe. Mother Corona asked Sister Cherubim Schaefer to prepare a concert for the occasion. A special welcome occurred on December 18, 1930.

The chorus and orchestra of the School Sisters of St. Francis gave a hearty welcome to Archbishop Stritch.

Welcome, Welcome!
With joyful hearts we greet thee,
And pray that God Almighty
May bless, protect, and guide thee.
Welcome, Welcome!

Compositions by Mozart, Beethoven, Haydn, Rachmaninoff, and Massenet were among 13 pieces performed. Schubert's "Ave Maria", with violin and soprano solos and chorus with piano and organ accompaniments, was one of the highlights for the archbishop, as well as Bach-Gounod's "Meditation" arranged by Victor Saar.

The archbishop's address formed an appropriate conclusion. He insisted that "the love of the aesthetic should be inculcated in the hearts of children; all beauty is just a shadow of God. We are to lead those entrusted to our care to the Highest Aestheticism—the Divine Beauty."

Mothers Stanislaus and Corona sat in the front row with the archbishop and were elated over the performance of their talented sisters. This was the first of many beautiful encounters with Archbishop Stritch. For his 25th ordination anniversary in 1935, Mother Stanislaus asked Sister Cherubim to prepare a concert. Both the music and the garland setting created and meticulously arranged by sister musicians was sheer delight to the audience. It was even rumored that Sister Cherubim had sprinkled perfume on the hundreds of handmade roses. The concert in the Rose Garden was memorable not only to Archbishop Stritch, but also to Mothers Stanislaus and Corona—both lovers of music and roses.

As Mother Stanislaus assumed the responsibility of steering the congregation in new directions, Mother Corona kept a low profile during the 12 years of Mother Stanislaus's administration. During her time as assistant, she must have made a conscious effort to learn the names of all the sisters. When she became Mother General, she was able to address each sister by name, not only in the United States, but also in foreign lands. She had an incredible memory that served her well.

To be sure, Mother Corona was a vital team member behind the scenes, as Mother Stanislaus began a new mission in China in 1931 with three sisters. When Mother Stanislaus became unable to travel long distances, she sent Mother Corona to China in the fall of 1936. The beautiful and inspiring account of her travels to the Orient appears in the following chapter.

The "needs of the times" and Mother Stanislaus' responses were challenging: St. Joseph Convent, sisters' retirement home, Campbellsport, Wisconsin, built during the Depression years, 1933; St. Labre Indian Mission in Ashland, Montana, opened with six sisters in 1933; St. Paul's Indian Mission, Hays, Montana, opened with four sisters in 1936. Also, in 1936, a juniorate for the sisters in temporary vows was established; Sister Confirma Ruhlman was appointed first director of junior sisters.

Not only was Mother Stanislaus concerned about missions in the United States, but her mind and heart extended far beyond to the European Province. The first mission at Tegucigalpa, Honduras, Central America opened with five sisters from Germany in 1932. Then in 1936, the European Province opened missions in West India among the Mohars; Rahata (St. Theresa) and Sangammer (St. Anne).

Mother Corona played a significant role in educational pursuits. Was she preparing for the future when she possibly would be Mother General? A School of Nursing opened at Sacred Heart Sanitarium in 1930 and was accredited in 1933 by the State of Wisconsin. The two-year St. Joseph Normal School expanded to a four-year program. The institution's name was changed to Alverno Teachers College. A four-year music program was established: Alverno College of Music.

Amid the joy of progress, Mother Corona suffered a personal loss in December 1934. Her surrogate mother, Aunt Agatha (Wirfs) Thome died.

Sadness did not derail progress. Alverno College of Music was then admitted to the National Association of Schools of Music in 1940. Also, Sacred Heart School of Nursing in 1940 established a psychiatric nursing rotation at St. Mary's Hill Hospital.

The building of St. Joseph Hospital, Beaver Dam, Wisconsin, was a challenge. Mother Corona initiated fundraisers for the institution, which was dedicated in 1938.

Sister Archelaus Markowski became novice director in 1939. Milwaukee's archdiocese held its first Liturgical Day in 1941, at the School Sisters of St. Francis motherhouse. Something dear to Mother Stanislaus was St. Francis Mission for African Americans in Yazoo City, Mississippi, where she sent four sisters in 1940. The spiritual director, Father Adolph J. Klink, was highly opposed to her doing so. His position as spiritual director gave him more authority in the community than if he were assigned as chaplain. However, Mother Stanislaus was adamant in her desire to serve the African American population in Mississippi.

The litany of accomplishments are praiseworthy and give witness to the great legacy of Mother Stanislaus. Although many sisters assisted in healthcare, music, and education to help bring her dreams to reality, she nonetheless had the strong and persistent leadership to make it all happen.

In preparation for the General Chapter of 1936, Mother Stanislaus called a special council meeting on December 17, 1935. The purpose was to elect two delegates to represent the United States Province and three for the German Province in the event that no one could come from there. An appended note to these minutes reads: "Later we learned that no delegates are to represent the Mother Provincial and two Sisters from the German Province. That would be uncanonical." With the January 6, 1942 chapter members' signatures is the notation: "Owing to the present war, the Provincial Superior of the German Province and her delegates were unable to participate." That year, the Chapter consisted of nine delegates.

To prepare for the 1942 Chapter, Mother Stanislaus consulted Father Ellis, S.J., who had been transferred from Marquette University to St. Mary College in Kansas. In her letter dated October 17, 1941, she sought advice regarding the election of delegates. She received an interesting response which foreshadows what was to come under Mother Corona's administration.

October 19, 1941

Dear Mother Stanislaus:

This is confidential, but it seems to me that the Sisters are not sufficiently represented at the General Chapter. This is not stated as a criticism, but as an objective fact. They should have a voice in the election of the delegates to the General Chapter. I think that it is time for you to think of dividing the United States into Provinces.

As things stand now, a small group controls all the elections, and while I have no doubt but that they are very worthy women, the mind of the Church is that the Sisters themselves should be represented by delegates whom they have elected themselves. The General Council has no right to elect delegates for the Sisters. You should have a Provincial Chapter for the United States, held perhaps during Christmas week, and at that chapter should be present all the superiors of houses having twelve or more Sisters who have active voice, as well as two Sisters from each such house, who have been elected by the Sisters of their community. All that the Provincial Chapter does is elect two delegates for the General Chapter.

The houses which number less than twelve members having active voice should be grouped together locally in groups of twelve or more and in the place appointed by the Superior General and her Council, they shall meet on an appointed day, and choose from this assembled group, one superior, and two Sisters who will be members of the Provincial Chapter. This is the mind of the Church.

It is quite possible that you are doing all this, and that I am making a mountain out of a mole hill. Perhaps it would be well for you to send me a copy of your Constitutions, if you care to do so, so that I may have a complete understanding of their provisions in regard to the General Chapter. It will be useful also when other points come up. Now please understand that this is merely a suggestion, and if it does not meet with your approval, just disregard it.

In the last analysis, you must continue to conduct your General Chapter as provided for by the Constitutions which the Holy See has approved. I know that you will pardon my frankness, since it has been prompted solely by interest in and desire for the well-being of your Congregation.

Sincerely yours in Christ

Adam C. Ellis, S.J.

Correspondence continued between Father Ellis and Mother Stanislaus. At the 1942 General Chapter, she was almost seventy-nine years old. Had she been re-elected, she probably would have considered dividing the United States into provinces. Membership grew to almost four thousand sisters under the leadership of Mother Corona before the first American Province was established in 1959. Decentralization became a necessity.

The first formal report of an administration was presented to the 1942 Chapter. Mother Stanislaus gave a brief, but impressive "account of her stewardship." Under the category of religious improvements, she prided herself in saying:

> The religious spirit has been promoted and
> quickened by the fostering of a more faithful
> observance of the common life, particularly as
> regards the spirit of poverty.

Other areas covered were: constitutional changes, membership, education, buildings and improvements, missions—domestic and foreign—and finances.

The membership of the Congregation was recorded as follows:

Senior Professed Sisters	1,641
Junior Professed Sisters	382
Novices – 1st Year	41
Novices – 2nd Year	55
Postulants	46
Aspirants	46

In her report, Mother Stanislaus stated:

> Despite the almost universal complaint on the part of
> religious congregations that vocations are declining at an
> alarming rate, our Congregation has been singularly blessed
> insofar as it has had an average of forty-eight vocations per
> year during the past six years.
>
> *Stanislaus*, Barbaralie Stiefermann, OSF

During the latter part of Mother Stanislaus' administration, her assistant, Mother Corona, assumed more responsibility. Age and physical limitations prompted Mother

Stanislaus to rely upon her just as Mother Alfons previously had done with Mother Stanislaus. To many sisters, it appeared as if Mother Corona was being groomed to be the next Mother General.

MOTHER CORONA
AS MOTHER ASSISTANT 1925–1942
PHOTO: 1930

MOTHER STANISLAUS AND ASSISTANT MOTHER
CORONA AT ST. ANTHONY FARM

TOP LEFT TO RIGHT
SISTER JUSTITIA BRILL; MOTHER CORONA WIRFS,
ASSISTANT; MOTHER STANISLAUS HEGNER, MOTHER
GENERAL; SISTER LORETTO THILL; SISTER DEODIGNA
SCHIRRA

FATHER ADOLPH J. KLINK AND DR. PAREDES
1939

CHAPTER FOUR

TRAVELS TO THE ORIENT

"Though we travel the world over to find the beautiful, we must carry it with us or we find it not." These words of Ralph Waldo Emerson can be applied to Mother Corona as she "carried beauty within her" in traveling to Japan and China during her time as Mother Assistant. Her awe-inspiring letter speaks for itself.

January 29, 1937

Dear Sisters,

It is a pleasure to comply with the wish of our dear Mother Stanislaus to give you a description of my visit to the Orient. I will tell you something of Japan and more about China, but will make no pretense of speaking authoritatively, since, after all, two months is but a short time wherein to gain accurate knowledge of a section of the earth as mystifying and paradoxical as China. I refer to China as a section of the earth since it comprises one-fourth of the earth's population—four hundred million people—people who differ from one another, not only in language and custom, but also in stature and physique, as much as the people of Europe differ from one another—for example, the Italians and the Dutch.

I sailed from Vancouver, on the SS. EMPRESS OF RUSSIA, September 5. The trip to Vancouver through the Canadian Rockies formed a delightful prelude to the wonderful voyage across the Pacific. From the train we viewed mountains—mountains bare and bleak, mountains thickly covered with spruce and hemlock, snow-capped mountains with their peaks in the clouds, lakes, rivers, waterfalls, glaciers—each a picture in itself but forming a gigantic whole almost too stupendous for the human eye and mind to grasp at one time. This picturesque scenery caused a succession of thrills, one greater than the other.

As our train neared Vancouver, new scenic beauties unfolded before us; mountains, rivers, forests, and lakes, but these were interspersed with villages, towns, and even cities. The only human touch in yesterday's picture was the hotel at Banff and the quaint little Swiss village, the latter the home of the mountain guides employed by the Canadian Pacific.

Vancouver, situated on a harbor bearing the same name, is a beautiful and attractive city. On the north side of the inlet lies a magnificent mountain range, two peaks of which, silhouetted against the horizon, have earned for themselves the striking name of "The Lions' Gate" because of their resemblance to couchant lions.

After completing arrangements for sailing, we made a hasty tour of the city, visiting among other places, Stanley Park, the residential and commercial districts, and Chinatown.

At 11:00 a.m. sharp, the SS. EMPRESS OF RUSSIA slipped away from her moorings to begin her trip across the great ocean. As the ties which bound us to land were broken, thoughts of the vast Pacific, dark and foreboding, flashed across my mind and a feeling, akin to fear, came over me. But only for a few moments, for immediately I was buoyed up by the thought that I was sent. I was going in the interests of our

Community, and God's blessing and protection would surely be with me. I knew, too, that the prayers of our dear Sisters would accompany me.

We made a stop at Victoria, the capital of British Columbia, about 4:00 p.m., and from there our route of travel was directly to Yokohama, Japan.

My two companions, both native Chinese, Sister M. Rosa of the Franciscan Sisters of Perpetual Adoration, La Crosse, Wisconsin, and Sister Maurice Clet, a Sister of Charity from Cincinnati, Ohio, proved themselves sociable and agreeable from the start. Both were newly-professed Sisters on their way to Wuchang, China.

The passenger list also carried the names of other Missionaries: Two Franciscan Fathers from the Cincinnati Province, one a native Chinese, Father Sylvester Cheng, O.F.M.; two French Jesuit Priests from Canada accompanied by a Brother and several students on their way to a China mission; and a French Redemptorist Father with four students enroute to Indo China. The seminarians are to complete their studies in their foreign field of labor in order to learn the language thoroughly and become acclimated.

Priests on board meant daily Mass and Holy Communion. We were fortunate, indeed, for, as I learned later, Holy Mass could not be celebrated on board the SS. EMPRESS OF RUSSIA on its next trip from Vancouver because of the stormy sea.

With the exception of a few cold, windy days, we had beautiful weather all the way and only on one day were we prevented from spending our time on deck due to the dampness caused by the salt sprays.

We reached a northern latitude of almost fifty-three degrees and were within sight range of the Aleutian Islands off the coast of Alaska, but, unfortunately, the dense fog interfered with the view. In crossing the International Date Line, we dropped Friday, September 11, from our calendar; on our homeward voyage, however, we picked up our lost day by duplicating Friday, December 4.

As we drew closer to Japan, the weather became warm, almost tropical. Our blankets and winter wraps were laid aside, the swimming tank was erected for the children, and the officers donned their white uniforms. On the morning of September 16, we steamed into the Bay of Tokyo on which is situated Yokohama, the chief seaport of Japan. This bay is enclosed by two huge breakwaters and a large iron pier; from the latter a railroad connects with Tokyo, the capital of Japan, seventeen miles away. It was almost noon when we were finished with the preliminaries attendant upon the landing of a vessel—namely, quarantine and immigration inspection.

Soon after landing we found ourselves on the way to Tokyo in a lean, swiftly-moving electric train, similar to the Chicago "L," but elevated only part of the way on embankments. Clusters of Japanese houses, low and unpainted, could not fail to attract notice as we moved along. The stations along the road were modern in every respect, but the signs or names of the places were printed in Japanese—a novel sight for an American. In Tokyo we received direction from the reliable Japanese Travel Service, and although our chauffeur spoke only Japanese, we were fortunate in having with us a Catholic gentleman, formerly of San Francisco, who spoke the English perfectly.

They took us to the Imperial Palace, to a number of government buildings, temples, parks, the Catholic University conducted by the Jesuit Fathers, and other places of interest. The War Museum, a building rich in architectural beauty, portrays the history of the Japanese wars in pictures; cannon and other artillery are also on exhibition. The lobby is most outstanding because of its native marble columns and variegated marble floor, ornate in design. The marble stairways are covered with white muslin, and before being granted admission, visitors must draw a pair of Japanese slippers over their own shoes. However, this surprise was not as great as the request to remove our shoes and put on a pair of heel-less slippers before we were allowed to enter a temple, the largest in Tokyo. Idols and ornaments of gold and bronze are displayed on the altars. The hangings are made of heavily-brocaded gold cloth. Costly silk tapestries adorn the walls and beautiful lanterns are suspended from the ceiling. I was quite startled to see a foreigner offer incense and ko-tow before one of the idols, but what impressed me most in this temple was the display of urns containing the ashes of prominent deceased Japanese. At the present time cremation is a law of Japan.

We also went to the business section of the city and were taken through the Mitskushi Department Store which may be considered a rival of the department stores in Chicago and Milwaukee. It even surpasses these insofar as it has a beautifully-arranged roof garden with trees, flowers, fountains, and garden benches for the convenience of patrons who find this a cool spot during the extreme heat of the summer. From this point we had a wonderful view of Tokyo and its suburbs. A high fence with long, sharp-inverted pickets encloses the roof garden, a safeguard made necessary in order to prevent suicides. The pagans of Japan prefer death to disgrace, and suicide is common.

The modest and simple manner of the beautiful girls employed in the store was very striking. In form, however, the Japanese are not so elegant. A large percentage are bandy legged, due to being carried astride their mother's back in their infancy. The custom of squatting, which is peculiar to the Japanese, is another cause for their having crooked legs. At the present time a movement is on foot to do away with both customs. In Japan the Emperor's word is law; his subjects adhere to him with the most steadfast loyalty—the predominant virtue of the race. Were the Emperor to issue an edict today abolishing a thousand-year-old custom, tomorrow no man, woman, or child under his dominion would think of following the old practice. This devotion and loyalty to the Emperor has unified the kingdom and is the secret of Japan's forward strides. In union there is strength.

It was nearing five o'clock when we bade farewell to the kind Japanese gentleman who had acted as our interpreter during the afternoon and who seemed pleased to have had an opportunity of reviewing his English. Before taking leave, Mr. Sakata pointed toward heaven and said to us, "Sisters, the next time we meet, it will be up there."

On the morning of September 18, we arrived at Kobe. The buildings of this city, too, are modern, and in order to give us a glimpse of real Japan, our guide took us to a village five hundred years old. The houses, small and unpainted, are built very closely together in irregular fashion. There is no place for vegetation, although here and there a tree has managed to survive. In the shopping district the streets are so narrow that a canvas is drawn from one roof to another across the street as a protection against the sun and rain. The stores are overloaded with merchandise of every sort and description, and we became aware of the fact that the Japanese know well how to crowd many people and many things into a small area.

In Kobe we visited a shrine or temple where Shinto Priests were officiating. Their vestments were of a beautiful blue and white silk; they wore a high black biretta and their shoes of wood were black and highly polished. We arrived toward the end of the ceremony and remained outside to watch the priests pass in procession on their way from the shrine. One remained in the building to serve rice wine to a number of gentlemen who had made a substantial offering.

We stopped at an old Japanese cemetery—slightly larger than a city lot—crowded with old tombstones. Members of one family are buried in the same plot of ground, one above the other. The cemetery in question is about five hundred years old, and the living descendants are able to trace their ancestry back to that period and even farther.

Our guide next took us to a government elementary school where we received a cordial welcome. We observed arithmetic classes, a manual training class for girls of sixth-grade age, a fourth-grade sewing class, and a first-grade singing class in which the tots were being taught action songs. Order and cleanliness prevailed throughout the school, and it was a pleasure to watch the four hundred children leave the building in a very orderly manner.

Toward the end of our tour we were taken up Mount Rocco, the highest in Kobe. Round and round we went, up and up, in our motor car, meanwhile gazing down into the ravines rich in vegetation or looking up at mountain peaks thickly covered with pine and other evergreen trees, until we reached the summit, three thousand feet above sea level. From this point we could view the entire city of Kobe, and across the bay we could see Osaka, the largest commercial city of Japan, as well as Kyota, the former capital.

The next morning found us surrounded by the beautiful islands of the Inland Sea—islands of every shape and size, some inhabited by fisher folk, and many terraced and cultivated to the very top. Throughout the day we lingered on the steamer deck, sailing in and out among these mountainous islands, eager to get the entire view. At dusk our vessel sailed between Shimonseki and Moji, both commercial cities situated on opposite islands. To see on either side of us, an electrically-lighted city with moving trains and vehicles created the impression of passing through fairyland. Oriental electric signs added to the picture, and there was present every evidence of busy city life.

On the following day, September 20, our vessel anchored at Nagasaki, Japan, and took on coal. It was a piteous sight to see women unloading the junks which carried the coal. These women worked steadily for several hours, and when finished, some washed their hands and face hastily in the dirty water of the sea before eating the scanty lunch they had brought with them.

At Nagasaki we visited the Cathedral, a simple structure built according to mission style; we also visited an orphanage conducted by the French Sisters of the Holy Childhood.

Soon we were again sailing the ocean blue enroute to Shanghai. Arriving there at 4:00 p.m., September 21, I bade farewell to my two companions and was directed by Father

Schulz, S.V.D., to the Convent School of the Sacred Heart, where accommodations had been provided. It was here that I experienced for the first time the sincere kindness of heart and the genuine hospitality which characterizes the missionaries throughout the Orient. Mother Nourry with several of the Sisters accorded me a hearty welcome. They surely have a knack for making a visitor feel at home.

Without delay I completed my plans for sailing to Tsingtao and arranged to leave the following morning on the SS. SANDVIKIN, a Norwegian ship sailing under English auspices. This gave me one free day in Shanghai of which I spent the morning with Mother Nourry, a veteran in the foreign mission fields of China and Japan. She is well-acquainted with our Sisters since they stop with her whenever business brings them to Shanghai; in turn, Mother enjoys spending part of the summer vacation in Tsingtao. This good Mother was happy to tell me all the good things she knew about our school. She thinks our Sisters are doing wonderful work in Tsingtao.

Of special interest was her account of the terrible earthquake which occurred in Japan in 1923. She was missioned in Tokyo at the time and had just completed her building program when the quake came. The work of years was annihilated with a single stroke, but this staunch woman, grateful to God for sparing the lives of the Sisters and the children, and full of confidence in His divine providence, with a courageous heart was ready to start anew. With the financial aid of the Japanese, who of their own volition offered assistance, the Sisters were able to erect even better buildings than they had before the earthquake.

While telling many interesting personal experiences, Mother Nourry showed me through the building, a school for foreign girls. We next went over to their little Chinese primary school. Immediately I was impressed by the perfect order and the studious attitude of the children who were clad in delph-blue gowns. The color seemed odd, but later I learned it is prescribed for the schools throughout China. High school boys wear a khaki suit similar to a scout uniform. Rich and poor children dress alike in school. Mrs. Chao, the principal of the Chinese school, is most efficient. She is a convert and has brought her husband into the Church.

In the afternoon, accompanied by the mother of one of the American pupils, I visited a middle school conducted by the Sisters of Loretto of Nerinx, Kentucky. From there we went to Zi-Ka-Wei to visit an orphanage in charge of the Helpers of the Holy Souls for the past seventy years. In this institution the Sisters devote their lives to the care of Chinese orphans who in their infancy were discarded by their parents. This practice is still common in parts of China. Each year hundreds of infants, especially girls, are thrown into the rivers or disposed of in some other way. Since it is known that the Sisters accept the infants readily, the relatives do not hesitate to bring them. The Sisters also employ coolies to pick up abandoned children and bring them to the orphanage. Many arrive just in time for baptism. The day I was there, the Sisters showed me about one-hundred-fifty tiny infants, each one neatly tucked under a red quilt in an individual crib.

In Zi-Ka-Wei I had my first rickshaw ride. The auto carried no license for the Chinese city, and for that reason the chauffeur waited for us at the city limits. I was somewhat surprised to hear the kind lady who accompanied me speak sharply to the rickshaw coolie when he insisted on more pay. When he was settled, she turned to me and said, "Don't be shocked, but we cannot let them take advantage of us. These coolies try to overcharge Americans, thinking the latter do not know better." However, I had been warned previously in this regard. If you give a coolie a dollar instead of a dime, he may press you for more in the belief that it is a good money-making opportunity. Consequently, tourists are instructed to give coolies no more than their due with perhaps a slight tip.

The next day found the SS. SANDVIKIN sailing the Yellow Sea bound for Tsingtao. Because of the yellow mud discharged into it by the Hwang-Ho, or Yellow River, the water actually is yellow for a considerable distance out from the land. All went well until the last day of the journey, September 24, when the sea became stormy and the small SS. SANDVIKEN pitched and rocked on the turbulent waters. On awakening that morning my thoughts were far from seasickness, for at this stage of the journey I felt immune. But, alas! I was not to be spared a taste of real seasickness, even though it was for only a few hours.

We entered the beautiful Tsingtao Harbor two hours behind schedule, or about five o'clock when the lights were beginning gradually to appear. The houses built on verdant hills and bluffs with their roofs of red tile and the majestic St. Michael Cathedral towering over all, form a picture strikingly beautiful. It was close to seven before we were ready to land. You can imagine my delight when I caught a glimpse of our Sisters on the wharf; they waved a welcome from afar. Soon the boat drew sufficiently near so that I could call each one by name. The girls of St. Joseph Middle School greeted me with the National Anthem of God's own country followed by a melody of God's other country. And there were cheers given in real American fashion! The strains of the STAR-SPANGLED BANNER and all that followed, elicited from an English passenger, the remark that that must be a real American and not a Chinese school even though the girls sang a Chinese song. Our meeting was indeed a happy one. Besides our own dear Sisters and students, Father John Weig, S.V.D., of the Catholic Mission, and Miss Gertrude Chen, the principal of our school, were present. The rest I will leave to your imagination.

Although I knew Tsingtao to be a modern city, I had never pictured it so beautiful. It is called the "Pearl of the Orient," and we are told its beauty is unrivalled in all China. It is the only Chinese city in which the streets are laid out according to a plan. Until 1897 Tsingtao was an insignificant fishing village, but the following year the city was leased to the Germans for ninety-nine years as part of the restitution demanded for the death of two Missionaries. In 1914, at the beginning of the World War I, the Japanese overpowered the German soldiers on guard there and took the city. It remained under Japanese control until 1922 when it was returned to China in accordance with the terms of the Washington Arms Conference. By special agreement, the Japanese retained certain rights; these often lead to difficulties and misunderstandings, but the Chinese usually give in so as to avoid trouble. Of the 270,000 residents, 13,500 are Japanese and 2,500 are foreigners.

I was surprised to learn that Sister M. Callista [Messmer] was recovering from a siege of severe illness which could have proved fatal; by the time I left Tsingtao, she was about her duties as usual. I found the other Sisters well and very contented with their missionary career. Of course, there was much to talk about, and I was plied with questions concerning our dear Mother M. Stanislaus and all the dear ones at home. It was a pleasure to find the Sisters so interested in whatever pertained to the Motherhouse. In turn, they had much to relate about China and their work in Tsingtao.

During the first few days of my visit, I observed the Chinese girls and was edified at their good conduct and studious manner. The enrollment is slightly more than two hundred, and the courses offered are those of a junior and senior high school. The Sisters acknowledge frankly that they would rather teach Chinese than American girls because the former apply themselves so well. Our school building, as most of you know, is a modern American structure, and after visiting schools in Peking, Tientsin, and elsewhere, I can truly say that not one of the middle school buildings I saw can compare with ours. The Sisters live in the school building just as do the Sisters at Alvernia and at Madonna high schools.

Our school must conform strictly to government regulations, and for this reason must have a Chinese principal; Miss Chen, who attended college in Cleveland, Ohio, and also Washington, D.C., is proving herself very capable. A number of subjects are taught by Chinese teachers. Science and physical education are being stressed throughout China, and each day the girls spend some time on the playground drilling under the direction of a well-trained gymnasium teacher. During my stay, a big athletic meet took place at a public playground, and our girls did remarkably well.

St. Joseph Middle School is regarded as one of the best of its kind in China. The three Chinese girls attending Mount Mary College in Milwaukee are proof of the good work being done by our Sisters in Tsingtao. Girls from Tsingtao, Tsinan, Tientsin, Peiping, and surrounding places comprise the student body; many of these girls are from upper-class families. In China, servants are employed even by families of the middle class.

There is scarcely a family without its amah or woman to take care of the children; in fact, in many families each child has its own amah who waits on the youngster hand and foot. As a consequence, it is not surprising that the Sisters find it somewhat difficult at times to get a girl to make her own bed and to help with the cleaning of the dormitories; but, regardless of their family background, all must and do submit.

Among the two hundred girls attending our school, thirty-three are Catholic, and of these, fourteen have been converted while attending the school. At present, a number are looking forward to the happy day of their baptism and others are patiently awaiting the permission of their parents to join the Church.

The devotion and religious fervor of these girls is admirable. The Catholic girls lead religious lives, and most of them receive Holy Communion every day. Morning and evening prayers as well as Communion prayers are said in common; visits to the Blessed Sacrament are frequent; and the Way of the Cross is made in common once a week. In every way they give evidence of being most sincere in the practice of their religion.

I have in mind a girl who, after she became acquainted with the teachings of our Holy Faith, went home one day and without mincing words, upbraided the family for their heathen practices. You can imagine that this caused quite an upset in the home, and the girl had to be warned by the Sisters. She was more zealous than prudent.

Another promising young lady was happy to tell me she had her father's permission to be baptized at Christmas. When asked if she intended to become a religious, she smiled and said she did but had as yet not mentioned this to her father. After she is a member of the Church, she will begin to coax for the second permission—namely, to enter the convent. This girl has a knowledge of English sufficient to enable her to read such books as LUCIUS FLAVIUS and THE WONDERFUL FLOWER OF WOXINDON, both by Father Spillman, S.J. Thus, more by example than by word, are the Sisters striving to bring the Chinese to Christ.

According to government regulations, religion may not be taught during school hours, but one of the Priests conducts a class in religion every Sunday. In a message to the Sisters, the Apostolic Delegate to China exhorted them not to become over-anxious in regard to the number of baptisms; for the present it suffices if these girls carry the lessons taught by the Sisters into their pagan environments. He recommended that the Sisters uphold Chinese customs. We had the honor of a visit with His Excellency during our stay.

While I am writing, I am thinking of two girls from Tientsin—sisters—who were converted through our Sisters and whose relatives were much opposed to their baptism. Now their father reads Catholic literature and prays the Hail Mary every day. They have high hopes that he will embrace the faith. Their mother and their aunt, the latter a medical doctor who spent nine years in the States, are also very kindly disposed toward the Sisters.

The music department of St. Joseph Middle School has developed far beyond expectation. Even though Sister M. Eustella [Bush] assists in the teaching of music, Sisters M. Fides [Bethke] and Eugenda [Kessler] have so many pupils that they are obliged to refuse new applicants. One little girl cried bitterly because the Sisters could not accept her as a violin pupil. The Sisters also have charge of a large mixed choir of which His Excellency, the Most Reverend George Weig, S.V.D., can be justly proud. The following appeared in the December 18, 1936, issue of *The Lumen*, a Peiping publication:

> 'On Wednesday, December 23, at 7 p.m. Eastern China time, the choir of St. Michael's Cathedral of this city and the pupils of St. Joseph Middle School are to give a Christmas concert which will be broadcast over the local station of the Min-chung Educational Bureau. The program will consist of hymns and selected parts of the Mass to be sung on Christmas. Brother John M. Peng, Principal of the Marist Brothers' School, will supplement the program with explanations in Chinese for the benefit of non-Catholic auditors.'

A thoroughly Catholic atmosphere envelops the entire Catholic Mission Unit in Tsingtao. The Most Reverend George Weig, S.V.D., the Vicar Apostolic of the Vicariate, is a man of high ideals. The beautiful new St. Michael Cathedral will be a perpetual monument to his zeal for the glory of God. The religious as well as the educational development of the mission must be a great comfort to His Excellency. One of his principal aims is to foster higher education among the Chinese, and the progress of St. Joseph Middle School is proof of the success which is attending his endeavors. At present, the Bishop is making plans for a middle school for boys to be conducted by the Brothers of Mary. He sees great possibilities for the future of China if the Church is successful in converting the people of the upper class because their example will influence the poorer classes.

Closely associated with the Bishop is the Reverend John Weig, S.V.D., pastor of the congregation. Father Weig came to

Tsingtao thirty-eight years ago when Tsingtao was a mere fishing hamlet; the growth of the city and his missionary zeal have kept pace. Now, after his strength has been well spent in the vineyard of the Master, Father Weig cherishes the hope of spending his declining years solely in the service of the poor and unfortunate.

At present, he ministers to a colony of lepers located several miles from Tsingtao. With the exception of four catechumens who are under instruction, every leper in the colony is a Catholic. When a new patient enters the colony, he is promptly informed by the others that he must take instructions because everyone there is Catholic. Sister M. Lucilla [Doffing], Sister M. Callista [Messmer], and I accompanied Father Weig on one of his bi-weekly visits when he hears confessions and distributes Holy Communion to the lepers. It was most edifying to note the devotion of these poor people as they knelt in the yard to make their thanksgiving. The chapel is too small to accommodate all at one time. When Father was finished distributing Holy Communion, he recited the prayers of thanksgiving aloud with the communicants; he had done the same with the prayers of preparation. Formerly, discontentment reigned among these unfortunate lepers and many committed suicide; now the peace and contentment of their souls is reflected in their faces. Father took us to see Anthony who was in a dying condition. When Father said, "Anthony will soon go to heaven; I anointed him this morning," the poor man looked up at us and smiled feebly. He was a terrible sight to behold. One of the lepers wrote the names of Jesus and Mary for us by guiding the brush with his mouth—his poor diseased hands are no longer able to steady the brush.

When we left, the lepers grouped around the gate and with smiles and bows, bade us farewell. We had our picture taken with the entire group and several asked Father Weig for one of the snapshots. In jest, one of the Sisters warned me not to show the picture at home or people would be afraid to come near me. Yes, leprosy is a loathsome disease and inspires fear and disgust, but the medical profession has established beyond a doubt that it is not as contagious as is commonly believed. Of course, it is necessary to take precautions, and in my case, I had even my shoes disinfected before entering my room. I was not afraid, but safety first!

The Catholic Mission of Tsingtao has certainly prospered and borne rich fruit. The Franciscan Missionaries of Mary, known as the "White Sisters," have a school for foreign girls as well as a dispensary which also serves as a small hospital. One of these Sisters regularly goes into the slums and villages to minister to the sick and the dying. I was told that she alone has baptized five thousand souls. Sister also visits the prisons, and on one occasion I was permitted to accompany her to an opium prison near Tsingtao. On that particular day she spoke to the prisoners—of course, in Chinese—about the Pope being the Vicar of Christ on earth. She carried with her a large picture showing Our Lord above, and the Holy Father and St. Peter's at Rome below. This picture was hung within view of the prisoners while she spoke. At the conclusion of her ten-minute talk, Sister said a prayer aloud and asked those who desired literature to come forward. A number responded. She also distributed medicine.

When Sister was ready to leave, one prisoner took down the picture, rolled it, and handed it to her; another took care of the door, both happy as school boys to be of service.

In these prisons, between thirty and forty men are lodged in a small room and since there were sixteen such rooms, it was necessary to repeat the instructions that many times. Sister made nothing of this; her one ambition is to bring souls to God. She told us of a prisoner who desired baptism, because, as he said, he was "in danger of death." The man seemed healthy and Sister could find no reason for hastening the reception of the sacrament. Then one of the other prisoners told her this man wanted to be baptized so that he could go straight to heaven after hanging himself. He is still among the living but is receiving instructions in the Faith.

Another part of the Catholic Mission of Tsingtao is a primary school for boys under the direction of native Marianist Brothers. The White Sisters conduct the primary school for girls. St. Joseph Middle School for Chinese girls is our portion of the unit, and it blends in harmoniously with the other activities of the mission.

The religious spirit in our school is most edifying. Each morning at six o'clock, the Sisters with the Catholic girls are in the chapel for Holy Mass and Communion. One of the servants serves the Mass while the others occupy the front pew. Chinese have a habit of chanting their prayers, and to a newcomer from America, this manner of praying is distracting. At first one is amused, later annoyed, and finally resigned.

Besides the Catholic activities mentioned, the Sisters from Steyl, Holland, have a chapel of Perpetual Adoration located near the seashore and within walking distance of our school.

The Franciscan Fathers have a rest house near the sea. "St. Bonaventure," as it is called, is a well-constructed modern building where tired and overworked missionaries can enjoy the benefit of invigorating sea breezes. Our Sisters, too, have their little nooks where, secluded from the inquisitive eyes of the passerby, they can watch the ebb and flow of the tide, enjoy the warm sunshine, and inhale the refreshing winds from the sea. Of course, since school is in session six full days a week with very few intermissions for holidays, the Sisters have few opportunities for such outings.

Each summer brings thousands of people to the shores of Tsingtao. On account of its mild climate, the city is a growing summer resort and several large modern hotels offer accommodations for tourists. One hotel, known as the Edgewater Mansion, is so constructed that each room has a private veranda. While we were being shown through, I casually remarked to the Chinese clerk in the office that the name reminded me of the Edgewater Beach Hotel in Chicago. Smilingly, he told me that the name was prompted by the one in Chicago. A man connected with the Edgewater Mansion also has an interest in the Edgewater Beach.

Tsingtao lies in the northern latitude of thirty-six degrees on a parallel with Tokyo and San Francisco. In summer, which begins about the middle of July and continues until the end of August, the temperature seldom rises above ninety-one, but the humidity is oppressive. In winter, the Fahrenheit thermometer seldom drops below twenty-three degrees. January and February are the coldest months, but even then, an extra outdoor wrap is not necessary in the sun. September and October are regarded as the most beautiful months of the year; to this I can testify.

Besides being a summer resort, Tsingtao is advantageously located as a distributing center and a port city.

The industrial development is due partly to the fact that large quantities of raw material from the Shantung Province can be conveniently transported to Tsingtao. This likewise accounts for the many factories, most of which are owned by the Chinese. The standard of wages is low, but the people are honest and hard working.

Through the kindness of the father of one of our pupils, I was taken through a large cotton mill where I saw cotton converted from the raw material into the finished product of thread or cloth, including the dyeing. Children who appeared no older than twelve or fourteen years were among the employees in this mill.

I also visited a needle and a match factory. In both places the employees work in dark, dingy, and poorly-ventilated rooms. In the match factory where children form a large proportion of the employees, the surroundings are particularly pathetic.

Tsingtao likewise has two egg condensing factories, both surprisingly clean. The process of condensing eggs is most interesting. Shipment of this commodity is made to all parts of the world, including the United States.

I was told by a gentleman of the School Board that China has a Child Labor Law, but because of the trouble with Japan, its enforcement is being delayed. Childhood in China is much like that in any other land, but in those sections where abject poverty reigns, half-starved youthful countenances plainly portray that these children have known little of childhood's joys and pleasures.

Factories operate seven days a week since Sunday is not observed in that pagan country. In the cotton mill, I inquired as to the salary and was told it varies from thirty to seventy cents Mex a day, or about nine to twenty-one cents in our money. It is true, the Chinese can live on much less than we; they require less for food, clothing, and home furnishings, but wages are very low, and the misery, poverty, and wretchedness in many parts is appalling. Nevertheless, the Chinese are a contented race and are satisfied to take things as they come.

Other places of interest in Tsingtao were the Seaside Park with its aquarium of tropical fish, the American settlement known as "Iltis Huk" where Americans of the larger cities have their summer homes, the abandoned German forts, the International Cemetery, the Japanese temple, the Shantung University, the Strand Beach, the Naval Pier, the Administration Building, and several schools and hospitals.

The German forts with their guns, concrete casements, and barracks are located in an advantageous position for guarding the harbor. The Germans devoted much labor and money to the development and fortification of Tsingtao and its surroundings and made the city practically what it is today. The hills and mountains of other parts of China are bare and bereft of vegetation, but not those at Tsingtao. Expensive fertilizer was imported, trees planted, and today verdant hills and bluffs greet the visitor as he enters the bay.

It was during the month of November that I visited the International Cemetery where lie the German soldiers who fell in 1914 when the Japanese took possession of the city. Red roses were in full bloom on their graves and I brought some home to Mother.

A visit to the Japanese temple was very interesting. This temple, built according to ancient style, has numerous archways called torii. A torii is an emblem of the Shinto religion.

The Japanese Catholics of Tsingtao have a neat little church in charge of the S.V.D. Fathers. Before entering, we were politely asked to remove our shoes but on second thought, the kind pastor, Father Babej, permitted us to keep them on. This removing of shoes is the Japanese way of keeping dirt out of a building.

Open air laundries, kitchens, restaurants, tailor shops, barber shops, and dental parlors are not uncommon sights in the streets of Chinese cities, even Tsingtao. A certain woman seems to have a monopoly on the corner near the school where she regularly sets up her portable tailor shop. The material is spread on the sidewalk to facilitate cutting; after a garment is cut, the seamstress seats herself on the little stool she carries with her and begins to ply the needle. Her laundry, which evidently was washed in the creek nearby before she began her tailoring, hangs on a line directly to the rear.

Frequently the restaurant owner carries his kitchen and dining room equipment on either end of his long shoulder pole. In the twinkling of an eye he can set up shop anywhere, and with the aid of his charcoal stove, begin the preparation of a meal which, taken from a Chinese standpoint of palatability, puts many a housewife to shame. With his forbidden-looking razor and without soap or cream, the barber, practicing his trade in the street is, indeed, a novel sight, but he is surpassed by the walking dentist—by no means painless—who goes about looking for customers among the crowds. A tooth is extracted, the mouth washed with a solution, and off goes the dentist in quest of further trade.

To watch the people buying and selling in the streets is truly amusing. I have heard it said that the only people who can beat the Jews in bargaining are the Chinese, who haggle over prices even amongst themselves. A minor transaction—such as, the purchase of a fish—which would take us only a few minutes, might take a Chinese merchant and his customer a half hour. Time means nothing to most people in China.

The cement walk in front of our school is used for the drying of peanuts, pumpkin seeds, vegetables, and other commodities. These articles are spread out, and the owner, like a shepherd, keeps guard close by. Pedestrians remain undisturbed over not being able to use the sidewalk; they simply take to the road and expect chauffeurs and rickshaw coolies to keep out of their way.

South of our school is a tenement settlement which I will term Chinatown; whether or not it is the correct name, I do not know. Every large city has a slum district; it is not surprising that Tsingtao should have its Chinatown.

I was desirous of obtaining a closer view of this settlement, and one day, in company with one of the Sisters, I walked through the narrow streets. Neglect and disease in human form came out to greet us. It takes little to attract a crowd in China, and soon men and women, young and old, appeared on every side, gazing at us in bewilderment. The misery, which always accompanies squalor, was everywhere apparent. We met vendors who advertised their presence by the sound of peculiar instruments. One of them reminded me of the Indian tom-tom. It was hard to realize that our beautiful school, with its neatly-kept surroundings, was scarcely a block away.

In the immediate vicinity of this Chinatown and, consequently, also of our school, is a theatre, and the Chinese music which forms part of their programs, gives free entertainment to our Sisters several times a week.

There are other slums on the outskirts of the city. I passed through some of them hurriedly but took particular note of the miserable huts which serve as dwellings.

The opposite extreme is the home of two of our students whose father is a retired lithographer of Shanghai. The beauty of their home, a modern two-story building surrounded by a park, is a sharp contrast to the poverty and disorder of Chinatown. On one side of the house a tile terrace overlooks the park. The oak-paneled parlor and dining room are furnished with substantial and massive furniture, including a built-in radio; the decorations are few, but costly and artistic; the dining room contained a cupboard for cut glass, and the adjoining room one for silver.

According to the fashion of the Chinese, we were invited for tea, but it proved to be a delicious Chinese luncheon, delicately and tastily served. The mother, a most charming hostess, took her place at the head of the table. The two girls took part in the luncheon and just beamed with joy in the thought that the Sisters were visiting their home. Immediately after the meal, the servant removed the beautiful white linen tablecloth together with the padding and replaced it with a lace cover; the chairs were put in place, the doilies on the back of the chairs arranged, and within a few moments, the room was in perfect order.

Our hostess took us to the second floor to see the bedrooms and sitting rooms, all beautifully furnished. The three individual bathrooms were of colored tile, one green, one amber, and one peach. The fixtures were of the same color, and everything was spotless. In the wardrobes, a row of gowns and suits hung in perfect order with shoes, well-polished, standing beneath. A table stood in a large open space at the head of the stairway, and the only son of the family, together with a cousin who makes his home with them, were preparing class work for the following day.

It is contrary to Chinese custom to take visitors to the kitchen, but we caught a glimpse of it when the waiter opened the door to bring in the food. The walls appeared to be of white tile and judging from the manner in which the meal was served, the kitchen was just as immaculate as the rest of the house.

I had occasion to visit other families in Tsingtao whose homes, if not as elaborate and costly as the one just described, were cozy and inviting, and bespoke culture and refinement.

I found Tsingtao a most interesting city but realized that if I wanted to see China at its best, I must make a trip to Peiping for, as the saying goes: "Unless you have seen Peiping, you have not seen China." On the way, we stopped at Tsinan and paid a short visit to the Franciscan Sisters of Springfield, Illinois, who have a hospital there. They received us with the usual Franciscan cordiality, glad to have visitors from America. We likewise visited the Sisters of St. Francis, Wisconsin, at Hungkialou, a suburb of Tsinan. The Sisters were pleased to have company from their home town, and we were just as happy to meet our Milwaukee neighbors. In spite of their many pressing duties, the Sisters made our three-day stay most pleasant; they treated us as one of their own. A new school building was nearing completion and a chapel was well under way. The seven years of labor and sacrifice of these good

Sisters are already bearing rich fruit in conversions and vocations to the religious life. Our interesting visit to Hungkialou will always remain one of the pleasant memories of the trip to China.

The large flourishing mission unit at Hungkialou is under the direction of the Franciscan Fathers with the Most Reverend Bishop Jarre as Prefect Apostolic. While there, we met His Excellency, the Most Reverend Paul Yu Ping (Yee Bin), the recently-consecrated Bishop of Nanking. His Excellency, a native Chinese, studied in Rome and up to the time of his consecration, was at the head of all Catholic education in China. Catholic Action flourished under his direction, and his thoroughly Catholic principles, coupled with a spirit of unswerving patriotism, have won for him the esteem and respect of his countrymen, Catholics and pagans alike.

From Hungkialou, we went to Tsinan and boarded the train for Peiping. We had no difficulty in traveling. The trains are fairly comfortable. Second-class passengers travel in compartments in Pullman sleepers. On two occasions, when a kind Chinese gentleman secured free transportation for us, we traveled first class, and for the sake of the experience, we tried out the third class over a short distance. It was most interesting. Missionaries usually travel third class, which means a great saving for them. On the train we lived on fruit, mostly bananas and persimmons. We went to the diner once. Hot tea is brought to the passengers as soon as they are comfortably seated, and my companion was amused when I insisted on pouring the first cupfuls out of the window. I had more reasons than one for doing so, but later when the cup was replenished, I enjoyed its contents. Real China tea, served in real China fashion—that is, without cream or sugar—is delicious.

Peiping—formerly Peking, the capital—remains the center of attraction in China, its past glory being recalled at every stop. In this city of palaces and temples, where mighty emperors once wielded the scepter of absolute power, we spent ten profitable and enlightening days and were accorded splendid hospitality by the Sisters of the Holy Ghost who conduct the Fu Jen, a middle school for girls in connection with the Catholic University. The principal of the school, Mrs. Chang, was formerly a teacher in our school at Tsingtao, and immediately she offered, with the assistance of her husband, to direct our tours through Peiping. Mr. Pie Lun Chang, being a teacher of English in the University of China, is conversant with our language. We were pleased to accept the kind offer of Mr. and Mrs. Chang, and with the utmost courtesy and consideration, they planned a systematic itinerary so that there would be no loss of time in seeing Peiping.

My first impression of this walled and moated city was one of disappointment, but the disappointment soon gave way to wonder and even to admiration. Massive walls, pierced by thirteen gates and surmounted by many-storied towers, surround Peiping and its cities within. The Tartar City which forms the northern part consists of three enclosures, one within the other, known as the Forbidden City, the Imperial City, and the Open City. The Forbidden City in the center, itself surrounded by a triple wall, comprises the throne rooms and the audience halls of the former emperors with their living quarters on either side. Today the palace has been converted into the great National Museum and contains relics of the past glory of the rulers of China. Many of the more costly articles have been taken to Nanking to be preserved in vaults during the impending danger of war with Japan.

The second, or Imperial City, was used by the guards in former days and is now used for commercial purposes.

The Open City, the third and outermost enclosure with its markets and stores, presents a living picture of industry and a desire for material gain.

The Chinese City grew up outside the southern walls of the Tartar City and is surrounded by a separate wall. The Manchus expelled the Chinese to this southern section, but after the fall of the Manchu Dynasty and the establishment of the Republic in 1911, the class distinction between the several "cities" largely disappeared, and the people of the different castes intermingled.

Along the south wall of the Tartar City lies the Legation Quarter, the site of the official residences of the foreign ambassadors, including the one from the United States. This section played an important part in the Boxer Rebellion of 1900 when the Chinese made a last desperate effort to expel foreigners. The Legation Quarter has its own administration.

Many of the buildings in the Tartar City of Peiping were the homes of Manchu princes and nobles and follow on a minor scale the plan of architecture used for the Imperial Palace— that is, a hall for religious ceremonies, a hall for audience purposes, and a private residence. This threefold building idea originated in ancient times, centuries ago, when the temple was the palace and the palace was the temple.

The spacious parks and once beautiful gardens of Peiping, formerly used exclusively by the emperor and his family, are now open to the general public. The Central Park is one of the finest and best-planned parks of the city and is famous for its altar of grain and agriculture. It contains many huge pots of large goldfish, some beautiful, but others unlovely and even grotesque, with large bulging eyes and peculiarly-shaped heads. I have never seen so many goldfish at one time and can testify that China is the land of goldfish.

The Winter Palace, known as the "Pei Hai" (Bay High) which means North Sea, is surrounded by lotus-strewn lakes. During the time of the emperors, these lakes were used for skating, skiing, and other winter sports. Rough places in the ice were made smooth by hot irons. A huge white dagoba towers above one of the main buildings. We climbed to its summit and were rewarded with a wonderful panoramic view of Peiping, particularly of the Forbidden City and its numerous buildings with their shimmering yellow tile roofs. The famous dragon screen with its eight tiled dragons, each of a different color, stands guard near the Winter Palace. The dragon is the emblem of China, and for this reason some of the catechumens do not approve of the representation of St. Michael stepping on the head of the dragon. To them it appears as though he were stepping on China.

About seven miles west of Peiping is the New Summer Palace built by the late Empress-Dowager when she was almost sixty years of age. The Old Summer Palace was destroyed by the British and French in the Allied War of 1860. The funds were low, but there was money on hand to build up a strong navy, and this money the Old Empress appropriated to carry out her building program. She erected a palace with buildings and courts most magnificent and enchanting. There are lakes, lotus ponds, rare trees, pavilions, mountains, bridges—among the latter the famous seventeen-arch bridge—in fact, nothing was lacking to make the palace a beautiful and attractive dwelling for the Empress of China. However, we are told it cannot compare with the exquisite and costly beauty of the Old Summer Palace. The new palace played a very important part in the history of China because in 1894, only a few years after it was built, China suffered defeat at the hands of the Japanese, primarily because her navy was weak. Had the navy revenue been used for its original purpose, in all probability China would not have been defeated. The palace is wittingly called: "A woman's fifty-million-dollar whim."

In the principal courtyards are large works of art in bronze—namely, incense burners, dragons, deer, birds, and fish; two huge bronze lions, cast about seventeen hundred years ago, grace one of the courtyards. The Chinese tell us that an emperor refused an offer of two million dollars for these lions. Many of these figures are covered with a wire netting to protect them from souvenir hunters.

At the top of the mountain, in back of the dwelling, stands a building known as "The Temple of Ten Thousand Buddhas," so named because the tiles of which it is made each represent a shadow niche with its seated Buddha. The renowned bronze cow, according to Chinese mythology, serves to keep the flood tides within their bounds. A covered gallery stretches through a mile of beautiful gardens with pavilions of marble, teakwood, and brightly-hued tile nestling among the pines on the hillsides.

The Summer Palace, now falling into decay, has been considered the crowning jewel of Peiping, but in point of architecture, the Temple of Heaven is considered superior.

This Temple of Heaven is a circular building with a triple-roofed tower covered with blue-glazed tiles and supported by teakwood decorated with red lacquer and gold. It is built on top of a triple-terraced marble altar, and the walls and carved lattice work are vermilion in color. The artistically carved ceiling is coated with gold and in the center contains the emblems of the emperor and empress—namely, the dragon and the phoenix. The emperor came to this hall—a hall, indeed, it is because there really is nothing in it—on New Year's Day to offer prayers to the gods for peace, blessing, and prosperity during the new year. The Chinese call it the Temple of the Happy New Year.

Not far from this temple is the Altar of Heaven where the New Year sacrifices were offered. This is a huge marble platform, well preserved, and beautiful to behold. It was remarked that this would be a suitable place for a Eucharistic Congress, the main altar to be erected at the top of this so-called Altar of Heaven. The space around the altar would be large enough to accommodate thousands. Who knows but the day will come when the one true God, in the Sacrament of His Love, will be adored and honored by His yellow children on the spot where pagan worship was once practiced. At present, the temple and the altar are nothing more than relics.

In Shanghai, the Sisters asked me to tell them something about Peiping, and I mentioned the Temple of Heaven. Immediately good old Mother Hayden whispered, "The temple of the devil!" with emphasis on the last word.

The Western Hills are famous for their temples and shrines. We went into the Temple of the Sleeping Buddha, a large bronze reclining figure twenty feet long occupying the last of a series of halls. Cupboards alongside the walls contain many pairs of enormously large shoes for the use of Buddha should he begin to walk in his sleep. Almost every temple is built in such a way that one must pass through two or more halls before reaching the main temple. Some of the halls contain heathen images; before the first is a large screen which obstructs the view from the outside. The purpose of this screen is to keep the evil spirit away.

To express a desire was to realize its fulfillment. Our kind friends knew we were eager to see the Great Wall of China and arranged the trip for Sunday, October 11. Bright and early we started out and alighted at the Green Dragon Bridge (Ch'ing Lung Ch'iao) near the Nankow Pass, forty miles from Peiping. Our party consisted of Mr. and Mrs. Chang, Sister M. Lucilla, and myself. Mr. Chang, as the protector of our little group, chose to walk; Mrs. Chang rode a donkey; while Sister M. Lucilla and I took a sedan chair to the mountain, ascending the wall on foot.

The first sight of the wall falls short of expectation, and one is inclined to ask why it is considered the "Eighth Wonder of the World." But, when weary and footsore, we paused for a respite after following its serpentine twists and turns, we began to realize why this stupendous piece of masonry has gone down in history as the greatest barrier ever constructed by human hands. It measures about seventeen hundred miles, or the distance between New York and Denver. The wall missed the aim of the builders to keep out the northern hordes, which at a later date, molested Europe, but nevertheless, it proved a protection against less powerful foes.

Construction of the wall was begun two hundred years before the birth of Christ, if not sooner, and continued in later centuries, the greatest part of the work being done in the latter half of the fourteenth century. When construction was begun in earnest, three hundred thousand troops, as well as all the criminals in the land, were pressed into service, and by the time the wall was finished, probably no less than one million persons had been employed in the work. It is said that so many workers died as a result of the hard task that their corpses were simply thrown into the embankment; this has given rise to the grim saying that the wall is the longest cemetery in the world. The width is sufficient to permit five or six horsemen to ride abreast, and the height varies from twenty to thirty feet. The mass of the wall is heavily-tamped earth faced on both sides with brick and at the base with stone. The mortar—its composition is now a lost art—is snowy white and binds the masonry firmly. All the material was carried up the mountains without the aid of labor-saving devices. The cubical content of the Great Wall at the Nankow Pass is estimated at 422,400 cubic feet per mile. The cost of the construction today would be at least $100,000.00 per mile.

The wall branches out into the different provinces of China like the tributaries of a mighty river, and though it has withstood the ravages of time remarkably well, it is gradually crumbling away. For the benefit of sightseers, however, portions of the wall, particularly near the Nankow and Kupehkow Passes, are kept in almost perfect repair. Turrets every hundred yards or so gave added protections, and it was in one of these that we chose to eat our picnic lunch. It was a real thrill to stand on the Great Wall and look down over the mountains.

A trip to the wall is often combined with a visit to the Ming Tombs, a burial place of thirteen emperors, which is not far away. However, since both trips could not be made in one day, we had to forego the latter. We were told the gateway, or pailou, at its approach is the most remarkable and finest piece of architecture in the country. This pailou was erected three and one-half centuries ago when Chinese building art had reached its culminating point. The marvels of architecture of which China can be justly proud are hundreds of years old. There are temples and pagodas dating back centuries before the time of Christ; it is this fact that makes Peiping so interesting. However, I shall not confine my account to a description of buildings and places, but will tell you something of the everyday life as seen in the busy streets.

I was surprised to find paved highways, carefully drained and well sprinkled, some one hundred feet in width. The side streets, on the contrary, are ill-kept and in a very unsanitary condition; they are not sprinkled, even during the dusty season. This explains why so many rickshaw passengers either tie a scarf over their mouth or hold a handkerchief to the face while riding through the streets of Peiping. The many trains of tawny-haired camels who with their patient, even trod, continually pass to and fro carrying heavy loads of coal from the mine to the bin. The loaded carts, the heavy wheelbarrows, and the thousands of human feet, all help to powder to infinite fineness the dust which continually pours in from the Gobi Desert. Peiping and its suburbs are noted for dust storms.

As I entered the Chien Men, the main street near the Forbidden City, I took particular notice of the large ornamental wooden arch of genuine Chinese architecture; a duplicate was not far away, for, according to Chinese art, everything must be arranged in pairs. This arch is known as a "pailou," or memorial arch; its original purpose being to commemorate loyal statesmen, virtuous widows, and other people of note, and it corresponds to the triumphal arches of Europe. However, the pailous in Peiping are mostly decorative.

It is intensely interesting and almost indescribable to watch the ever-changing scene of human activity passing in and out of the large city gates. Automobiles, cabs, rickshaws, and bicycles hurry past slowly moving catafalques and wedding sedans; Peking carts, wagons, and wheelbarrows intermingle with perambulating merchandise marts and thousands of pedestrians, some of whom are accompanied by specimens of livestock. The picture is a rather humorous spectacle to Westerners like ourselves.

It is difficult to decide which are more numerous, rickshaws or bicycles. Street cars are rare. I noticed only one street car line in Peiping—a little green car running down a lane close to the place where we were staying. The rickshaw takes the place of the street car or tram as it is called in China. A coolie will paddle along all day carrying his passenger from one place to another for a few cents.

There is nothing uncommon about the bicycle except that occasionally the onlooker is awestruck at seeing a cyclist guide his wheel with one hand and with the other carry a piece of furniture or balance a high stack of loose articles.

Automobiles are not so numerous, but up-to-date cars are ever present on the main streets. It took some time to become accustomed to the traffic regulation of keeping to the left.

Accidents on the crowded streets are rare because of the severe punishment inflicted on a driver who injures a person. This is not saying, however, that chauffeurs are not reckless. Pedestrians saunter through the streets regardless of vehicles, expecting chauffeurs and rickshaw coolies to give them the right of way. Is it surprising that one is annoyed by the continuous honking of horns made necessary by these "jay walkers?"

The Peking cart, the predecessor of the rickshaw, is a small springless wagon drawn by horses or donkeys. It jolts and tosses its occupants from side to side as it passes over paved roads and also unpaved ones filled with deep ruts—ruts all the deeper because of the narrow truck wheels, purposely made narrow to prevent an accumulation of the sticky mud during the rainy season. Not infrequently, the cart driver walks alongside the horse carrying a long bamboo pole with which he prods the animals when necessary. Other forms of Peking carts provide the driver with a front seat.

Horse- or mule-drawn wagons pull through drifts of Peking dust, bricks and trunks of trees, though often the wagons are drawn by men. It is not at all unusual to see three men pulling a wagon loaded with heavy tree trunks. Modern motor trucks have a long way to go before they can replace the coolie; the machine age applies only to the West.

The wheelbarrow is a very important means of conveyance throughout China. In some interior places it is the only vehicle used and is employed to carry not only commodities, but also passengers. Sometimes the wheelbarrow is arranged on the order of a bus—that is, with a seat through the center—to provide accommodations for six or eight people. One interior town of more than a million inhabitants conveys all outside commodities from the place of purchase to their destination by means of wheelbarrows. A band from the shoulder to the handles often relieves the strain on the hands of the human "beast of burden," who must push superhuman loads over great distances. While lifting or pushing a heavy load, laborers frequently sing or hum; they select their own melody, make up the words, and repeat the homely chant over and over again.

Another largely used method of conveyance is the shoulder pole, usually of bamboo, by means of which vendors carry their wares, laborers their tools and material, and old men their cages when they take their homely birds out for an airing. There is nothing unusual about a person walking down the street carrying a bird in a cage; nor is there anything remarkable about a man keeping guard over his pet confined in a cage on a walk close by.

In connection with the street activities, we must not lose sight of the cooks, shoemakers, barbers, dentists, and others, ever ready to open shop any place and every place, wherever they can secure trade; and picture besides this the numerous shops and outdoor stands loaded with every variety of merchandise and crowded with a multitude of clerks ready and eager to serve a customer.

In Peiping we met a Miss Liu, a prospective postulant, who has charge of one of the government foundling homes. Miss Liu holds a college degree from the I.H.M. Sisters of Monroe, Michigan. It was a sad sight again to see the poor little children—many of them sick—who had been discarded by their parents. When someone wishes to dispose of a child, he merely opens the door of an aperture built into the wall and places the baby in the cradle found hanging there. The weight of the child automatically causes a bell to ring in the house of the gateman who comes and takes the child to the orphanage.

We accepted Miss Liu's invitation to meet her mother and other relatives, and I had my first Chinese dinner in her home in company with Sister M. Lucilla. The plate set before us was smaller than an ordinary saucer. Besides the chopsticks, we were given a spoon with which to help ourselves should the former prove out of the question. I suppose you are wondering which we used! The hostess kept our plate replenished and rolled pieces of the famous Peking duck into the pancake prepared for that purpose, handing it to us with chopsticks. To refuse any dish is considered a breach of etiquette; however, you are not expected to eat everything offered. Chinese menus consist of beef sinews, pig nerves, shark fins, sea cucumbers, bamboo shoots, turtle dove egg soup, bird's nest soup, century-old eggs, boluses, noodles, rice, dumplings, lotus-seed pudding, precious-eight pudding, watermelon and pumpkin seeds, and a variety of other meats and vegetables. As many as thirty courses make up a banquet. The Chinese dishes are rich and prepared with infinite care, and one is forced to marvel at the patience and time their preparation entails. No labor-saving devices are employed, and it would be sad for the country if they were ever introduced.

Upon inquiry I was told that no special form of table etiquette is required. Anything we foreigners do is all right. Allowance is made for our ignorance. This was expressed by a guide in another connection when he said in pigeon English: "'S' all right, 'S' all right; you dunno no better."

Miss Liu's mother and brothers are fervent Protestants, but she is a devout Catholic. The mother is trying to do missionary work among her friends, but she is beginning to see the beauty of the Catholic Faith. One of the brothers, a teacher in a Presbyterian middle school, passed a remark to the effect that there is more depth to the Catholic than to the Protestant religion. When the boluses, a sort of biscuit, were passed at the table, mention was made about removing the outer layer because it detracts from the appearance of the food, although the contents, a combination of ground meats and vegetables, are very palatable. To this the brother replied, "This food is like we should be—much better inside than out."

Miss Liu's is a real Chinese home. The furniture, hand-carved and beautiful, is several generations old. Her great-grandfather was very wealthy, and, according to custom, whatever is left of the wealth is handed down from generation to generation until there is nothing left. Miss Liu's generation must work for a livelihood. An elderly aunt, the deceased father's sister, makes her home with them and she has a perfect right in the home. The family must support her. Several of the boys are married, but they all live in the same compound with their mother. The compounds of the private citizens, with their courtyards, secluded gardens, and covered verandas, have a special charm and fascination of their own. Architecturally they have little of interest to offer since they are one-storied buildings all constructed on the same plan and in the same style. Ordinarily a compound is the home of an entire relationship, thus forming a clan. As each successive son marries, a new dwelling is added, and when the compound is filled, lot decides which member should establish a new compound.

One day during our stay in Peiping, we had occasion to witness a large funeral procession, that of a former statesman. A funeral is usually an eventful day for the beggars because it means a good meal, and for a few hours, a decorated green cloak thrown over their own ragged apparel. To them is assigned the task of carrying the catafalque, draped in red-brocaded silk, as well as paper effigies of servants, animals, and furniture which they believe will serve the deceased in eternity and be a hint to the gods as to his station in life. Artificial paper money is burned with the effigies.

Streamers of white flowers, representing life everlasting, were fastened to long poles and carried in the procession. Scrolls bearing complimentary remarks about the departed one were likewise borne aloft on long poles, while his picture was carried in a paper shrine. Several corps of priests, some from the Llama Temple, took part in the procession while, at intervals, a number of bands played doleful tunes.

According to custom, the mourners were dressed in white; the sons and grandsons walked before the hearse, in a semi-circular enclosure of cloth resembling unbleached muslin; the wife, daughters, and grand-daughters rode behind in individual Peking carts. Soothsayers usually set the date for burial, hence interment seldom takes place at once; in the meantime, the body is kept in a vault. The dead are not buried deep in the ground, but just a little beneath, and a cone-shaped mound is built over them; foodstuffs for the deceased are often placed on the graves. Farmers and their families are buried in their own fields. When passing in a train, one receives the impression that China is one vast graveyard because of the many graves all along the way. Superstition is so much a part of pagan China that it has left its traces on the countenances of many people, and one is saddened at the thought that paganism still holds sway over millions of souls. It is hard to understand how intelligent people, such as the Chinese are, can believe in such practices.

Peiping being the greatest educational center in China, we made use of the opportunity to get first-hand information regarding the educational status of the country. We visited the Catholic University, the University of Peking, the Chin Hwa, the Yenching University, and the National Normal School, as well as a number of middle and primary schools. The enrollment in the universities was on an average of eight hundred students each. I was astonished at the well-equipped university buildings, especially the science laboratories and libraries.

The Catholic University, under the direction of the S.V.D. Fathers, is making rapid headway. The University has extended the biology, physics, and chemistry departments to keep pace with the ever-increasing demands of the government to educate the students thoroughly along scientific lines. Much of the apparatus used in the science department is made in their own machine shop. A Chinese mechanic is able to make almost any ordinary apparatus from a catalog picture; neither patent nor copyright laws of other countries affect China. American textbooks are reprinted and sold by the hundreds, and our publishing companies can do nothing about it.

Each major science department has its own special library, but, of course, the students also have access to the general libraries.

In the medical department of the Catholic University, a French doctor with his Chinese assistant demonstrated the process of making a serum to counteract the spotted typhus which formerly made serious ravages among the missionaries. It was fascinating to watch the experiment, but I would not attempt an explanation. Suffice it to say that the brain of a guinea pig and the intestines of a louse play an important part in the preparation of the serum which has reduced to a minimum the death rate from this dreaded disease. No missionary need die of spotted typhus unless he refuses to be inoculated with this serum.

Library science is also being stressed in China. I was quite thrilled at the National Library when I picked up a card and noted that the books are cataloged according to the system used by the Library of Congress in Washington, D.C. Later I learned that this system is used in other universities throughout the country. A beautiful new library building in connection with the University of Peking has recently been completed. The librarian had just returned from the United States after completing a thorough course in library science. Almost all the university libraries provide large reading rooms, one for English and the other for Chinese literature. These rooms are usually well-occupied. Another room is devoted to newspapers of various countries. Often the newspapers are hung over a stand in the center of the room, and it is interesting to observe a row of students standing on each side busily engaged in absorbing the news of the world. Newspapers are also posted on street corners for the benefit of pedestrians who are able to read.

Our visits to the middle and primary schools were also very interesting. English is taught in all the middle schools, and it was amusing to read some of the English sentences illustrated on the blackboard. Of course, were a Chinaman to observe one of us teaching Chinese, he would have his laugh, too. Hygiene and Civics are being stressed in all the schools, middle and primary, and already the results are apparent. I made notes as we went along, but to go into further detail would make my account too lengthy. In every school we found teachers and pupils hard at work and eager to advance. China is making rapid strides educationally since 1905 when the old Empress Dowager issued an edict abolishing the antique examination system and ordering the establishment of schools for the teaching of "western learning." An ever-increasing number of China's sons and daughters is receiving a higher education. The percentage of illiteracy is very high, and it will be many years before a sufficient number of schools can be founded and teachers trained to educate the masses. However, the studious atmosphere that permeates the institutions of learning speaks well for the educational future of the nation. Another obstacle which is slowly being removed is the belief that girls do not need an education. Not many years ago a Chinaman regarded the girls of his family as non-entities. If he had only one son and three daughters, he would tell an inquirer that he had one child and three girls.

Mayor Shen of Tsingtao is outstanding in his efforts to further education. At the present time, he is particularly stressing educational methods in the primary schools and adult education. With the assistance of a member of the school board, he supervises the night schools for grown people. By having the buildings occupied during the day by the children and in the evening by the adults, he is utilizing them to the greatest possible extent. His great problem is how to reach the masses living in the villages and on the outskirts, mostly poor factory laborers. He is grateful to our Congregation for assisting Tsingtao, in particular, to reach a higher level of education.

One of the last places we visited in Peiping was the John D. Rockefeller Foundation, a large, well-equipped, up-to-date hospital with which is connected an important medical college. Just as Rockefeller accumulated his wealth by his conservative manner of living, so he believes in disposing of it conservatively—that is, in a way that will do the most good. Instead of giving small amounts to many, he came to the conclusion, through counsel with others, that it would be best to give a large amount to help the sick in neglected parts of the world, and China came under this heading. The result was the Rockefeller Foundation. I was astounded at the order and system with which this place is operated. The kitchen, both in its foreign and Chinese departments, is a model of order and cleanliness. In the offices of the Social Services Bureau, we were shown their American methods of keeping records. The buildings are well constructed and modern in appearance with just enough of the Oriental touch to make them attractive to the Chinese.

Our kind benefactors, Mr. and Mrs. Chang, would have been pleased to show us more of the city with its vast store of historical and educational wealth, but time would not permit us to remain longer. We were thankful for the opportunity afforded us and carried away from Peiping a valuable lesson on the passing of all things earthly. Once the pride and glory of a mighty empire, Peiping, with its abandoned palaces and neglected gardens, presents a sad spectacle of ruin and decay. Palaces of former princes and other members of the nobility have been sold to foreigners; famous temples have been converted into barracks and police stations; historic places have become modern restaurants and tea houses; parks, once exquisite places of beauty, have been permitted to deteriorate into places of wilderness; ancient cypress trees have been cut down and sold for kindling wood. It is beyond comprehension how the Chinese, formerly so attached to their own culture and customs, could consent to this wholesale destruction of ancient art. In view of such indifference, the outlook for the cultural future of the country is not good.

On our return trip from Peiping, we stopped at Tientsin, primarily to meet a Miss Hsia, the principal of a large and progressive middle school.

Miss Hsia, a member of our school board in Tsingtao, is deeply interested in all that concerns St. Joseph Middle School.

With a graciousness born of Chinese culture and refinement, she took us through her institution. Kind but firm, Miss Hsia's outstanding character has a wholesome influence on the young people of Tientsin who are fortunate enough to come under her jurisdiction. A woman such as she is capable of doing wonderful things for God and His Church.

Through the thoughtfulness of Miss Hsia, we were directed to several other schools, among them a large normal and a Protestant middle school. We also met Doctor Chung, the aunt of two Tsingtao students, who, together with Mrs. Chung, the girls' mother, showed us through the city of Tientsin. They took us through the various concessions of the leading nations, to two hospitals, and to the Nankai University. When we left for Tsingtao on the evening train, we felt we had covered considerable ground in a day and a half. Our hasty tour of the city was well described in a letter Doctor Chung wrote to her nieces. She said: "We flew around like people in the moving pictures."

During the remaining time of my visit, I was happy to be with our own dear Sisters in Tsingtao. Together we spent a day in the historical mountains of Laoshan thirty-five miles away. The mountains with their waterfalls and vegetation are superb. The air is considered equal to that of the Alps, and no other place in the Far East affords rundown people better possibilities to regain their health and strength. The outing to Laoshan was most delightful and special thanks is due to Mr. and Mrs. Cheng and their daughter Marianne, who accompanied us and made the necessary provisions for the trip. James Cheng, a son of the family, is a student at Marquette University, Milwaukee.

On another occasion we visited the beautiful little Tsingtao Island, which lies a short distance out in the harbor.

We crossed over in a junk, which in itself was a novel experience.

The Sisters were eager and anxious to make my stay as pleasant as possible. The principal of our school, Miss Chen, as also the teachers and the parents of some of the girls, left nothing undone to have me carry back to the States happy memories of my visit to China. Naturally, there were greetings from every side to Reverend Father Klink, whose many friends in Tsingtao want him to know that they remember him and are eagerly looking forward to the time of his next visit. Then there were greetings from our dear Sisters to one and all. They have not forgotten their fellow Sisters in America and request you to remember them and their missionary endeavors in your prayers. You would be surprised how many of you they mentioned by name. Of course, the Sisters sent very special greetings, accompanied by expressions of love and gratitude, to our dearest Mother M. Stanislaus, whom they all love and revere.

Soon it was necessary to complete arrangements for our homeward journey, and accommodations were secured on the SS. PRESIDENT LINCOLN which would bring us to San Francisco.

We left Tsingtao on November 13, the nameday of our dear Mother M. Stanislaus. Because of Mother's feast, the Sisters and girls sang hymns during Mass, and Reverend Father Weig was kind enough to give Benediction. Tommy, the cook, surprised us with a beautifully-decorated cake in honor of the occasion. He is a specialist in making cakes and other delicacies too. He takes his recipes from an English cook book.

On the way to Shanghai, we detoured in order to stop at Chumatien, a town on the Peiping-Hankow Railroad. A Sister of the Holy Ghost and a native Chinese Priest met us. In this vicariate, the Bishop, as well as all Priests, are natives. The Sister directed us to the Bishop's cart which she explained had been sent expressly for us. It was a Peking cart drawn by a horse and without a running board or steps to make entrance convenient. Finally, we were seated in the cart with bag and baggage stacked in the rear, and Sister M. Lucilla sitting on a little platform with her back to the horse and facing me. The driver walked alongside the horse, while the Priest who had met us rode in a rickshaw close by. The unpaved roads were anything but even, and we were tossed and jolted as we rode along. However, I don't suppose it was as bad as being transported in a wheelbarrow. At Chumatien, we again were accorded splendid hospitality. We were glad to have made the visit because it gave us an insight into real missionary life in China.

Our final stop was at Hankow which, together with Wuchang and Hanyang, forms the Tri-City known as Wuhan, situated near the junction of the Yangtze and Han Rivers. Hankow is a modern city, so much so, that the driveway along the river reminded me of the Lake Shore Drive in Chicago. Hankow is one of the most important cities in China and one of the richest shipping ports of the world. The Yangtze is navigable for the greater part of the year, even for ocean liners.

In Hankow we stayed at the International Hospital conducted by the White Sisters. We were surprised when a young lady called on us, for we were unacquainted in the City. She had met our Sisters in Shanghai, and when asked how she knew we were at the International Hospital, she answered, "Sister, don't you know there is no secret in China." This girl voiced what I had noticed on several occasions. She was eager to enter a convent, but her father, although a good Catholic, wanted to force her into marriage. She put up a fight and won; nevertheless, she felt sad about the whole affair. She placed her car at our disposal and accompanied us across the Yangtze to Wuchang.

We crossed in a ferry and had as a co-passenger Bishop Gubbels, O.F.M., of Ichang, a vicariate up near the Yangtze gorges. His Excellency highly recommended the young lady who accompanied us, saying she is of a religious and wealthy family in Hankow. In Wuchang, we spent an afternoon with the Sisters from La Crosse, Wisconsin. Mother M. Dominica, who had commenced the mission, had died a few weeks previous. The Sisters conduct a flourishing primary school for boys and girls, a catechumenate, and a dispensary. In the catechumenate, women and girls from the interior are instructed in our Faith. They remain with the Sisters for about three months and return to their villages after baptism. It is interesting to watch some of the Chinese women with bound feet—a practice which is dying out, although it is still being followed in some interior places—hobbling to services, or to see a lady in church praying devoutly while a little child is scampering about on the floor.

People with the most loathsome diseases come to the dispensary for relief. The Sisters are handicapped in their work through lack of dressings or bandages. They showed us the pitiable device they are using as a substitute—namely, a thin piece of muslin sewed to a piece of newspaper and fastened with strings. Sister Francis Therese, a native Chinese and a real M.D., and Sister M. Laetitia, a registered nurse, are in charge. Almost daily, dying infants are brought to the dispensary; the Sisters send many to heaven by means of the sacrament of baptism. They promised to name one for Mother M. Stanislaus, one for Sister M. Lucilla, and one for me; recently we received a letter saying that little Stanislaus, Lucilla, and Corona have been sent to heaven with strict orders as to what they should tell God in behalf of those whose name they bear. We really would have missed something very much worth-while had we omitted a visit to Wuchang.

On the following morning, November 19, the day of our departure, the Sisters took us over to Hanyang where the Sisters of Loretto have a large catechumenate for girls. Again, we were enlightened and edified. The Sisters teach the girls the art of making beautiful embroidery, specializing in vestments and other church goods. The cheerful manner of the Sisters could not fail to make an impression on any visitor. In spite of hardships and sacrifices, they are always hopeful.

The Superior of the Sisters of Loretto was eager to have us meet Bishop Galvin, who conducts a catechumenate on a large scale through a group of reliable young women. This group is the nucleus of a native community of Sisters. His Excellency took special delight in showing us his night school, a rather dingy room which has recently been improved by the addition of two or three electric light bulbs. The Bishop personally teaches catechism to adults at night.

Returning to Hankow about noon, we hastily took lunch and prepared for our departure. The White Sisters were exceedingly kind, not only at this point of our journey, but in other places as well. It was always most edifying to see these white-robed figures kneeling before the exposed Blessed Sacrament in their beautiful white chapels which form a vital part of all their institutions.

The distance between Hankow and Shanghai—six hundred fifty miles—was quickly covered. Sister M. Justin [Welch] was awaiting us at the Convent of the Sacred Heart in Shanghai where once more we were greeted with the friendly smile of Mother Nourry. A telegram, too, was awaiting us stating that the SS. PRESIDENT LINCOLN would not sail until November 25. This was a disappointment, but we made use of the intervening days to visit the institutions of the Sisters of St. Vincent de Paul, who conduct an orphanage for foundlings, a home for aged men and women, a regular hospital, a hospital for prisoners, an isolation hospital, and an insane asylum. It was inspiring to see so many native Chinese Sisters quietly moving about in the discharge of their respective duties.

This large institution is one of several founded by a wealthy Catholic Chinese, Loa Po Hong of Shanghai. To tell you about this benevolent gentleman would require pages, but you will get an insight into the nobility of his character when I relate how he came to found these institutions. A man suffering from a contagious disease was found on the street by Loa Po Hong, and in vain he sought admission for the patient in various hospitals. Finally, he took the unfortunate man into his own home with the resolve to do something for such poor beings. Today, thousands are benefiting from the charity of Loa Po Hong who has been especially honored by the Holy Father.

After going to several other places, there was little time left for us in Shanghai—Shanghai, the great commercial and industrial center of China and possibly the most cosmopolitan city of the world for almost every nationality on earth, is represented there. It is now situated on the Whangpoo River, although at one time it was directly on the sea. (Shanghai means "on the sea.") The foreign consulates, banks, shipping offices, hotels of the world-famed "Bund" looking out upon the Whangpoo present a picturesque scene. A number of large, modern, and well-organized department stores, similar to those in our large cities, add zest to shopping tours.

The Whangpoo River at Shanghai with its ships of every kind and description, from stately ocean liners to the Chinese junks and sampans, offers a striking contrast to the quiet and dignified harbors of San Francisco and Vancouver.

Before leaving Shanghai, we had the pleasure of meeting Mr. Jermyn D. H. Lynn, a prominent lawyer and the father of Miss Helen Lynn, formerly of our school in Tsingtao and now a student of Mount Mary College, Milwaukee. Mr. Lynn spoke of the high regard in which the Chinese hold the Americans, and said that to be an American is passport sufficient to get into China. They like the Americans because we are not so "grabby." Our country relinquished its concessions in China, helped them to regain Tsingtao, gave freedom to the Philippines, and erected the Chin Hwa College in Peiping with the Boxer Indemnity Fund. This admiration for American people and things is very noticeable, and one regrets that other nations are not equally as friendly in their relations with one another.

In Tsingtao, we had met the parents and relatives of Miss Lois Wang and Miss Gertrude Wong, who together with Miss Lynn, form the Sheng Kung trio at Mount Mary College. Sheng Kung is the Chinese name for St. Joseph Middle School. Lois's brother and sister-in-law, Mr. and Mrs. Chao Wang, have been faithful stand-bys since the foundation of the school. The father of Gertrude is a successful banker in Tsingtao. He came personally with Gertrude's mother and sister to convey special greetings.

Finally, on the evening of November 24, we boarded the SS. PRESIDENT LINCOLN and in the early hours of the following morning, the vessel quietly slipped out of Shanghai Harbor. We stopped at Kobe, Japan, long enough to permit us to visit the wonderful Japanese school conducted by the Religious of the Sacred Heart in Obayaski. Located in the mountains, the school is surrounded by luxuriant vegetation and overlooks the bay. Mother Meier, who is in charge, is doing wonderful work on behalf of the Japanese.

Another short stop was made at Yokohama, and we used the opportunity to make a brief visit to the commercial museum, the post office, and the shopping district.

While sailing between Shanghai and Kobe on November 26, we had a wonderful view of Fujiyama, the sacred mountain of Japan, which is frequently the subject of Japanese art. Heavy fogs often obscure the view, but on the day we passed, the mountain was in view during the entire morning. Its snow-crested top, glistening in the sun, was plainly visible; even the ridges in the snow were discernable. The snow line was very acute, while the rock beneath the snow line looked purple in color. As the moving vessel gave us ever-different views, the beauty of Fujiyama became more and more apparent, and the whole made an unforgettable picture. The paintings and drawings of Fujiyama which we see are not exaggerated.

During the first day out of Yokohama the ocean was rough, and an elderly missionary doctor who was traveling against the advice of his physician, fell and suffered serious injury when a huge wave gave the vessel a severe jolt. In an attempt to save her husband from falling, his wife sustained a broken arm. The doctor died a few days later and was buried at sea. This was a new but sad experience for us.

On account of the marine strike, there was a feeling of anxiety among the passengers since they did not know just what to expect upon landing in San Francisco. The officers tried to break the monotony of the voyage in various ways. One evening the passengers were invited to appear for dinner in Oriental attire. Some came beautifully-gowned in Chinese costumes, others in gorgeous Japanese kimonos, and a few in Philippino and Hindoo dress. A Chinaman connected with Ringling Brothers had purchased circus costumes and outfitted himself and a few friends for the occasion. On the whole, the affair was a novel and interesting sight, and all present seemed to enjoy the dinner party.

There is just one more point I will mention in connection with our ocean voyage, and that is Sister M. Justin's birthday. It seems the stewards have a knack of finding things out. On the evening of Sister's birthday, a nicely-decorated cake with eight lighted candles was set on our table, while some of the ladies close by began to sing: "Happy Birthday to You," in which the whole assembly joined. Of course, Sister arose, made a bow, and a second one, and then shared the cake with her neighbors. It was all very nice, but I was thankful that my birthday was some months away.

On the morning of December 10, we reached the end of our voyage. The weather was ideal and the beautiful sight that met our eyes as we passed through the Golden Gate made us feel that, after all, "The Queen of the Earth is the Land of my Birth, my own United States." We were thrilled with the beauty of it all. Our vessel passed beneath the new Oakland Bay Bridge, which crosses the longest stretch of navigable water ever bridged. A kind lady who lives in San Francisco was eager and happy to point out the various buildings which make up the attractive skyline of San Francisco. St. Ignatius Church stands out prominently between two hills, and nearby is the college conducted by the Religious of the Sacred Heart. We also passed close to Alcatraz, or the so-called "Devil's Island," where Al Capone is imprisoned.

The rumors regarding the marine strike, which had disturbed more than one passenger, proved untrue. On landing, all passed off in a quiet and orderly manner. We remained in California until the 13th when we started our cross-country trip to Milwaukee.

Sister M. Lucilla, Sister M. Justin, and myself were three happy Sisters when our beloved convent home came into sight. Truly the best part of any journey, no matter how interesting, is the homecoming. We were accorded a hearty welcome by our dearest Mother and the Sisters. Then began a series of detailed accounts which is still unfinished.

My visit to China is now a memory, but one that will never be effaced. As a result, I hope that the light of Faith may be brought to some soul now groping in the darkness of paganism. The Church is making headway in China—the latest statistics show about 3,000,000 Catholics—but considering the vastness of the field, the progress is slow due to a dearth of laborers and a lack of funds. The good which could be done is unlimited. A Brother of Mary aptly expressed this idea when he said, "Only the sky is the limit to the good which could be accomplished if more missionaries and money were available." The present is regarded as the seeding time; most of us will not live to see the harvest. The Chinese are a thinking race and, moved by the self-sacrificing example of the missionaries, many feel that there must be something to a religion which molds such heroic characters. But not all of us are called to the foreign mission field; the vast majority are needed at home; but if St. Theresa of Avila by her prayers and sacrifices brought as many souls into the Church as did St. Francis Xavier by his missionary endeavors, we may hope to share in the merits of the missionaries, at least in some degree, if we strive earnestly to assist them in prayer and good works.

In closing, let me thank you, dear Sisters, for your greetings and good wishes, but more especially for the many prayers you said to implore God's blessing upon the journey. I am deeply grateful. May God reward and bless you!

Lovingly,

Sister M. Corona, OSF

* * * * * * * * * * * * * *

Mother Corona's thoughts often tiptoed back to her wonderful time in China. Little did she realize the sadness that awaited her when she would become Mother General. After Japanese occupation in Tsingtao, the sisters were placed in concentration camps. The country was in terrible shape. On October 1, 1949, Chinese Communist leader, Mao Zedong, declared the creation of the Peoples Republic of China (PRC). It was a sorrowful day in 1949 when Mother Corona recalled all the sisters who had come to know, love, and serve the people of China for 18 years.

CHAPTER FIVE

THE GENERAL CHAPTER - 1942

The Most Rev. Moses E. Kiley, D.D., President
Rt. Rev. Roman Atkielski, Chancellor

Members of the Chapter
Mother M. Stanislaus [Hegner], Retiring Superior General
Mother M. Corona [Wirfs], Assistant & First Councilor

Councilors
Sister M. Alexander [Fiecke]
Sister M. Loretto [Thill]
Sister M. Charity [Reiter]
Sister M. Deodigna [Schirra], General Secretary
Sister M. Justitia [Brill], General Procurator

Delegates at Large
Sister M. Winfrida [Hopp]   Sister M. Amanda [Schoenenberger]

Because of the World War, the Provincial Superior and her
two delegates were unable to participate.

_____

PROCEEDINGS
Veni Creator Spiritus
Orations
Holy Ghost
Immaculate Conception
St. Joseph
St. Francis
Election Proceedings

Unobtrusively His Excellency entered the Chapel, and in a brief address, announced to the Community—tense with the solemnity of the moment—the outcome of the election.

ELECTION ANNOUNCEMENT

Three years ago, I had the honor of being in Rome for the election of the Holy Father. It was a very solemn occasion. All the members of the hierarchy were present and many others, even those who were not of the household of the Faith. On that occasion, after the election took place, the Senior Cardinal Deacon appeared on the balcony of St. Peter's and announced that he had a message of great joy for the bereaved Church without a head. He said, 'Now we have one—Eugenio Cardinal Pacelli—has been elected Pope and has taken the name of Pius XII.'

This morning we had an election, and I announce to you that you have a new Mother General—

Mother M. Corona

Mother M. Amanda [Schoenenberger]	Mother Asst. & 1st Councilor
Sister M. Alexander [Fiecke]	Second Councilor
Sister M. Loretto [Thill]	Third Councilor
Sister M. Charity [Reiter]	Fourth Councilor
Sister M. Deodigna [Schirra]	General Secretary
Sister M. Justitia [Brill]	General Procurator

This is the result of our election this morning.

I wish to thank your Mother General particularly for what the Congregation has done for the Archdiocese and pray that this Community may continue to serve God in a manner pleasing to Him; that all may fulfill the obligations each individual assumed when she made profession; and that all will persevere, no matter what happens, so that you may take your place among the virgins who follow the Lamb withersoever He goeth.

May the blessing of Almighty God, the Father, the Son, and the Holy Ghost descend upon you and remain ever with you. Amen."

SOLEMN BENEDICTION

by

His Excellency, The Most Rev. Moses E. Kiley, S.T.D.

Deacon...Rev. Anthony Wisniewski

Subdeacon...Rev. Placidus Meyer, O.F.M.

Assisting in the Sanctuary

Rev. Leo Wedl

Rev. Pancratius Pfaffel, O.S.B.

Rev. Harold Herbst

Rev. John Bertram

Music

Adoro te...Gregorian

Tantum Ergo.............................Sister M. Cherubim [Schaefer]

Holy God...Traditional

Congregation

PROGRAM OF FELICITATION

Processional..Savino
Orchestra

Address..Sister M. Augustine [Scheele]

Candle Light..Cadman
Chorus

Septet Op. 20 (First Movement)....Beethoven—Sr. Cherubim [Schaefer]
Orchestra

Song of Thanksgiving...Alletson
Chorus and Orchestra

Hymn of St. Cecilia...Gounod
Violin – Sr. Imelda [Spitzer]
Orchestra

Psalm 150..Franck
Chorus and Orchestra

ADDRESS – SISTER M. AUGUSTINE SCHEELE

With the announcement by His Excellency, our Most Reverend Archbishop, of the results of the election, thoughts have come crowding in upon our minds, and sentiments flooding our souls—thoughts of the past and thoughts of the future.

The past bursts upon our vision, flashing before us events of the Community over a period of years, covering several decades. There we behold in bold relief our dear Mother M. Stanislaus serving us these many years as Mother General and previous to that as Mother Assistant. This service will go down into the annals of the Community as being eminent for its spirit of tenderness, sympathy, kindness, motherly solicitude, selflessness, generosity, and spirituality. It is engraven deep and firm in the hearts of each and everyone of us, there to remain as a cherished memory bidding us to diffuse its spirit.

Mother Stanislaus's administration is remarkable not only for its spirit; it is extraordinary in the achievements Mother effected in everyone of the Community's fields of activity. Particularly outstanding is the spirituality Mother stimulated through the many opportunities she provided for our advancement towards perfection. But this is not the time to recount what is so well known to all of us. Nor is it the time to attempt to describe in detail the feelings of appreciation, gratitude, and love which at this moment almost overwhelm us. They are too deep for utterance. God alone can know how dear Mother Stanislaus is to our hearts. May He assume our debt to her and recompense her, for only He can give her a reward proportionate to her service as head of the Community. May He grant us the privilege of her continued presence in our midst for many years to come! She shall be an inspiration to continue the many good works she so zealously initiated.

As we glance into the future, our spirits, made heavy at the realization of the expiration of Mother M. Stanislaus's term of office, become lightened at the thought of having as our new Mother General, Mother Corona. With her as our Mother and guide, we face the future with a feeling of hope and a sense of security. The many beautiful qualities Mother manifested as Mother Assistant have won her our affection, admiration, and respect. Her proved competence as an administrator inspires our fullest confidence in the effective execution of her new office. Her patience, kindness, calmness, serenity, self-sacrificing spirit, and motherliness stimulate in us filial devotion and loyalty. Her genuinely religious spirit compels our complete trust in her spiritual guidance. God be praised and blessed for providing us with so worthy and competent a successor to our dear Mother M. Stanislaus!

The office of which Mother Stanislaus has been relieved and to which Mother Corona has been newly-elected carries with it, we realize, many and grave responsibilities and a heavy burden. We promise you, Mother Corona, to help you bear this burden and to put forth every effort to make it as light as possible. We pledge you, as your spiritual daughters in Christ, our cooperation, support, and loyalty in times of adversity and in times of prosperity, in days of sorrow as well as in days of joy. But realizing how weak and infirm even the best of our efforts are, we promise to pray continuously that you may have the constant support of Him in whose hands, as the Introit of today's Feast of Epiphany tells us, is the kingdom and power and dominion. May He manifest Himself to you and lead you on as He did the Magi of old. May, not only this first day, but every day of your administration be an Epiphany. And thus, together with you, our Mother and guide, we shall follow the light that will lead us to the Eternal Bethlehem. There we shall contemplate the beauty of God's majesty for all eternity. And there we shall bring our gifts which our lives spent entirely in His service (God help us that they may be so) have acquired— gifts of gold—our love, of frankincense—our adoration.

God bless our mothers, Mother M. Corona and Mother M. Stanislaus! May He bless our new Mother Assistant, Mother M. Amanda, the members of the Council, the General Secretary, and the General Procurator!

CANDELIGHT

You are like a blessed candle,
Burning through life's night,
Gently useful, softly radiant,
Always giving light.
Light which sweetly is reflected
In each passing face,
As of candles calmly burning,
In a holy place,
In a holy, holy place.

Candles, dearest one, burn brightly,
To the very last,
Giving till their all is given,
And the night is past.
You are like a blessed candle,
Beauteous in the night.
Life grows late but you grow dearer,
Always giving light,
Always giving, giving light.

--C.W. Cadman

On January 6, 1942, Mother Corona sent the following letter to the sisters.

January 6, 1942

My dear Sisters,

The General Chapter which convened at the Motherhouse today—His Excellency, the Most Reverend Moses E. Kiley, D.D., presiding—elected the following officers:

Mother M. Corona [Wirfs]	Superior General
Mother M. Amanda [Schoenenberger]	Assistant and First Councilor
Sister M. Alexander [Fiecke]	Second Councilor
Sister M. Loretto [Thill]	Third Councilor
Sister M. Charity [Reiter]	Fourth Councilor
Sister M. Deodigna [Schirra]	General Secretary
Sister M. Justitia [Brill]	General Procurator

It is with deep regret that we omit the name of our dear Mother M. Stanislaus from this announcement, but it was her earnest request that she be spared the responsibility of office. Her noble and beautiful example, especially during the weeks immediately preceding the election, will always be a source of inspiration to those who must now carry on the administrative work which she performed so efficiently and well. The Congregation owes a debt of deep gratitude to Mother M. Stanislaus, and this debt will be paid—at least in a measure—by prayer. May God reward and bless her as only He can do. She will ever be a guiding star to the Community, especially to those who have had the happiness of living close to her.

Your prayers are also requested by the newly-elected officers, who will strive to carry on the ideals of the three great women who have laid the foundation of our beloved Congregation—

Mother M. Alexia [Höll]	the Foundress
Mother M. Alfons [Schmid]	the Builder
Mother M. Stanislaus [Hegner]	the Organizer

In our humble way, we shall go steadily forward even though the star of hope is somewhat dimmed by world conditions. We count on your loyal support and prayers so that God may direct our actions according to His good pleasure, and that we may deserve to abound in good works.

Sincerely,

Mother M. Corona, OSF

MOTHER M. CORONA

CIRCA 1946

CHAPTER SIX

WORLD WAR II

Mothers Alexia and Alfons endured many hardships in their administration due to World War I. Mother Stanislaus dealt with the Great Depression when she assumed office. Mother Corona began her administration during the turbulent times of World War II, which began in 1939 and ended in 1945.

President Franklin Roosevelt called December 7, 1941, "a date which will live in infamy." On that day, Japanese planes attacked the United States Naval Base at Pearl Harbor, Hawaii Territory. The bombing killed 2,300 Americans. This happened one month before Sister Corona was elected as Mother General and greatly affected her time in office.

Mother Corona's four-page letter to the sisters dated March 12, 1943 contained the following paragraph:

> I am sure you are praying for world peace and for all who are in distress and sorrow on account of this terrible war. Continue to implore God's help for the men in service and frequently during the day breathe a fervent prayer for the dying and the wounded. Remind the children again and again to be unselfish in offering their prayers and good works for those in affliction. Make special intentions for the welfare of our Country. Attendance at Holy Mass should be recommended to your pupils, for it is through the Holy Sacrifice that the wrath of God will be appeased. It is not sufficient to merely tell the children to come to Mass, but a special effort ought to be made to teach them how to participate in the Mass effectively. The rosary, too,

is a beautiful prayer, and has brought untold blessings upon entire nations. You were asked sometime ago to offer frequently during the day the Precious Blood to the Eternal Father, and I was pleased to hear from a number of Sisters that they are continuing this practice. We live in difficult times, but God will protect and bless us if we place our trust in Him.

Another excerpt of a letter, dated April 9, 1943, dealt with various effects of the war. Imagine the difficult emotions of German sisters in America, with family members suffering in Europe.

My dear Sisters,

We are seriously considering the advisability of having all the Sisters come to the Motherhouse for retreat this coming summer. Traveling is expensive and difficult, and, besides, our Government requests that unnecessary trips be avoided. It would not look well for large groups of Sisters to be traveling to and fro; restrictions as to the number of sisters allowed on the train on one day have already been made in some instances, and such restrictions may be increased as time goes on. There is also the question of provisions. A small group with ration books can more easily obtain what is necessary.

Another matter to be taken into consideration is the Victory Garden. From far and near letters are coming from the Sisters inquiring if they should plant a garden. In every case I have advised them to raise as much as they possibly can and even to go beyond their immediate needs by providing for the winter. I am told that fruit jars with rubber rings are still available, but it will be necessary to buy them now because they will soon be off the market. Home canning will affect not only a saving but also relieve the Sisters of much anxiety when necessary purchases cannot be made. We are told that the ration bureau intends to make further cuts in the individual allotments. Last year the Sisters of the Madonna High School, Aurora, raised sufficient in their Victory Garden to provide vegetables for their summer needs which included three square meals a day for the aspirants of St. Joseph Convent, Milwaukee, for six weeks. And not only that, but they were able to can 650 quarts of vegetables from their own garden.

Mother Corona sent this enclosure to all the missions.

WAR RATION BOOK 3

Application cards for War Ration Book 3 are being distributed by letter carriers. They are to be filled out and mailed immediately. If you are not appointed to remain on the mission, give the address of the Motherhouse and we shall see that the book reaches you. Please carry your ration books whenever you leave the mission. If you come to the Motherhouse, deposit the books with Sister M. Justitia and call for them before you leave.

The following taken from a Government bulletin is timely and should be thoughtfully read:

Meats, fats, oils, cheeses, canned fish. Red stamps A through H have expired; J through K remains valid through June; L becomes valid June 6.

Extension of rationing to all cheeses and cheese products, except cottage, bakers' and pot cheese, will take place early in June as a move to conserve indicated short supplies of milk.

Processed foods. Blue stamps A through F have expired; G through J remain valid through June 7; K through M will continue good through July 7.

Expired red or blue ration stamps can breed black markets, and housewives who have not used up those stamps should destroy them.

Sugar. Stamps No. 13 in War Ration Book One is valid for 5 pounds through August 15. Stamps No. 15 and No. 16 are good for 5 pounds each for use in home canning. Housewives who require more than 10 pounds for canning may apply at local ration boards.

Coffee. Stamp No. 24 in War Ration Book One is valid for 1 pound, which must last through June 30.

Extra ration points may be allotted to individuals and some types of eating establishments in isolated areas that have little access to unrationed foods.

Shoes. Stamp No. 17 in War Ration Book One, good for one pair of shoes, expires June 15. Stamp No. 18 becomes valid June 16. No expiration date has been set.

Portions of Mother Corona's letter of May 15, 1943 are as follows:

> We are living in times when all people, including religious, are called upon to set aside their own desires for the general good. What we do for the sake of patriotism is small, indeed, when compared with the hardships and sufferings endured by the men in service—and let us remember that they are suffering for our protection. In turn, we ought bravely to accept the disappointments and privations which naturally accompany a state of war, and by our willingness to cooperate, help in some measure to bring about an early peace.
>
> It is very necessary, dear Sisters, to go against self and follow the safe path of obedience. A religious who forms a habit of always having her own way becomes unhappy when obliged

to give up her cherished desires, and goes from bad to worse, sowing the seed of dissatisfaction in the community. Thank God, our sisters in general are docile and eager to win for themselves the blessings of interior peace and real happiness which result from an honest effort to carry out the orders and wishes of superiors, but from time to time it is well to be reminded of the danger of self-will.

That you may gain the merit of the vow and give edification to the Sisters with whom you live, I ask all of you, dear Sisters, to accept your appointment in the right spirit, be it agreeable or not. Show yourselves genuine religious, and I guarantee you will spend a happy and profitable summer. Those not appointed for summer school will enjoy an old-fashioned vacation—sewing, studying, reading, planning for the coming year, organizing notes and school work which have accumulated—and, of course, they will want to spend some extra time in prayer. They will also want to enjoy plenty of sunshine and fresh air which will be a tonic and do more for them than medicine. If you work in the garden, be careful not to stand or kneel on wet ground or to work under the hot noonday sun. Each one must know how to safeguard her health.

On October 2, 1943, Mother Corona focused her thoughts on St. Francis of Assisi, the peacemaker.

My dear Sisters,

Pax et Bonum – Peace and everything that is good! This was the favorite greeting of our Holy Father St. Francis, and it is my greeting to you today. This year more than ever before, the Franciscan world is turning to our holy founder in a nationwide St. Francis Day Peace Observance. The Poor Little Man of Assisi is considered the great peacemaker, and during our days of war and universal unrest, it is most fitting to call to mind his works and virtues, and to strive to imitate him in his life of prayer and penance.

She ends her three-page letter with the following:

> In writing this letter, I borrowed largely from the FRANCISCAN HERALD AND FORUM which abounds in soul-stirring articles on the spirit of St. Francis, whose simple and humble yet beautiful and rich life brought about a complete reform in his time, and whose spirit, if taken on individually, will bring about a similar reform today. Each and everyone of us must begin with ourselves; those about us will imbibe the spirit, and, before long, there will be groups of well-meaning people following in the footsteps of our Seraphic Father. The words penance, self-renunciation, and change of heart may sound hard and uninviting, dear Sisters, especially in a feast day setting, but the spirit of penance never diminished the joy and cheerfulness of heart which were characteristic of St. Francis. The Franciscan spirit is the cheerful giving to God of everything, great and small, and this cheerful giving brings peace and joy to the soul. There can be no peace in the individual heart, in the family, in the community, or in the nation unless the spirit of unselfishness predominates. If we wish to contribute our share toward bringing peace to the world, let us follow the Franciscan way of doing it.

Not only did Mother Corona focus on problems in America, she had grave concern about the sisters in Europe as this excerpt from her February 12, 1946 letter indicates.

> I have been in communication with Mother M. Catherine, European Province, during the time she visited Switzerland. I wish I could send food and clothing to all of you, but with the best of will that is not possible—at least not now. I have sent clothing to our dear Sisters in Holland, and we are all happy over the fact that the packages reached the Sisters.
>
> God bless you all. Please pray for us as we do for you. After I hear that this letter reaches you, I will write again.

Excerpts from the following post-war letter from Sister M. Lea Beck dated April 11, 1946, Frankfurt-on-Main, gives only a glimpse of the hardships, dangers, and sacrifices the sisters in Europe endured during the war. These sisters had the backing of an entire community praying for them, as well as their own spiritual reservoir of faith, hope, and Franciscan joy amid destruction all around them.

I had the chance to get to the Motherhouse in Erlenbad and to talk matters over with Rev. Mother Catherine, especially all about the building of our new home. We have not yet got the license, since the house is destroyed to 80%; workmen and material are still lacking. I wonder if it ever can be built up again. You and your influence are our only hope. Now we only have the good news, that we are not living in the boiler-room of our neighbor's house (also half burnt) anymore. From Sept. 12th, 1944, till May 1st, 1945, we were camping there, and in this dark hole (mostly with candle-light all day long), we had to eat and sleep. We first spent a lot of time digging in the ruins, in order to gain back what hadn't been entirely destroyed: the large hearth, dishes, pots and other articles and you can imagine the hallooing whenever there appeared some trifling thing we had saved. Being true children of 'Bruder Immerfroh,' we bore our lot patiently and gladly. In order to help those who did not know how to find a place where they could take their meals, we arranged poor and scantily in the cellars a kitchen, a scullery, a dining room, a store-room and a wash-kitchen. But finally, the attacks of bombs and fire were unendurable and lasting day and night, so that nobody could leave the cellars anymore. It was hell we went through—never to be expressed in words!

We shall never forget those last days! What a relief it was, when at last, on April 28th the American troops marched in. How we rejoiced and bid them welcome: 'Three cheers for the Red, White and Blue,' I shouted, on their entering our basement. 'O.K.' they said, 'You sisters need not fear anything.' We treated them with wine and they left, thanking for such reception. If ever we prayed, we learned it in those past times of war, dear Rev. Mother! And, we shall never cease to thank God the Almighty for His great goodness and protection!

Now we could go to church again. It was just in 'Holy Week' and you might well imagine our inmost feelings when singing the 'Hallelujah' on Holy Saturday morning, tears running down our cheeks. After the Holy days, I hastened to look out for a new house and home. The houses were mostly all destroyed, or badly damaged. One we discovered, that was empty and only a little bruised: it was the house of the Nazzi-Ortsgruppe, who had fled, leaving everything behind them. How they had hated and persecuted us!! The municipal-office-men let us have the house with all it contained. We took possession of it at once and began to move in on May 1st, 1945. The Nazis and troops had left it in an indescribable condition and it took us fully four weeks to get it somehow clean, so that we could take in boarders. We then had the new home consecrated, so as to drive away all Nazi-spook.

Since about half a year we are allowed to fetch the food-remains in an American mess-hall, and owing to this, we could feed many children and old people, who needed help badly. We feed about 100 to 120 people daily, 28 of which are house-inmates.

Lengthy letters continued to go back and forth between Mother Corona and Mother Catherine concerning a variety of problems. The following is an excerpt from Mother Corona's letter, April 1946.

We notice the effects of the terrible war—in fact, we feel them more now than during the conflict. It is impossible to purchase even necessary things including food, clothing, and equipment of every kind. There is also a great shortage of labor, repair and building material, and the situation threatens to become worse. The flour allotment has been cut 25%. There is not enough grain to feed the cattle, and this means less meat and butter; the farmers cannot buy even chicken feed so eggs, too, are rather scarce. We try to grow as much as we can in the line of vegetables, and so far cannot complain, but we cannot be choicy either. Our sacrifices in comparison with yours are slight and scarcely worth the name. When we do sit down to a well-filled table, we often feel reluctant about partaking of what is set before us because our dear Sisters in Europe cannot share it with us. We must accept the trials as they come, although I do not think we can call them severe trials. The Sisters have enough to eat, but it is a perpetual headache for those who must provide the necessities of life to make ends meet.

Nonetheless, as soon as there is a possibility, we intend to send food to you. We are already trying to gather clothing for you and the Sisters, but some articles can be purchased only in small quantities at a time or not at all. The Sisters have made underwear, skirts, and other things for the dear Sisters in Europe, and we are awaiting the day when we can send everything on. Our supply of serge dwindled during the war. Many religious communities had to purchase and use whatever material was available because serge was not to be had. We were fortunate that our supply lasted until this year's distribution of clothing, and the Sisters have enough for another year. We managed to get enough serge to make the habits for the reception class and new habits for those in the profession class, but from now on we will have to watch for opportunities to buy a bolt of serge here and there or we will have to use other material for habits, too.

The religious garb worn by the School Sisters of St. Francis was in jeopardy because of the war. The Order was forced to take the white stripe out of the veil because the material was hard to obtain, and even the starch supply was running low. In December 1946, the sisters walked into chapel with a new soft veil of light material known as "nun's veiling." The starched collar was replaced with a celluloid one. Of course, Mother Corona petitioned the Sacred Congregation in Rome to make all these changes in the habit.

Materials for crucifixes, cinctures, and rosaries were in short supply. Medals for the large rosaries worn by sisters were not to be had. The scarcity of beads for the rosaries also posed a problem. In fact, Mother Corona obtained jaboncilla beads from the Oblate Fathers in Texas. This is a soap bead, the fruit of a plant. One of the sisters in Campbellsport bore a hole in them with an electric drill, and thus, the sisters continued to wear the rosary—though smaller in size.

Mother Corona received a letter from Sister Bonifacia in Holland. The sisters there were happy with the clothing and food sent to them. The congregation managed to send veils, collars, and shoes, but not habits and scapulars.

Amid this three-page dismal letter to Mother Catherine in April 1946, Mother Corona welcomed Spring.

> The cherry and pear trees in our garden are in full bloom, also the ornamental crab bushes. The sight is beautiful. I hope this weather will continue so that we will have plenty of fruit. Last year we had an early spring, too, followed by severe frost, with the result that the crop of early fruits was small.

Dear Mother Catherine sends another letter to Mother Corona begging for help.

Obersasbach, Oktober 28th 1946

My dear Mother Corona!

Today I come as a petitioner to you, dear Mother. It is hard to be obliged to beg, but the thought of the responsibility I bear for our Community encourages me to appeal on your kind and motherly heart.

Conditions are growing worse from day to day. The harvest of this year may be called a falling-out and potatoes, the main food of most of the people, are very scarce also, so that many are suffering from hunger. I am sorry to say, that we are also in great need of food, especially for our young people for they never can appease their hunger. The allotment is very small, and our family is very big. We are in all about 225 persons, sisters, pupils and teachers, to be supported every day. The children are losing in weight right along. Good Sr. M. Laurentia and the Sisters in Switzerland would gladly provide for us, but the export of the nourishing food is forbidden since a few weeks.

We would be very happy and grateful if you dear Mother could help us in sending some nourishment:

beans	grit, farina
peas	corn maize
oats	flour
rice	fat

Through the Catholic Welfare of the U.S.A. or the Schweizer Nothilfe, things can be sent directly to us. May God reward your kindness is our daily prayer for you. I wonder if you received my last letter? The boxes you kindly send to us have not arrived yet. I shall write to you soon again.

Hoping you are in good health I am with kind regards to you and all the sisters, espc. your staff.

Your ever grateful and loving,

Mother M. Catherine, OSF

Mother Corona was not only dealing with the wrath of war on our sisters in Europe, but also the delays in travel to Central America, and the Communist takeover in China, as indicated by the following letter:

November 23, 1946

Dear Mother Catherine,

Your letter of October 28 arrived on November 20, and it shocked me to learn that the parcels of food that have been going out from here almost continuously have not reached you. We have you and the Sisters in mind almost constantly and want to do everything we can to help you. We have what might be termed a small 'shipping department,' where the Sisters are doing their utmost to get packages out to you and to the relatives of our dear Sisters.

When we learned that the French Zone was open, we lost no time in sending packages to Erlenbad. We also ordered twenty 30-pound packages of food from C.A.R.E., 50 Broad Street, New York 4, New York. These packages should reach you any day if they are not already in your hands. There was a coast-wide maritime strike—that is, the men who operate the boats on all the seas which bound the United States refused to work. We were told that in New York the depots or deposit stations were overflowing with gift packages to such an extent that the walks were littered with parcels which had been held up by the strike. So, if there was a time when you did not receive anything, it must have happened during that period. The strike has been settled on the east and the south coasts.

Sister M. Rosaria [Kessler] was delayed here for a month on account of the strike—there were no boats sailing between the United States and Central America, and there was an embargo on all shipments. The embargo was lifted shortly before Sister sailed, so her large shipment could be handled promptly. I am so happy because the Sisters do need the things that are being sent to Honduras. The west coast, that is California, is still strike-bound.

We have four missionaries ready to sail for China, but they cannot leave until about two months after the settlement of the strike because the vessel on which they have their reservations must make a trip to China and return before they can sail. Our Sisters are scheduled for the fourth voyage, and the vessel has not yet made the third voyage. Our neighbors, the Sisters of St. Francis, are waiting in San Francisco since early September. They were to sail on September 15. Because of these abnormal conditions, delays and disappointments are bound to result.

In the same mail with your letter, I received one from Sister M. Eustella [Bush] in China telling me how terrible conditions are there, and how fortunate they are to receive large supplies of food from the United States Navy for distribution among the poor. They receive cases and cases of food and medicine, and Sister is happy to send them to the interior for the relief of starving missionaries and their charges. At the same time, our dear Sisters in Tsingtao are being provided for. So, in spite of all the misery, the Sisters at least have food. If only there would be some way of my dear Sisters in Europe being thus cared for.

The same mail also brought a letter from a poor Priest in India telling me about his poor, starving people, and what confusion and disorder are being created by the Communists. It makes one's heart ache to think of present conditions the world over, and no one seems to be able to do anything to bring about relief. We have this consolation—namely, that a loving Providence watches over all, and in God's own good time peace and order will be restored. It remains for us to do all the good we can and to keep our own souls pleasing to God. Come what may, no one can do us any lasting harm. If God be with us, who can be against us?

You mention that good Sister M. Laurentia [surname unknown] and the Sisters would gladly provide for you. I am wondering if you are aware that we sent more than 200 packages of food to Sister, besides a large shipment of clothing just for the Sisters? So far, we have disposed of about 700 pounds of coffee and 500 or 600 pounds of sugar in smaller quantities in parcels which went to Europe. This does not include Holland. We did not send much food there because the Sisters wrote that they could manage on what they received from the people; however, since they needed clothing, we sent them clothes.

Sister M. Berchmann's [Schmidt] note of September 16 arrived on October 24. The only way we can send food and clothing to you is in the 11-pound packages (5 kilo) as stated on the clipping which was attached to Sister's note. No large shipment will be accepted. As soon as we hear from Caritas Verband or the Catholic Welfare that we may send larger cases, we will be one of the first to do so. I sent you the letter which I received from Monsignor O'Boyle of the National Catholic Welfare Conference last spring in answer to my request that some of the articles we donated to the general drive be diverted to you. Veils and veil material were sent to Sister M. Laurentia. We have no Psalm Books, and it would not seem advisable to print them now since the book is to be changed. Even if we wanted to print them, we could not get the paper required. There is a great shortage, and the paper we are able to secure is of a poor quality.

Please write me a letter as soon as you receive some of the parcels we sent. We have been advised not to send farina and flour because it is liable to get wormy enroute. Only recently have we been able to purchase rice, and we are sending some to you. Other commodities such as sugar, meat, lard, butter, and the like are both difficult to obtain and very expensive.

Mother M. Corona, OSF

All avenues were explored to get relief for the sisters in Europe.

December 21, 1946

War Relief Service
National Catholic Welfare Conference
350 Fifth Avenue
New York 1, New York

Gentlemen:

We have a provincial house which numbers about one thousand Sisters, who are in great need of food and clothing. We have been sending 11-pound parcels in great numbers, but considerable time, labor, and postage is involved.

The purpose of this letter is to inquire if your office would be able to accept larger shipments of food or clothing or both for delivery to our Sisters in Europe. We would regard this as a great favor because the Sisters are in such need and it seems impossible to get sufficient help to them by means of the 11-pound packages we have been sending.

We sincerely trust you will be able to assist us in making larger shipments. The postage thus saved would enable us to give further help to the poor in Europe.

With gratitude for your kind consideration of this inquiry, we are

Sincerely yours,

THE SCHOOL SISTERS OF ST. FRANCIS

Mother Corona sought help for the sisters through the French Embassy.

December 31, 1946

The French Embassy
Washington, D.C.

Your Excellency:

Our Sisters in Baden, Germany, are in great distress due to the shortage of food and clothing. About one thousand Sisters are connected with this provincial house of our Congregation. These Sisters care for poor, neglected children, nurse the sick and infirm, teach catechism, conduct Kindergartens and sewing schools, and perform domestic work in students' homes and seminaries. Our Congregation is an American foundation, and this house in Baden is a subsidiary of the Motherhouse here in Milwaukee.

The Sisters are in great need of help. They must feed 225 persons daily. This number includes, besides the Sisters, students and others whom the Sisters are trying to help. We are making every effort to assist them by sending 11-pound packages as is permitted, but for an institution of that size, it is difficult to send an amount of food and clothing that would cover their minimum needs. As for us, a tremendous amount of work and time is involved in the packing and sending of these small parcels and the writing of the many tags required, not to mention the cost of postage.

The purpose of this letter is to respectfully petition Your Excellency to seek permission from the French Government to ship our supplies of food and clothing in larger boxes. Your sympathy for the poor and suffering will, we trust, prompt you to grant the favor so ardently desired. It will be reciprocated by a remembrance in the prayers of the Sisters.

Respectfully yours,

THE SCHOOL SISTERS OF ST. FRANCIS

Mother Corona received the following disappointing response:

January 13, 1947

Dear Mother Corona,

Thank you for your letter dated December 31, 1946, in which you bring my attention to the situation of your Congregation in Germany.

I fully understand its needs and I can assure you that the French Government, by opening its zone to packages despite the frightful shortage of freight cars and locomotives, makes every possible endeavor to help the needy people of Germany. However, the size and weight of packages sent from the United

States is not within the competence of the French Government, but of the American post-office. The same regulations apply to packages sent to France: their size and weight is limited to 11 pounds.

May I suggest that you get in touch with the American Postmaster General who might be in a position to help you.

Very truly yours,

Jean Beliard

In a letter to the sisters dated February 5, 1947, Mother Corona wrote the following:

Word has come to us from Mother M. Catherine that parcels from here are arriving almost daily since January 6. A package sent on December 6 arrived on January 6. Before the French Zone was open, we sent many 11-pound packages to Switzerland and later larger packages. It was with some difficulty that the Sisters in Switzerland managed to get the things over, but, in spite of delays, the goods finally reached our needy Sisters in Germany. While I am writing this letter, one arrived from Erlenbad telling me of the many packages that are pouring in from the Motherhouse and from our missions. Mother M. Catherine expresses her gratitude most heartily. She is very happy to be able to give her sisters and all connected with her house sufficient and substantial food at least for a while. She expressed special thanks for the warm clothing for the Sisters. Thanks to all who contributed toward this relief. I am listing the missions from which packages were received:

Aurora	Milwaukee, St. Matthias	St. Paul, Iowa
Bloomfield	Milwaukee, St. Rita	Saukville
Forest Park	Naperville	Waumandee
Fremont	Olean	Wheaton
Glen Ellyn	St. Martin, Wisconsin	Winsted

> It will relieve your mind to know that your parcels arrived. I told Mother Catherine that for the present she could notify us, and we, in turn, would inform you of the arrival of your parcel. This will save postage and paper; of the latter, they have very little. Later you will hear from her personally.

The aftermath of World War II was the beginning of an era defined by the decline of all great powers except for the Soviet Union (USSR) and the United States of America. Allies during the war, the USA and the USSR became competitors on the world stage and engaged in the Cold War (1947-1991), so called because it never resulted in overt, declared war between the two powers but was instead characterized by espionage, political subversion, and proxy wars. Western Europe and Japan were rebuilt through the American Marshall Plan, whereas Eastern Europe fell under the Soviet sphere of influence and eventually an "Iron Curtain."

The Cold War also saw a nuclear arms race between the two superpowers. Part of the reason the Cold War never became a so-called "hot" war was that the Soviet Union and the United States had nuclear deterrents against each other leading to a mutual destruction standoff.

A final plea for prayers in Mother Corona's letter of February 5, 1947 indicates a fear of Communism taking over in America. After World War II, Catholic churches and schools nationwide prayed for the "conversion of Russia."

> Pray for the poor people of Europe who have very little food, insufficient clothing, and no fire during these cold days. And while we pray for those in need, let us ask God to have mercy on our beloved country and spare us from the horrors of Communism.
>
> Lovingly,
>
> Mother M. Corona, OSF

In another letter dated March 26, 1947, the suppression of Communism was still a topic of grave concern.

> I shall close, dear Sisters, with an earnest plea for prayers for the suppression of Communism. Often meditate on the fact that the best way to prevent the spread of this evil with all its horrors and misery is to begin with self-improvement. Each one of us must strive to become a better person, more God-fearing, more God-loving, more charitable and kind. We must never lose sight of the obligations of our holy vows—more detachment from material things—from pleasures, love of ease, self-will, and other forms of selfishness. We will go a long way toward helping to convert the little world in which we live if we begin with ourselves in imitating our great St. Francis, who in his humility, poverty, and simplicity brought about a great reform in his time.
>
> Lovingly,
>
> Mother M. Corona, OSF

The aftermath of World War II also saw the use of Communist influence in Southeast Asia, with the People's Republic of China, as the Chinese Communists emerged victorious from the Chinese Civil War in 1949. Regretfully so, this is when Mother Corona withdrew the sisters from China after 18 years there.

One good consequence of the war was the allies' creation of the United Nations, an organization for international cooperation and diplomacy. Members of the United Nations agreed to outlaw wars of aggression in an attempt to avoid a third world war.

CHAPTER SEVEN

WAUPUN MEMORIAL HOSPITAL

Planning for a 50-bed community hospital at Waupun, Wisconsin, began with a committee of citizens in 1943. By 1944, a fund of $26,500 was on hand, $25,000 being a donation from the Shaler Company. Land for a hospital was donated to the city by citizens Matt Rens and George Landaal; the city provided an additional plot of land.

Hopes for federal aid for a hospital were thwarted in 1946 because of existing hospitals in the nearby communities of Fond du Lac, Beaver Dam, and Ripon. In 1947, George Hutter, whose construction company had built St. Joseph Hospital in Beaver Dam, suggested that the Waupun community contact the School Sisters of St. Francis about erecting a hospital.

In 1949, Mother Corona agreed to have the congregation erect and staff a hospital with accommodations for 100 patients. The hospital was incorporated under the title Franciscan Sisters Hospital Incorporated.

The Record of Proceedings is as follows:

The first meeting of the incorporators and members of the FRANCISCAN SISTERS HOSPITAL, INC., was held at St. Joseph's Convent, 1501 South Layton Boulevard, Milwaukee, Wisconsin, on the 14th day of June 1949, at 9:30 o'clock A.M....

There were present:

Rev. Mother M. Corona [Wirfs], Mother General

Sister M. Clemens [Rudolph], Mother Assistant General and First Councilor
Sister M. Deodigna [Schirra], Secretary General
Sister M. Justitia [Brill], Procurator General
Sister M. Loretto [Thill], Superior of the hospital at Waupun, Wisconsin
Sister M. Jutta [Hollenbeck]

Also present were:

Rev. Adolph J. Klink
E.H. Hallows, Attorney for the Corporation

The meeting was organized by the election of the Rev. Mother M. Corona as chairman and Sister M. Deodigna as secretary.

Funding for the hospital building came from the following sources:

$300,000 from Waupun
$150,000 from the City
$10,000 from the town of Alto
$25,000 from Shaler Industries
$1,000 from the town of Chester

and donations from many individuals and businesses.

The School Sisters of St. Francis provided $1,231,626 through a direct grant and long-term loans paid off from hospital income.

All business transactions had to be approved by the archbishop and/or the Sacred Congregation of Religious in Rome, now known as the Congregation for Institutes of

Consecrated Life and Societies of Apostolic Life. The School Sisters of St. Francis is a pontifical order; therefore, approvals are often channeled through Rome, depending on the amount. When Mother Corona requested a $4,000,000 loan for two high schools, Archbishop Kiley said, "You have to go through Rome." The following request sent to Archbishop Kiley regarding Waupun Memorial Hospital is an example of such requests.

The Most Reverend Moses E. Kiley, S.T.D.,

The current interest rate of the Northwestern Mutual Life Insurance Company is 3 ¾%, but they are offering us a 3 ½% rate. The company could not make a lower rate, but the flexibility of their terms makes it easy for us to save interest.

According to the Northwestern proposal, we need not draw out any part of the $750,000 first mortgage loan on the Waupun Memorial Hospital or the $1,250,000 loan on the Sanitarium and other buildings until August 1, 1952, and the latter until December 31, 1952. During these periods, we may withdraw part or all of the loan and pay interest on the amount withdrawn. After that, to April 1, 1955, we make regular semiannual payments with the privilege of making optional payments once a year equal to 10% of the principal. After April 1, 1955, the company will permit us to decrease the principal in unlimited amounts. The charge for holding the money is ½ of 1%.

With the sanction of Your Excellency, we would very much like to accept the proposal of the Northwestern Mutual Life Insurance Company, and humbly ask for the desired permission.

With kindest greetings and sentiments of profound respect, I am

Your Excellency's humble servant,

Mother M. Corona, OSF

With such requests for loans, is it any wonder that the many letters Mother Corona sent to the sisters often requested money. Given the sisters' meager salaries at that time, the miracle is that the congregation was able to sustain itself, while at the same time promote apostolic works in health care and education. It was truly a modern version of the multiplication of loaves and fishes.

The hospital represented a unique kind of cooperation. The townspeople were principally of the Dutch Reformed and Protestant churches. Catholics were a minority. Before the building had begun, there were rumors of opposition to the sisters, but this did not happen.

The success of fundraising drives is evidence of the relationship between the two religiously different groups. Newspaper accounts of the cornerstone-laying in 1950 and dedication in 1951 attest to the interest of the local people in the hospital and the cooperation between Catholics and Protestants. At a combined civic and religious ceremony, His Excellency, the Most Reverend Moses E. Kiley, Archbishop of Milwaukee, laid the cornerstone of the hospital on June 25, 1950. The hospital was placed under the patronage of St. Maria Goretti, who was canonized by Pope Pius XII, on the same day the cornerstone was laid.

In 1952, the hospital was the beneficiary of the legacy of Ella Martin, who had designated that her estate be given to the city of Waupun for foundation and maintenance of a municipal hospital. Amelia Chamberlin had likewise bequeathed $5,000 to the city for a non-sectarian hospital. Both of these cases were successfully argued in favor of the money going to the Franciscan Sisters Hospital.

Waupun Memorial Hospital Edition, 1951 of *The Waupun Leader-News*, featured a photo of Mother Corona with the cutline:

> Mother Corona is the Mother General of the School Sisters of St. Francis, St. Joseph Convent in Milwaukee. Mother Corona made the decision to build the hospital in Waupun and has made the final decisions and approved all plans for the hospital. It is expected that she will attend the blessing of the Waupun Memorial Hospital on July 5, 1951.

The same newspaper bearing the headline: "Many Unusual Features Found in Waupun Memorial Hospital" states the following:

> Completely modern from the basement to the penthouse is the best description of the Waupun Memorial Hospital.
>
> No cost has been spared by the School Sisters of St. Francis in making the hospital as pleasant, convenient, and up-to-date as is humanly possible.

Another article in the same publication states "One of the most attractive buildings in Waupun is the new Waupun Memorial Hospital."

Mother Corona loved marble as is evident in the buildings she built during her administration. Alverno College has a beautiful marble foyer and its Immaculate Mary Chapel is predominantly marble. St. Joseph High School in Kenosha, Wisconsin, is another example of her passion for marble. It is no surprise that Italian marble lines the foyer of Waupun Memorial Hospital, with a memorial plaque on the left wall as the outstanding feature. The lobby is paneled in oak. The hospital is faced with Goshen brick with a dark trim, and an oval drive, 20-feet wide, black-topped surfaced, leads from Beaver Dam Street to Elm Street.

According to *The Waupun Leader-News*:

> One of the most costly items in the hospital is the private lavatory and toilet which adjoins every adult patient room. The toilets have been added for patient convenience and comfort at a large additional cost to the hospital construction.

There is no doubt Mother Corona had the ability to interlace beauty with practicality and her hopes that the buildings would endure for generations.

Construction began in 1949 and Waupun Memorial Hospital was opened in July 1951. Within its first year, the hospital admitted over 2,300 patients, and thereafter, the patient census rose.

After the hospital was built, members of the congregation were sent to Waupun for hospitalization when needed, unless there was an emergency.

I have a personal story to tell regarding Waupun Memorial Hospital. I was a patient for a condition known as achalasia of the esophagus (a constriction of the esophagogastric junction). The most discouraging factor about this affliction was that no doctor at that time in the United States knew how to treat it, so I suffered for five years with this condition. I went to numerous competent doctors in Chicago and DuPage County. Finally, I was sent to Waupun Memorial Hospital by Mother Clemens, Assistant to Mother Corona, in 1956, where six doctors held a staff meeting with me present.

I listened to each doctor express different diagnoses with the final word from the chief of staff who wanted to do exploratory surgery. I strongly objected and would not sign the consent paper.

The director of nurses reported me to Mother Corona as being "a young, obstinate sister who refused to take the suggestion of the chief of staff." To my surprise, Mother Corona called me the next day. She wanted to know what I had said to the doctor. My reply was, "When you cut me open, you're not going to remove anything, or insert anything into me. You have to get my system to function properly. Surgery is not going to work." Mother Corona listened; there was a brief, silent pause. Then I asked, "Mother Corona, would you sign the papers if six doctors each had a different diagnosis and wanted to do an exploratory?" She emphatically said, "No." The matter was dismissed. The following year a doctor from Vienna came to Northwestern University/Passavant Hospital in Chicago and did a procedure that cured me without surgery. Later, a World Congress was held in Munich, Germany, to teach doctors about this condition.

While under observation, I did enjoy that summer at Waupun Memorial Hospital amid beautiful trees, shrubbery, flowers, and well-groomed lawns that Mother Corona so strongly advocated in her plans for the hospital. At the doctors' requests, I was periodically asked to walk with patients suffering from depression through this nature wonderland.

In the 20th anniversary booklet of Waupun Memorial Hospital, the opening remarks of an article are as follows:

> How does Waupun Memorial Hospital happen to be owned and operated by a Roman Catholic order of nuns?

The opening of its doors almost 20 years ago, July 11, 1951, was termed by one reporter, 'a triumph in interfaith cooperation.'

The article continues emphasizing interfaith cooperation.

The Franciscan Sisters were at first doubtful about the cooperation they might expect to receive in such a strongly Protestant community. But after Mother M. Corona, superior of the order, and a group of nuns visited with community leaders, including representatives of the churches, they were persuaded that the people would give whole-hearted cooperation.

In a letter to the sisters dated May 22, 1980, Sister Lauretta Mather, President of the School Sisters of St. Francis, states:

For over a year we have been in discussion about a possible transfer of ownership of our hospital in Waupun. The hospital is at a point of strength, but our discussions were focused around two realities:

a) The fact that this hospital is the only acute care hospital which we sponsor. The increasing complexities of health care management, as well as the benefits to the hospital of being associated with a group that has more than one acute care hospital, leads us to the conviction that our hospital would have a more secure future under new sponsorship.

b) Our financial requirements related to retirement costs have made it necessary to realize some substantial amounts of money from the sale of an institution. We have had discussions about a transfer of ownership of Waupun with General Legislative Assembly delegates, with some of our sisters in health care, with our sisters presently employed at Waupun, with several religious orders, with the Board of

> Directors of our hospital, with Archbishop Weakland, and with the Sacred Congregation for Religious.

The conditions upon such a transfer of ownership were the following:

1) To maintain this hospital as an acute care facility serving the people in Waupun.

2) To ensure that the employees do not suffer from this transfer (in particular, to ensure that their retirement benefits are protected).

3) To ensure that the values associated with a Catholic hospital are continued.

4) To make provisions that Waupun's civic community can continue to have a participative role in the operation of the hospital (as they do through the School Sisters of St. Francis' structure of a Board of Directors).

5) To realize a financial return to the School Sisters of St. Francis.

Ownership of Waupun Memorial Hospital was transferred to the Sisters of St. Agnes in Fond du Lac, Wisconsin, August 1981—September 1981. Continued provision of health care services to the citizens of rural Wisconsin in the Waupun area still thrives today under Agnesian HealthCare.

WAUPUN MEMORIAL HOSPITAL

ERECTED BY THE SCHOOL SISTERS OF ST. FRANCIS,
THE CITY OF WAUPUN, THE TOWNS OF ALTO AND
CHESTER, AND THE RESIDENTS OF THE CITY OF
WAUPUN AND THE TOWNS OF ALTO, CHESTER,
TRENTON AND WAUPUN.

IN TRIBUTE TO THE SERVICE MEN AND WOMEN OF
BOTH WORLD WARS, AND THE IDEALS FOR WHICH
THEY FOUGHT AND DIED, FOR THE CARE AND
TREATMENT OF THE SICK, WITHOUT REGARD TO
RACE, COLOR OR CREED.

DEDICATION PLAQUE IN HOSPITAL LOBBY

CHAPTER EIGHT

ST. JOSEPH HOSPITAL

St. Joseph Hospital in Beaver Dam, Wisconsin, was built and staffed by the School Sisters of St. Francis in response to a request from Archbishop Samuel A. Stritch of Milwaukee in 1936. The archbishop received petitions from influential Catholics in the Beaver Dam community requesting such a hospital. Archbishop Stritch then approached Mother Stanislaus, who responded to the need. Mother Corona was her assistant during this time.

Lutheran Hospital was already in existence at the time but was too small to meet the needs of Beaver Dam and the surrounding communities. Planning began in 1936, construction in 1937, and the opening in 1938. This was the first general medical-surgical hospital of the School Sisters of St. Francis.

In 1955, Mother Corona was asked to remodel St. Joseph Hospital and add a five-story wing expanding the capacity from the original 65 beds to 125. The new addition was opened in 1960, the end of Mother Corona's administration.

The major fund-drive planned in 1958 to support the new addition was given over to Foley Associates, Inc., a professional fundraising group from Rochester, New York. The drive failed primarily because of lack of rapport between the Foley group and the local people. The Foley group was dismissed, and the fundraising was turned over to the local people.

In 1966, under the School Sisters of St. Francis leadership of Sister Francis Borgia Rothluebber, various boards were created to consider all aspects of a merger between St. Joseph Hospital and Lutheran Hospital. After much discussion, discord, breaking off of talks, and then resumption of them, the merger was accomplished in 1972, and the new corporation was known as Beaver Dam Community Hospitals, Inc. With that, control of the hospital by School Sisters of St. Francis changed to a Board of Directors. Sisters were to remain on the board for 15 years after the consolidation, which was the period for repayment of the debt to the School Sisters of St. Francis by St. Joseph's Hospital. The debt was assumed by the new corporation.

The consolidation proposal was a response to the need for comprehensive and regional health planning and a desire to maintain a full-range of hospital services in Beaver Dam. The first documented talk of the merger appears in 1967, when St. Joseph's felt it advisable to close its obstetrical department because of the small number of patients and to work out a cooperative program with Lutheran Hospital. The merger received impetus when it became evident that regional planning for hospitals was becoming a reality.

The following paragraph indicates the struggle of agreement with all parties concerned.

> Because of the stalemate in negotiations and refusal of Lutheran to accept two proposed offers from St. Joseph's, a Hospital Consolidation Study was organized in late 1970. The composition was four members of the St. Joseph Advisory Board, four from the Lutheran Board of Trustees, and four from the community at large. This became known as the 4-4-4 Group. The task of the group was to investigate all possible approaches to future health care in the area with

emphasis on consolidation, merger, cooperation, and sharing of services.

The tensions that accompanied the merger are well documented. Both groups held out tenaciously for what they considered their rights. There seemed to be little tendency to move from their positions.

After two years of deadlock, consolidation of the two hospitals was finally approved in May 1971 and became effective in March 1972. The new corporation became Beaver Dam Community Hospitals, Inc.

* * * * * * * * * * * * * *

When Mother Corona assumed office, there was another hospital on the horizon. On November 22, 1944, she and Mother Amanda, her assistant, consulted Milwaukee's Archbishop Moses E. Kiley regarding the following:

> The possibility of our erecting a hospital in West Allis rather than in the town of Greenfield. His Excellency was heartily in favor of West Allis but warned us to make the city 'come across.' He was not at all opposed to our having chosen O'Meara & Associates, St. Louis, as our architects, and encouraged us not to worry about criticism because we did not favor a Milwaukee firm. He added that we must have a man who is experienced in hospital building. When Mother mentioned that Mr. Brust will erect the addition to the hospital at Beaver Dam, the Archbishop said that is a small undertaking compared with the new hospital, which he called a 'gigantic' work. He mentioned that the land we purchased could be used for the community.

On May 22, 1945, Mother Corona sent the following letter to Archbishop Kiley.

May 22, 1945

Most Reverend and dear Archbishop:

Some time ago I informed Your Excellency that we should like to give the name 'Alverno' to the new hospital which at that time we intended to erect on the fifty-acre plot purchased between 39th and 43rd Streets. However, since later developments took us into West Allis, it seems more expedient to give the hospital another name in order to preclude possible confusion and difficulty in the future when the Alverno College buildings will be erected on the fifty-acre plot. We have, therefore, decided to call the new hospital 'The Madonna Hospital.'

The City of West Allis donated a fourteen-acre tract of land between 88th and 90th Streets on West Lincoln Avenue. The officials of the City will be ready to give newspaper publicity to the proposed hospital plans sometime next week, and we wanted Your Excellency to have the foregoing information beforehand.

With greetings and sentiments of profound respect, I am

Your Excellency's humble servant,

Mother M. Corona, OSF

In June 1945, Archbishop Kiley responded to Mother Corona with the following:

June 8, 1945

Dear Mother Corona:

The name you have selected, the Madonna Hospital, meets with my approval. I hope that the City of West Allis

---

succeeds in fulfilling its pledge to the hospital. So many times, promises are made and not fulfilled.

Wishing you and all the Sisters every grace and blessing you and they desire, I remain

Sincerely yours in Christ,

Moses E. Kiley
Archbishop of Milwaukee

Mother Corona had a meeting with Archbishop Kiley on March 12, 1948. The meeting clearly indicates the prospective buildings that she was hoping to become a reality. The report of that meeting reads as follows:

1) The proposed hospital at Waupun

2) The Alverno College building project

3) A financial drive for the proposed Madonna Hospital in West Allis

4) The high school in Whitefish Bay

Re: Waupun – When the Bishop inquired what the City of Waupun would do toward the building of a hospital, Mother Corona explained to His Excellency that the people have pledged themselves to give $300,000, of which $250,000 has already been collected, and the lease of a site for an indefinite period of time. The Archbishop cautioned Mother to get a clear title to the land; to purchase it outright, so that those who follow would have no reason not to bless us. In the end, however, he admitted that a long-time lease might be satisfactory.

Re: Alverno College – His Excellency also consented to our going ahead with plans and the construction of Alverno College on the Fischer estate. His Excellency advised that we put up a worthwhile building, one that will form part of a larger unit, and to build large enough, looking to the future and a finished product.

Re: Financial drive for the proposed Madonna Hospital in West Allis – The Archbishop also approved of our plan sponsoring a drive for the building of the Madonna Hospital in West Allis. Mother Corona told the Archbishop that we have had a competent lawyer go over the abstract and establish a clear title to the property given us by the City of West Allis. This was done by a friendly suit which terminated in our favor.

Re: Lastly, Mother Corona touched on the matter of a high school in Whitefish Bay. The Archbishop said it is understood that we would take it over, since we have charge of St. Monica's [on adjacent property]. Mother Corona asked if it would be a co-educational high school like Messmer, and the Archbishop said, 'Yes.' Mother Corona said if it is possible, we would prefer a girl's high school like Alvernia. His Excellency agreed that would be the better plan, but it is more than difficult to get teaching brothers for the boys, and he went on to add that our Sisters were doing a wonderful piece of work with the boys and girls at Pius XI High School. Of course, the Bishop said this high school project is in the distant future and need give us no anxiety at this time.

In discussing our building program, the Archbishop asked how we stood financially, and Mother Corona told him what we have on hand and how we plan a bond issue for the construction of Waupun.

After numerous meetings from 1944 to 1949 regarding Madonna Hospital, the following was documented in the Day Book, September 9, 1949.

Mr. E.H. Hallows, our attorney, prepared a deed whereby the property donated to us by the City of West Allis for the proposed Madonna Hospital is ceded back to the

City. After the deed was executed in duplicate, it was returned to Mr. Hallows, who will deliver it to the City Attorney.

The Common Council of West Allis went to work, and, in 1961, the seven-story West Allis Memorial Hospital opened. There was also a request to Mother Corona to build a hospital in Port Washington. Neither she nor her successors chose to build that hospital.

What happened that Madonna Hospital did not materialize when a fund drive was to be launched? Mother Corona must have changed her mind due to a lack of money and personnel, especially since St. Joseph High School in Kenosha and Alverno College in Milwaukee were already in the planning stage.

What happened to a possible high school in Whitefish Bay? The Sinsinawa Dominicans opened Dominican High School in the fall of 1956.

One can only imagine the expansion of health care and education the School Sisters of St. Francis could have done, had there been more money and more sisters.

ST. JOSEPH HOSPITAL
BEAVER DAM, WISCONSIN - 1938
WITH ADDITION IN 1955

SACRED HEART SCHOOL OF NURSING
CLASS OF 1956

CHAPTER NINE

MARIAN HALL

During Mother Corona's administration, many girls after eighth grade were interested in becoming sisters, then known as aspirants. After completion of their high school, they then became postulants for one year followed by two years of novitiate. This was followed by several years living in temporary vows as junior sisters. Each stage had a formation program that prepared the aspiring candidate for religious life and a ministry of service in the church and society. Accommodations at the motherhouse were stretched beyond its capacity due to the influx of vocations. Again, Mother Corona used her problem-solving skills. It was time to move the high school group (aspirants) to another building.

Mother Corona and Mother Clemens spoke to architect John Brust on November 19, 1953, about a hall for aspirants to be built on the 29th Street and Orchard Street corner. Brust informed Mother Corona that he was having problems securing the services of a surveyor. Finally, by August 6, 1954, engineers had begun the work.

The groundbreaking ceremony for the new aspirancy was held on September 8, 1954. Mother Corona, Mother Clemens, Sister Deodigna, Sister Justitia, and others, including Sister Viola Blissenbach and Sister Patricia Cullen, were present. The following month, cement for the foundation was poured. A newspaper clipping on December 17, 1954, stated that the construction of a new $700,000 building to include eight dormitories, gymnasium, and chapel had begun. Mother Corona announced that the building would accommodate 160 young women and was expected to be finished by August 1955. Brust and Brust were the architects, and Ed Steigeswald & Sons, Inc., were the general contractors.

On March 1, 1955, plans were made to have a statue of Our Lady of Fatima (2nd apparition) at the entrance of Marian Hall. Work continued at a rapid pace. The Day Book indicates that on February 2, 1956, Mother Clemens and Sister Justitia toured Marian Hall building. They were pleased with the elevator, floors, ample washing and bathing facilities, and spacious gymnasium.

An interesting feature of the building that attracted a lot of attention was the placement of windows. During the planning period, Father Adolph J. Klink, who was the spiritual director of the motherhouse at that time, exerted his power and influence in having narrow, horizontal windows placed up toward the ceiling so that the "aspirants would avoid all worldliness in gazing out the windows." This was a topic of conversation among the sisters for many years.

May 18, 1956 was the big day. The happy aspirants moved into Marian Hall. The notation in the Day Book the following day stated, "The aspirants who moved into their new quarters last night slept very well. Everyone is delighted with their new living accommodations. Our prayer now is that we will fill the building with aspirants."

On June 13, 1956, Archbishop Albert G. Meyer officiated at the reception ceremonies at St. Joseph Convent. Seventy-four postulants received the habit that day. Archbishop Meyer gave a beautiful and inspiring address to all present. There were 80 priests in attendance. After the services, His Excellency, in company with Father Adolph M. Klink (nephew of Father Adolph J. Klink) and Father Donald N. Weber, as well as Father M. Patrick Cremer, SCJ, cross-bearer, and two acolytes, walked to Marian Hall to place the cornerstone and dedicated the new building. Father Klink offered the first Mass at Marian Hall on June 22, 1956. Mother Corona, Sisters Deodigna and Justitia were present, as well as teachers, senior sisters, and representatives of the aspirants.

For the next ten years, Marian Hall was the residence of lively teenagers aspiring to be sisters who attended high school classes at St. Joseph Convent. At the end of 1966 school year, the aspirancy closed. Many factors entered into this decision. Changes in the church and religious communities were a factor. The idea of young girls making long-term commitments after eighth grade was questioned. Also, at that time, more options were opened to young women.

In the spring of 1969, renovations were begun to convert the building into a residence for retired sisters who were ambulatory and capable of self-care, a much-needed facility at that time.

On June 1, 1969, Sister Leona Riedy moved from Alverno College to become the first coordinator of Marian Hall. Sisters Hadumar Bolte and Syra Niesyto were still in residence, having served as seamstresses and gardeners during the aspirancy days. The first new residents were Sister Cyrillus Kremer and Sister Amor Lehn, arriving on June 18. During the month of June, in typical School Sisters of St. Francis manner, cleaning and equipping the 24 bedrooms, the dining area on the third floor, the kitchen in the basement, the offices, lounges, library, and storage areas on the first floor, were the important tasks. The five sisters in residence during June walked to St. Joseph Convent for daily Mass and meals. By August 1969, Marian Hall was in full operation.

The sisters who resided at Marian Hall were primarily retired or semi-retired. Most of them did some kind of work outside the residence. In some instances, this was paid, part-time employment, while in other cases, it was volunteer work in the vicinity. For several years, the sisters did contract work for a hosiery company. Most sisters helped with the work of the house.

In September 1990, the decision to allow for intergenerational living was put into effect. At that point, Marian Hall ceased to be a retirement home; however, the vast majority of sisters residing there continued to be of retirement age.

Through the passage of time, the Marian Hall building was no longer conducive to the aging residents. After all, it was built for teenage aspirants. Much renovation and updating were needed in the building itself. Consequently, a blessing and farewell was held on September 15, 2002 at 6:00pm. The sisters who lived at Marian Hall moved to other facilities of their choice in the Milwaukee area.

On February 4, 2003, the U.S. Province Corporate Board, namely, Sisters Therese Thoenen (Provincial), Adilia Milligan, Kathleen Kunze, and Helen Butzler (Treasurer), accepted the proposed purchase of Marian Hall by Nativity Jesuit Middle School (now known as Nativity Jesuit Academy). The final contract for the sale of Marian Hall was completed by June 2003.

The Nativity Jesuit Middle School renovated Marian Hall at an estimated cost of $4,000,000 and opened the site to a day school for Hispanic boys in September 2004, which is still vibrant and alive. The first remodeling the Jesuits did was to install new windows so that the students would have light and could peer out the windows and praise God for trees and flowers. Little did Mother Corona realize when she built Marian Hall fifty years before that her passion for education would continue on to Hispanic boys who are groomed to become competent and compassionate leaders dedicated to the service of others.

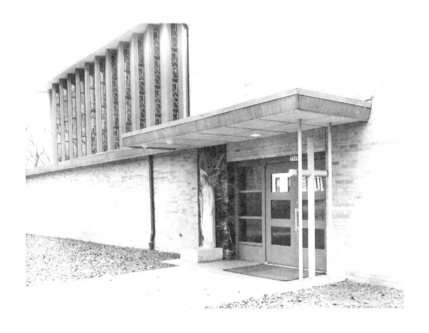

MARIAN HALL – 1954

MARIAN HALL – 1954

CHAPTER TEN

ST. JOSEPH HIGH SCHOOL

The pastors of the Kenosha area parishes made their request for a Catholic high school during the years 1947-1950. The cost for a suitable building was estimated at $1,000,000. Archbishop Moses E. Kiley, of Milwaukee, requested that the entire sum be available before the building began. He warned that there was a shortage of priests and sisters. He also wisely said that secondary education costs would triple by 1970.

In 1950, pastors of Kenosha parishes again requested a centralized Catholic high school. Archbishop Albert G. Meyer, Archbishop Kiley's successor, was eager to help but was also concerned about financing and staffing. By 1953, the School Sisters of St. Francis had accepted the archbishop's offer to staff the school, now estimated to cost $2,000,000. The archbishop required the parishes to have at least one-fourth of that amount on hand before building began.

When the initial fund-drive began in 1955, the estimated cost had risen to $3,000,000. The parishes pledged $2,000,000; School Sisters of St. Francis pledged $500,000. It was hoped the remaining $500,000 could be raised in the city of Kenosha. A kick-off rally for $500,000 from the total city of Kenosha was held August 21, 1955.

On September 8, 1955, Archbishop Meyer turned the first spade for the $3,000,000 high school on a ten-acre plot. The high school was to provide accommodations for 1,600 students, with a possible expansion for 2,000. Notes and mortgage were signed October 19, 1955, and the title: St. Joseph High School, Inc. On April 5, 1956, construction began.

From the very beginning, the proposed high school appeared to be on shaky grounds according to the following letters.

MARSHALL & ILSLEY BANK
MILWAUKEE 1, WISCONSIN

January 20, 1956

Rev. Raymond G. Leng
c/o Our Lady of Mt. Carmel Church
2210 55th Street
Kenosha, Wisconsin

Dear Father Leng:

In re: St. Joseph High School Loan

As requested by you in our conversation last night, I am listing herein the parishes in Kenosha who are participating in the above loan together with the amounts they requested. I have also indicated the amount each parish owes to St. Joseph High School (the signer of the Mortgage) covering the stand-by fee for January 1956:

	Participation In Loan	Stand-by fee for Jan. '56
St. Anthony's	$ 90,000.00	$ 90.00
St. George's	175,000.00	175.00
Holy Rosary	162,000.00	162.00
St. Mark's	250,000.00	250.00
St. Mary's	156,000.00	156.00
St. Thomas Aquinas	200,000.00	200.00
	$ 1,033,000.00	$ 1,033.00

Marshall & Ilsley Bank
   1/10 of 1% of $ 310,000.00 $ 310.00
Northwestern Mutual
Life Ins. Co.
   1/10 of 1% of   723,000.00   723.00
                 $ 1,033,000.00 $ 1,033.00

The above figures for stand-by fees will be the same each month until such time when funds are withdrawn from the lenders. At that time, we will be pleased to advise you the percentages to be charged each participant parish. If anything further is desired, kindly advise me.

MEMBER FEDERAL RESERVE SYSTEM

Archbishop Meyer's letter to Mother Corona expresses concern and worry.

April 5, 1956

Dear Mother Corona:

Enclosed you will please find a letter, which has been sent to all the members of the board of St. Joseph High School of Kenosha. I presume that one copy is sufficient for you and the other sisters, members of the board.

Pursuant to the various negotiations which the architects, Pfaller and Pfaller, had especially with Sister Justitia, we informed the Willis Construction Company that it had been awarded the general contract on a negotiated basis.

It was my understanding from the assurances of the architects, that the School Sisters of St. Francis had given them the assurance that they would be willing to bear the costs above the two million mark promised and pledged by the parishes of Kenosha. I would be very happy to have this assurance for the sake of the record in the form of a letter from yourself. Naturally, I am deeply grateful for this assurance, as I have given much thought and worry to the whole project. It is one, however, that seems to be most important for the good of souls in the Kenosha area, and I am sure that dear St. Joseph will see us through.

With every assurance of my blessing and best wishes, I beg to remain

Very sincerely yours in Christ,

Albert G. Meyer
Archbishop of Milwaukee

Mother Corona's response to the Archbishop is also filled with uncertainties.

April 14, 1956

The Most Reverend Albert G. Meyer, STD
Archbishop of Milwaukee

Most Reverend and dear Archbishop:

This is an acknowledgment of Your Excellency's letter of April 5. We wish herewith to renew the assurance given in our letter of May 23, 1955, that our Congregation is willing to assume that part of the cost of the proposed St. Joseph High School, Kenosha, over and above $2,000,000, and the amount realized on the civic drive.

No commitments have ever been made to the architects concerning our part of the cost, but at various times Sister M. Justitia has discussed plans and the selection of contractors with them. About Easter time in a lengthy discussion with Sister M. Justitia, Mr. Mark A. Pfaller emphasized the importance of starting building operations soon. Sister agreed with him and later, in giving me a report of the conversation, informed me that Mr. Pfaller expected her to telephone him regarding my reaction. Since there was still uncertainty as to the selection of contractors and the approximate cost of the building, I did not feel that anything definite could be arrived at. I replied that it was not within our jurisdiction to say when building operations should start but agreed that it was of importance that the work begin soon.

Again, we assure Your Excellency of our hearty cooperation in whatever you may approve in connection with the proposed St. Joseph High School. When I learned of the mounting cost without knowing what the final figures might be, I became anxious and worried lest we assume a financial obligation which we would not be able to meet. At the present time, we are negotiating for a large loan to cover the indebtedness of our entire building program and hope to secure the money at a comparatively low rate of interest. When negotiations are further advanced, we intend to seek the advice and help of Your Excellency, confident you will assist us in obtaining the required ecclesiastical permission to make the loan. We join Your Excellency in imploring the assistance of our holy patron, St. Joseph.

> With hearty greetings and profound respect, I am
>
> Your Excellency's humble servant,
>
> Mother M. Corona, OSF

By December 7, 1956, parishes already stated problems of meeting their pledges. In 1957, School Sisters of St. Francis promised to pay $200,000 to St. Joseph High School, Inc. Payments were to be made monthly as is evident in the following correspondence.

> March 29, 1957
>
> Reverend and dear Father Leng:
>
> Today we mailed to the Kenosha National Bank checks for $200,000. We will arrange to send to the Bank at the end of each month funds sufficient to cover monthly certificates until $750,000 is paid.
>
> Sincerely yours in Christ,
>
> Sister M. Justitia

The fund-drive collected only $40,948.50 of the $500,000 the planners had hoped to raise. After expenses, $38,000.00 was presented to St. Joseph High School, Inc. On August 9, 1957, the saga began; parishes did not pay what they had pledged. The School Sisters of St. Francis were straddled with picking up the slack.

August 9, 1957	
Parishes paid	$ 500,000
SSSF paid	$ 718,500

October 18, 1957	
Parishes paid	$ 997,900
SSSF paid	1,052,000
Mortgage loan	559,776
Miscellaneous	50,121
	$ 2,659,797

January 15, 1958	
Parishes paid	$ 997,900
SSSF paid	1,314,000
Mortgage loans	740,000
Miscellaneous	50,271
	$ 3,102,171

March 15, 1958	
Parishes paid	$ 997,900
SSSF paid	1,472,000
Mortgage loans	740,000
Miscellaneous	51,271
	$ 3,261,171

Archbishop Meyer dedicated and blessed St. Joseph High School on September 16, 1958, when over 200 priests and sisters were present. More than 1,000 persons attended the impressive ceremonies, which began with a procession from the east academic wing of the high school through ranks lined by the student body to the main entrance. Ceremonies then moved to the main entrance of the school after which the archbishop made a tour around the huge structure. He was utterly amazed at the state-of-the-art St. Joseph High School.

The Kenosha Evening News, September 16, 1958, reported the following:

> Ceremonies then moved inside to the main lobby where local priests assisted in the blessing of scores of rooms in the building. The rites were concluded with the placement of a large crucifix in the lobby of the building.
>
> The procession then adjourned to the outdoor athletic area of the building where a Solemn Pontifical dedication Mass was said by Archbishop Meyer for more than 1,000.
>
> The school choir under the direction of Sister M. Rosemarie Kinsey assisted in singing the Mass.

In the archbishop's homily, he paid tribute to the following:

> Revs. Altstadt and Leng and to the pastors of Kenosha's parishes whose work and cooperation in meeting a two-million-dollar assessment made possible the school.
>
> He singled out the School Sisters of St. Francis and Mother Corona, mother general of the order, for their contributions both in money and personnel to staff the school.
>
> Literally without Mother Corona's help and the School Sisters of St. Francis, the school would never have become a reality.

Then Archbishop Meyer addressed his remarks to the student body.

I exhort you to make a sustained and concerted effort to make St. Joseph High School a place to become a disciple and a learner, bringing out your latent talents. Your industry will reflect itself in self-discipline and the opportunity to go forth in the world to serve as better citizens to your community.

After Mayor Eugene Hammond extended congratulations on behalf of the city to all who made the project possible, Rev. Leslie A. Darnieder, principal, expressed appreciation to the School Sisters of St. Francis and the community. Rev. Ralph Altstadt, pastor of St. Mark Parish, spoke on behalf of the pastors of Kenosha's parishes, tracing many problems encountered from the beginning and then went on to say:

> Today we witness the results of the archbishop's zeal to get things done. We are grateful to him and to the School Sisters of St. Francis who have contributed nearly $2,500,000, plus 30 sisters to staff the school.

Monsignor Edmund J. Goebel, Superintendent of Schools, confined his remarks to the growing trend for more and more lay teachers in parochial school systems. His final remark was:

> In St. Joseph High School you have appointments and facilities hard to equal in all the schools I have seen in this state and other areas. I urge you to use them well.

Mother Corona told the audience the School Sisters of St. Francis were grateful for the opportunity to staff the school and thanked the archbishop, priests of Kenosha parishes, people of the city, the architect, and contractors who assisted in bringing the school to reality. Her final statement was:

It is our cherished hope that St. Joseph High School will
help its students know the truth and appreciate the good.

At the time the school was opened, it was determined
that the archbishop would appoint the principal, Father Leslie
Darnieder, who would also make assignments for priest
instructors, appointed by the archbishop, and any lay teachers.
The Mother General was to appoint the vice principal, Sister
Mary Schmaderer, who would make assignments for the
sisters. The sisters would control the school finances. The
financial responsibilities and the decentralized administrative
responsibilities led to some misunderstandings over the years.

The financial saga of the high school continued
immediately after the memorable dedication. On
September 19, 1958, a letter was sent to the archbishop stating
the cost estimate to be $5,000,000. The parishes continued to
default on their loans as School Sisters of St. Francis made up
the deficit. Ironically so, the people in Kenosha, who had been
accustomed to free tuition in elementary school, thought the
sisters were making big money now that they were asked to pay
tuition for high school.

December 31, 1958	
Parishes paid	$ 997,900
SSSF paid	2,026,622
Mortgage loan	858,955
Miscellaneous	53,056
	$ 3,936,535
June 1, 1959	
Parishes paid	$ 997,900
SSSF paid	2,037,503
Mortgage loans	1,005,000
Miscellaneous	53,058
	$ 4,093,461

On April 27, 1962, the Board of Directors of St. Joseph High School, Inc. met with Archbishop William E. Cousins, successor to Archbishop Meyer, for the purpose of dissolving the building corporation. All assets reverted to the Milwaukee Archdiocese. The archdiocese transferred title to the assets of St. Joseph High School, Inc. to the School Sisters of St. Francis.

The following year, the Wisconsin Province was formed. Later, under the leadership of President Sister Francis Borgia Rothluebber, St. Joseph High School became the responsibility of the Wisconsin Province, but the General Council retained "custodianship." This was the only School Sisters of St. Francis institution in the United States for which a province was responsible.

In 1968, the Wisconsin Province, under the provincial leadership of Sister Coleman Keeley and first councilor, Sister Agnes Marie Henkel, developed and initiated a feasibility study on the St. Joseph High School. John Conway Associates, Inc. was commissioned by the province to do this study. A Board of Advisors and a Board of Trustees were formed, the former being very short-lived. Finally, in 1969, the school was leased to the Board of Trustees; the Wisconsin Province was to represent the lessor (School Sisters of St. Francis) in all matters indicated on the lease agreement with the lessee (St. Joseph High School). All indebtedness of the Board was subject to the approval of School Sisters of St. Francis. The financial picture did not begin to turn around until the parishes' fund-drive of 1970-1971; $240,000 pledged on a three-year timeline. North Central Accreditation conducted an evaluation 1971-1973. St. Joseph High School received an "A" rating. The School Sisters of St. Francis set the standard for high-quality, Catholic education that still exists today. The transfer of ownership of

St. Joseph High School to the Archdiocese of Milwaukee for $1.00 took place on July 1, 1991. A formal ritualization of transfer took place September 5, 1991.

What effect did this arduous process have on the sisters of the Wisconsin Province? Members of the province, as well as former teachers at St. Joseph High School, interviewed for this publication had at that time great fear and stress that the community would have to declare bankruptcy because of the financial drain of St. Joseph High School. Sister Coleman Keeley, Provincial of the Wisconsin Province, asked a number of sisters in 1969 to apply for jobs in public schools because, as she said, "We need the money."

On May 1, 1969, St. Joseph High School of Kenosha, Wisconsin, Inc. was incorporated as a Wisconsin not-for-profit corporation to operate the high school. The Board of Trustees, 14 members, had to be shocked as they reviewed the financial records.

Mother Corona managed to launch this ship and kept it afloat during her administration. Sister Agnes Marie Henkel worked unceasingly in the 60s, 70s, and 80s to bring this financial sinking ship safely to shore. The sisters interviewed said they owe a debt of gratitude to her for her savvy business acumen, her tenacity, patience, and perseverance in bringing the financial saga to an end. Sister Agnes Marie successfully navigated St. Joseph High School's transition to an archdiocesan school with a Board of Trustees.

Barbara A. Kluka, a former student of St. Joseph High School, exemplifies Mother Corona's hope as is evident in the statement that follows:

My parents valued Catholic education. In 1958, I graduated from our parish school, St. Anthony of Padua. In the spring of that year, I registered to attend St. Joseph High School, which opened in September 1958. I puzzled over the meaning of 'credits,' a weighted scale of scholastic performance, and what it would be like to have Franciscan sisters, rather than the Dominicans at St. Anthony, in the classroom. I didn't puzzle for long. I soon was excited about new courses, demanding teachers, and hundreds of students in the same school.

The most important academic thing I learned was communication, oral and written. The School Sisters of St. Francis taught us to do our best always, and start over, if necessary. That atmosphere served me well as I went on to Alverno College, UW-Milwaukee for a master's degree, and Marquette University Law School. The foundation I received at St. Joseph High School set my values and work ethic as a high school teacher, practicing attorney, and Wisconsin Circuit Court judge. I am eternally grateful.

Laurie McKern, a volunteer at St. Joseph Catholic Academy, gave a recent update on the school.

Similar to many other regions of the country, Catholic school enrollment in the Kenosha area declined from 1990 through 2008. In an effort to sustain and grow Catholic education in the area, St. Joseph High School once again led the way. Working with the Archdiocese of Milwaukee and local parishes, the St. Joseph High School Board of Trustees created a community-based preschool through high school Catholic educational community called St. Joseph Catholic Academy.

Officially opened on July 1, 2010, on two proximate campuses, SJCA is supported by ten local parishes and has grown to be the largest private school in the area. With its comprehensive focus on academic, moral, social, and spiritual development throughout a student's entire educational journey, SJCA has strong outcomes that validate its unique educational model.   SJCA has the highest graduation rates, the highest average ACT scores, and the highest AP pass rates in Kenosha County.   Even more importantly, every SJCA student from the youngest preschoolers to graduating seniors is committed to serving God, others, and the community.   Centered in Christ, St. Joseph Catholic Academy builds scholars, leaders, and stewards who will transform the world.

Always revering its heritage, SJCA holds the School Sisters of St. Francis close to its heart, with Sister Sylvia Leonardi teaching at St. Mark School, Kenosha, since 1974, and presently teaching religion at the SJCA Lower Campus, and Sister Louise Bernier serving as a member of the SJCA Board of Trustees.   In addition, SJCA recently honored the School Sisters of St. Francis at the May dedication of a new grotto built on the school grounds.   The School Sisters of St. Francis have left an indelible mark not just on St. Joseph Catholic Academy, but on Catholic education in the area.

After 60 years, Mother Corona's legacy lives on.   "It is our cherished hope that St. Joseph High School will help its students know the truth and appreciate the good."

ST. JOSEPH HIGH SCHOOL
KENOSHA, WISCONSIN
1958

CHAPTER ELEVEN

RYAN MEMORIAL HIGH SCHOOL

Ryan Memorial High School was named after James Hugh Ryan, Archbishop of Omaha Archdiocese from 1935 to 1947. His dream was that an archdiocesan-sponsored high school would be built to further the mission of the Church. After Archbishop Ryan's death, his successor, Archbishop Gerald T. Bergan, carried out Archbishop Ryan's dream and requested the School Sisters of St. Francis, the local parishes, and the community to assist in making Ryan Memorial High School a dream come true.

On November 2, 1954, Archbishop Bergan sent Mother Corona an official letter inviting the School Sisters of St. Francis to accept Archbishop Ryan Memorial High School. The letter stated that the Archdiocese of Omaha would deed to the School Sisters of St. Francis 30 acres of land and would provide substantial financial assistance toward the construction of the school.

In a letter dated January 5, 1955, Archbishop Bergan wrote to Mother Corona, "I do wish to put in writing my heartfelt gratitude to you for accepting the new Archbishop Ryan Memorial High School in Omaha." He went on to say, "It will be a magnificent institution. The priests and people in that section of the city have been looking forward to such a school for over 50 years."

One year later, this letter was sent to the archbishop.

February 8, 1956

The Most Reverend Gerald T. Bergan, D.D.
Archbishop of Omaha

Most Reverend and dear Archbishop:

This letter concerns the proposed Archbishop Ryan Memorial High School, Omaha. Our enthusiasm for the project has not abated, but we are not financially able to assume a debt of $2,000,000. After checking and rechecking our financial resources, we see no alternative but to defer the construction of the Omaha high school building indefinitely. We are obliged to make a large loan to meet the obligations of our present building program, and fear to encumber our Congregation beyond this point, for the interest on this loan will be tremendous.

Mr. Leo A. Daly and Associates, recommended by Your Excellency, have proved themselves highly efficient and pleasant to work with. We expect from them herewith completed plans about February 15, and we are concerned about having permitted the work to progress this far. Although we did expect more financial help from the Archdiocese of Omaha when we accepted the school, still we were willing to cope with the situation by means of a loan when Your Excellency informed us of your own financial situation. In face of present circumstances, we find that with the best of will, we are financially unable to assume this debt.

We sincerely regret that we cannot continue with the building at the present time, but in all sincerity, we must say that we are not financially able to do so. We shall continue to pray that the Lord will open the way for the proposed Archbishop Ryan Memorial High School in South Omaha.

With sentiments of profound respect and deep regret, I am

Your Excellency's most humble servant,

Mother M. Corona, OSF

Shortly thereafter, Mother Corona sent another letter to the archbishop emphasizing the financial situation.

> March 13, 1956
>
> The Most Reverend Gerald T. Bergan, D.D.
> Archbishop of Omaha
>
> Most Reverend and dear Archbishop:
>
> We are very much concerned about the plans for the proposed Archbishop Ryan Memorial High School.
>
> The Leo A. Daly Company expects to have these plans complete on or before March 19. As yet, we have not informed them of our financial status, hoping that a way of raising funds for the construction of the building may be found. Very successful fund-raising campaigns have been brought to our notice. We are interested and willing to staff the school but are financially unable to assume a heavy debt in connection with the construction. May we humbly seek the advice of Your Excellency?
>
> With kindest greeting and sentiments of profound respect, I am
>
> > Your Excellency's humble servant,
> >
> > Mother M. Corona, OSF

Archbishop Bergan immediately sent a reply to Mother Corona explaining his financial plight in the archdiocese.

> March 15, 1956
>
> Dear Mother Corona:
>
> Your letter of March 13th is with me, and I felt that your former letter really needed no answer inasmuch as it was stated so definitely that the new South Side High School would have to

be postponed indefinitely. It was quite a shock to me, as I thought all matters were arranged satisfactorily even though I realize that it would be quite a burden for some years upon the School Sisters of St. Francis.

It is true that there have been several successful drives in the various dioceses during the past few years. However, as I told you, within the last five years I have assessed the parishes of the Archdiocese one and one-half million dollars for Saint Vincent's Home for the Aged and one-half million dollars for our new Junior Seminary. In addition, all the parishes in South Omaha have had a building program of their own with a new church or school, or a large addition to the latter. That program has been followed in almost every parish in the city and it is just impossible for the Archbishop to levy another assessment against these parishes.

The Sisters of Mercy built their new Motherhouse at a cost of two and one-half million and also a new high school for one thousand girls at over a million dollars; Creighton Prep will build a new high school for one thousand boys and the Servants of Mary have just opened a new high school for three hundred girls. The Archdiocese did not give them any direct help on these projects. In a practical sense, I think the following would be feasible. We really at this time, do not need a high school for fifteen hundred pupils. It will take a long time to fill it and a school for one thousand would be very adequate for a number of years to come. The Leo Daly Company is a very fine firm, but perhaps should be carefully watched lest the building would be too expensive. They are absolutely honest and as in the case of the recent Cathedral Grade School, they built a building at a very cheap price. We do not need gold door knobs in South Omaha and with proper supervision, there would be much saving. The new Mercy High School for one thousand girls and a convent of fifty-four rooms was built this year at a cost of one million two-hundred thousand dollars. The new Creighton Prep is supposed to cost the same amount of money without a residence for the faculty. It seems to me that we should be able to build an adequate high school with convent for one million five-hundred thousand dollars.

Suppose the adjoining parishes would pay for half the cost. While it would not be easy, I believe with some persuasion, even though they have debts, the priests would cooperate. In all honesty, I think this is a fair proposition under the circumstances. The high school will be yours and in time will produce revenue and vocations. I suppose some member of the Daly firm will be in Milwaukee Monday with the first drawings. I would ask you to discuss the problem with him and ask him what lowest basic price he could build a high school for, for one thousand, with an adjoining convent for a sufficient number of sisters. This will give us a basis for further consideration.

We need the high school very badly and would like very much to have your community own it and direct it. So many of your sisters have come from this Archdiocese that I know they would be immensely pleased if the School Sisters of Saint Francis would accept this new high school.

Will you kindly consider this matter before your Council and let me know your opinion in the problem.

With all best wishes, I am

Sincerely yours,

G.T. Bergan
Archbishop of Omaha

Once again, Mother Corona's big heart and fervor for education figured out a way to allow the construction of the high school to move forward. Ryan High School opened its doors to 284 freshmen on September 2, 1958. The headlines of the archdiocesan newspaper, *The True Voice*, February 27, 1959, "Ryan Opening 'Slow' But Few Complained" continued to explain:

Take a beautiful new $2,225,000 high school not quite completed; add 300 freshmen from 22 South Omaha parishes. Then, just to make it interesting, throw in a lengthy carpenters' strike and mix well.

This was the recipe here early in September 1958, when Archbishop Ryan Memorial High School opened its doors at 60th and L Street.

Sister Rita Wermes was the first principal; Father Edward Shad was the first superintendent. The opening of the school before completion resulted in more than a little inconvenience according to Father Shad.

Incoming students had only the third floor of the sprawling three-story structure available for classroom space. The cafeteria, gymnasium, and locker rooms weren't ready either.

This meant that for two months students had to bring their own lunches. It also meant that football players had to go home after practice before they could shower.

But as they look around them today at their bright, cheerful surroundings, there probably isn't a single student or teacher who would say the inconvenience wasn't worth it.

The dedication of the school occurred on March 1, 1959. *The True Voice*, February 27, 1959, featured this headline, "Archbishop Bergan Will Bless New $2,225,000 School in South Omaha." Honored guests included the mayor, governor, superintendent of Omaha city schools, commissioner of education, the archbishop, Father Shad, and Mother Corona. After attending the dedication, Mother Corona wrote the following letter to Sister Rita.

Dear Sister Rita,

Our visit to Omaha on the occasion of the dedication of the new Archbishop Ryan Memorial High School will never be forgotten. God truly was lavish with His blessings. Everything was perfect from the time we left Milwaukee until we returned, tired and happy on Monday evening. The weather was ideal and the roads good, so we decided to drive all the way home.

You have a beautiful building and above all a wonderful apostolate. May the latter bear rich fruit both for time and eternity.

With a hearty 'May God reward you!' for all you did to make our visit pleasant, I am

Your loving,

Mother M. Corona, OSF

Fourteen School Sisters of St. Francis lived in the convent at the opening of the high school. Sister Darlene Hoch was one of the sisters who enjoyed teaching home economics. She said, "The pastel colors used throughout the school were cheerful, plus the building was designed in such a way that there was so much natural light, which was conducive to teaching and learning. Ryan High School was an impressive sight situated on a high tract of land. I loved teaching at Ryan and cried when we sisters had to leave in 1983."

Since a grade was added each year, the enrollment increased by about 300 annually, until all four grades were served at the school. Soon Ryan became the largest Catholic high school in Nebraska, reaching its peak enrollment, 1,111 students in 1962.

In April 1975, the School Sisters of St. Francis concluded an agreement with the Archdiocese of Omaha changing the status of Ryan Memorial high School from that of a private school to an archdiocesan school. The School Sisters of St. Francis, however, still retained ownership of the school.

Ryan was fully accredited by the State of Nebraska as a Class A school before 1970. In addition, the school enjoyed AA Classification, the highest level of accreditation offered by the State of Nebraska, from 1970-1983. This classification could only be attributed to the standard of excellence and innovation by the School Sisters of St. Francis.

Initially, Ryan's program was typical of most high schools of that period, but in 1966, the school adopted modular scheduling. In 1971, it adopted open scheduling. For much of its existence, there were no letter or number grades. Students had the choice of completing courses at varying speeds. This non-traditional program was unpopular with many students and their parents. Although the school's program had again become more structured, the trend toward decreased enrollment could not be stopped.

To make matters worse, in 1968, the Archdiocese built Daniel Gross High School about three miles from Ryan High School. The two schools competed for the same student population. Furthermore, there was a population shift from the south side of Omaha, where Ryan High School was located, to the west side. By 1971, enrollment dropped significantly. Thereafter, it continued to decrease or plateau until September 1982, when it dipped to 333 students. The school was plagued by financial problems, which were alleviated only by funding efforts. Church and community support diminished. By 1982, rumors that the school might close spread throughout the city;

enrollment dropped even further. The decision to close Ryan High School was publicly announced in January 1983. The building was sold to the Archdiocese of Omaha for $1.00 in March 1983. Legal documents were signed on June 30 of the same year. The final day of classes was May 25, 1983, and the last class graduated on May 29th.

Sister Elizabeth Heese joined the faculty in 1963, as a chemistry and Spanish teacher. She then left Ryan to establish a new smaller Catholic high school in rural Nebraska, but she said, "I carried with me the rich lessons and outcomes from what I had learned at Ryan about setting up a positive and engaging school environment."

In 1980, she returned to a much smaller Ryan High School as its principal. At that time, she did not know she would be its last principal. Sister Elizabeth described the closing of the school as follows:

> The final days of Ryan High School were a mix of hectic activities to complete programs for graduation, registration for the next year for a very different kind of school, and a mounting grief for the great loss that was felt by all. However, students and staff alike rose to the occasion and found hope and many silver linings. These included: Ryan had served well in the community for 25 challenging, but very good years; many students who loved the program found that they had enough credits to graduate early and get their diplomas from Ryan after all; students responded to the many challenges they were facing with maturity and great love; and many teachers would be able to keep their jobs and continue serving there, at least for a few years. In the midst of our grieving, we decided to celebrate what would have been Ryan's 25th year!

Sister Mary Diez expressed the following:

Being part of the first class in 1958 was a unique experience. The school admitted only freshmen that first year and so, in effect, we were the 'seniors' all four years. That meant heartbreak, as we lost most athletic contests for the first two years; but it also meant pride in beginning the traditions and being the 'first' in every new effort. The sisters were a big part of the experience of the school. We had some priest teachers (mostly part-time for religion, but a couple full-time including a wonderful social studies teacher and debate coach); there were only a few lay teachers. What I most remember is the quality of the teaching. Our teachers demanded a lot of us, engaging us in critical thinking and creative projects. Music, art, and drama were strong areas, as I have come to understand marked all School Sisters of St. Francis high schools.

Sister Jane Russell gave her recollection of Ryan Memorial High School.

I came to Archbishop Ryan High School as a senior in the fall of 1961, when my father was transferred to Offutt Air Force Base in Bellevue, Nebraska, south of Omaha. I was happy to be back in a Catholic school atmosphere, after two and a half years in a Georgia public high school that had felt very Protestant. At Ryan, it was nice to know that my excellent math teacher, Sister Mary Fred [Dostal], was a believing Catholic Christian—reinforcing my trust that our faith did make sense to intelligent modern people. The students were also generally friendly, helping me through the awkward situation of trying to make new friends in one's last year of high school.

I loved most of my teachers at Ryan that year. My favorite was Sister Pacis Roth, the brilliant, quirky English teacher who pranced around the room acting out Ophelia's swooning madness, or whatever the lesson was. She was also the first teacher to suggest that I could write poetry as well as read and analyze it, a revelation for which I am eternally grateful. Father William Kelligar taught a great course in Foreign Relations (mock U.N., anyone?), while we plodded through *Mater et Magistra* with Father Vernon. The Physics course I wanted was not being taught that year, but the school compensated by giving me an art class I thoroughly enjoyed.

Even though I was commuting by bus from ten miles away, I managed to take advantage of a couple of extra-curricular activities. Roped in by my friend Mary Diez, I helped with a couple of debate tournaments, serving as a timekeeper or scorekeeper or something. Mainly, though, I tried to find my inner Thespian by trying out for two theater productions. My Georgia accent proved an asset in the choral speaking pageant (written by Sister Pacis) commemorating the centennial of the Civil War. For our senior class production of *Much Ado About Nothing*, on the other hand, I did not land an on-stage role, but was drafted as one of the two 'assistant directors' helping Sister Sienna [Schwerzler]. This peripheral 'go-fer' position at least got me involved in the play and gave me another taste of the theater arts. It also gave me additional out-of-the-classroom contact with many sisters who were helping behind the scenes, showing a picture of sisterly camaraderie which, I found very attractive.

Liking the sisters at Ryan helped me face a question which I had pushed out of my mind while attending public school: did I have a religious vocation? I wasn't sure, but Father Tony in the guidance counselor's office encouraged me to discuss it with Sister Pacis, who encouraged me to give it a try. I wound up being one of seven young women entering the School Sisters from Ryan in 1962. At least Mary Diez and I have found our life calling here!

My first mission was to go back to Ryan and teach Spanish in January, 1967, to replace a sister who had health issues. On the one hand, it was nice to be familiar with the building, the ethnic surnames, and many of the teachers, especially since I had less than 24 hours to prepare; on the other hand, it was very strange to try to step into a peer relationship with some of my own teachers, both sisters, priests, and lay teachers.

Even Fortune 500 Companies come and go. It's unfortunate that a high school that had such promise would close after 25 years. However, the school fulfilled Mother Corona's wish, "to bear rich fruit both for time and eternity." Cardinal Blasé J. Cupich of the Chicago Archdiocese is a 1967 graduate of Ryan Memorial High School. Sister Mary Diez, President of the School Sisters of St. Francis, an international order, was in the first graduating class, 1962. Sister Jane Russell, also a School Sister of St. Francis, graduated in 1962 and is an associate professor of theology at Belmont Abbey College in Belmont, North Carolina.

RYAN MEMORIAL HIGH SCHOOL
OMAHA, NEBRASKA, 1958

CHAPTER TWELVE

ALVERNO COLLEGE

Pressures to have young sisters complete their professional training and obtain their college degrees before being sent out to teach were mounting. State teacher certification requirements and, in 1936, Milwaukee's Archbishop Samuel Stritch's insistence on sisters' education before being sent on mission, forced Mother Stanislaus Hegner to initiate a new educational system for the sisters. She asked Sister Jutta Hollenbeck, head of the congregation's educational program, to develop a teachers' college from the existing St. Joseph Normal School. Like the Normal School, it was to be located in the motherhouse and serve the members of the congregation and those in formation. The college was incorporated in 1936 and immediately began to function with a faculty of School Sisters of St. Francis. Originally to have been a three-year program leading to a diploma, which would entitle the holder to a Wisconsin teacher's certificate, actually became a four-year program, known as Alverno Teachers' College.

Alverno College was the result of a merger of three institutions of higher learning of the School Sisters of St. Francis: Alverno Teachers' College, Alverno College of Music, and Sacred Heart School of Nursing. The transition in the Teachers' College began in 1946 when the purpose of the college was changed from teacher education to liberal arts. The name change to Alverno College was already noted in 1947. In 1950, under the leadership of Mother Corona, the merger of the three institutions took place and accreditation by the North Central Association of Colleges and Secondary Schools was granted in 1951.

From 1942-1948, Mother Corona was president of Alverno College. An excerpt from the opening address, September 13, 1942, Mother Corona stated the following:

> It is to your advantage to use the minutes, the hours, the days that are at your disposal now to prepare yourself for the great work ahead. The better that you are prepared, the more knowledge you acquire, but first and foremost, the more you work at your interior spiritual life, the greater will be the blessings God will bestow upon your work and the more good you will be able to do.

Another significant statement from the opening address follows:

> If what we do emerges from what we are, our doing increases our being, but, if our doing is an end in itself, the longest life lived filled with the most frantic doing is a futile one.

In 1948, Mother Corona opened Alverno's doors to lay women. The following letter was sent to all the sisters.

> My dear Sisters,
>
> With the coming semester, which begins on January 21, Alverno will open its doors to lay women. Perhaps you know of a young lady who may be interested—a girl of the parish in which you are working or a relative. We do not expect many to enroll now, but it is advisable to give out the information so that those who wish to enter here in September can enroll early.
>
> Boarding accommodations are limited as are also our facilities for social activities until we have a college building.

However, the girl who enrolls at Alverno will be given every opportunity for intellectual, religious, and social development. A few girls have been enrolled and they are happy and contented here. They seem to enjoy the peaceful atmosphere of their school and are not slow in telling others how glad they are to be students of Alverno College. Those who are looking merely for social enjoyment, will be disappointed, but the students who are eager to study and make progress will find the set-up ideal. Of course, there will be sufficient recreation and social activity, but not on a major scale. The few girls who have been in attendance went forth animated with the spirit of Alverno and carried its message to the outside world. There is so much good to be done and so many souls to be won for Christ, that the more zealous apostles we can recruit, the more help we will have in the tremendous work which lies before us.

Do what you can, dear Sisters, to interest good girls in our College—girls who are both morally and intellectually fitted; that is, those who rank in the upper half, preferably in the upper quarter of their graduating classes and those who are eager to make themselves good Christian leaders.

I should like to hear if you have any prospects for this semester or for next fall. For full information regarding enrollment, courses, etc., have the applicant write to the Dean, Sister M. Jutta, OSF, 1413 South Layton Boulevard, Milwaukee 4, Wisconsin.

Your loving,

Mother M. Corona, OSF

Already in 1944, Mother Corona was bound and determined to build a college. She and her assistant, Mother Amanda, consulted Archbishop Kiley regarding the purchase of the Fischer Estate for a hospital and college site. The property consisted of 50 acres; consequently, there would be plenty of room for both institutions.

The 50 acres was formerly part of a sprawling, picturesque farm owned by the late Wilhelmina Caroline Fischer, whose frame farmhouse, now known as the "White House" which houses some of the sisters who teach at Alverno, still proudly stands on the campus.

A crystal, clear lake stocked with fish was once a physical beauty of the wooded and lush farmland. Old-timers said the lake stemmed from a deep underground spring which fed the lake and originated from the cold water of Lake Michigan. Because of the construction of a roadway that became Forest Home Avenue, the lake disappeared.

The Fischer family's herd of cattle grazed on the farmland only a few years before Alverno College's cluster of buildings was erected.

The purchase of the Fischer farm in 1944 by Mother Corona is worthy of notice. The Day Book records the following:

> May 13, 1944
>> We paid a $1,000.00 option to the Fischer Brothers on the Fischer Estate between 39th and 43rd Streets.

> July 1, 1944
>> A payment of $24,000.00 was made on the purchase of the Fischer Estate today.

> October 5, 1944
>> We engaged Steinhagen & Steinhagen to arrange for a topographical survey of our property between 39th and 43rd Streets. Mr. Steinhagen said he would begin next week.

> October 25, 1944
>> Judge Jacques and Mr. Charles A. Koubeck delivered the deed for our newly-purchased

land—the Fischer Estate. The final payment of $25,000.00 was made, and the deed, opinions, insurance policies, tax receipts, and other important papers in connection with the completion of the purchase were handed over to us.

What is more interesting is the following statement given to the Alverno Archives on July 30, 2008.

I, Sister Katherine Mary Kramer, was assigned to work with Sister Edmund Klingenbeck in the Registrar's Office during the summer in the mid-40s. Alverno was still housed at the motherhouse, but it was common knowledge that property for the college was being sought. One afternoon towards the end of summer school, Sister Jutta Hollenbeck announced that property southwest of the motherhouse had been purchased. The Fischer brothers would not sell their farm to a religious organization. Consequently, Mother Corona Wirfs gave the money to John Svoboda (known as 'Hill John'), one of the maintenance men at St. Mary's Hill Hospital. He bought the Fischer farm and then sold it to Mother Corona for one dollar.

An article in the *Milwaukee Journal*, August 18, 1950, verifies the fact that the farm was purchased by John Svoboda.

Mother Mary Corona, OSF, superior general of the School Sisters of St. Francis, announced Thursday that construction would start October 1. The college will accommodate about 800 students. The religious order, which operates Sacred Heart Sanitarium, 1545 S. Layton Boulevard, purchased the property, a former farm from John Svoboda, 1445 S. 32nd Street, for $50,000.

Even though construction of the college did not begin until 1950, Mother Corona wanted to be sure she had the land on which to build. Timing was important to her, not only regarding Alverno College, but many other business ventures, especially the establishment of provinces. Timing was part of her business acumen and foresight.

The hospital never materialized probably due to lack of finances and personnel. Also, the Felician Sisters built St. Francis Hospital on the south side in 1956. St. Luke's Hospital, also on the south side, built its new hospital in 1950 and additional wings in 1957 and 1958. The competition forced Mother Corona to focus on building a reputable college on the south side.

The *Milwaukee Journal*, December 15, 1950, featured the following article, "Start Preparing Site for Alverno Buildings."

> Surveyors have started work for the new Alverno College for women, to be completed within the next two years on a wooded 50-acre plot of land between S. 39th and S. 43rd Streets, about a block and a half south of W. Oklahoma Avenue.
>
> Originally estimated to cost three million dollars, the building total is now 'undetermined,' Mother Mary Corona, OSF, superior general of the School Sisters of St. Francis, said Thursday.
>
> The general contract at a figure near four million dollars has been awarded to the James McHugh Construction Co., Chicago. An application for a building permit was received by the city building inspector's office Thursday.
>
> The college will accommodate 800 students. The present Alverno College will be taken over for use by the motherhouse of the order, St. Joseph's Convent, 1501 S. Layton Boulevard.

In a letter to the sisters dated March 16, 1950, Mother Corona expressed her strong sense of mission and concern for the future. Alverno College to her was the future, no matter what the cost.

> We must support and educate a large group of young people who are preparing to teach the children of the parishes in the future. We must have a building wherein to educate these prospective teachers, and construction costs are very high. However, there is no alternative. We must build. It is all for Christian education, and the parishes reap the benefit therefrom.

Another reason Alverno College became a dire necessity is strongly indicated by the following letter from Archbishop Kiley.

> June 16, 1951
>
> Dear Mother Corona:
>
> The Congregation of Religious is not in favor of granting Religious permission to attend secular universities, particularly in these times when these are practically all pagan.
>
> If Marquette University does not provide the courses to attend for which you are asking permission for
>
> Sister M. Emelinda Erkens – Library Science
> Sister M. Niceta Ruby – Library Science
> Sister M. Delia Gross – Art
> Sister M. Antoine Trimberger – Geography
>
> I grant them permission to attend these courses at the Milwaukee State Teachers College. It is understood that these Sisters are thoroughly grounded in their faith so that it will not in any way be impaired as a result of the remarks of the professors whose courses they will follow.

> Wishing you every grace and blessing you desire, I remain
>
> Sincerely yours in Christ,
>
> Moses E. Kiley
> Archbishop of Milwaukee

The transformation of the farmland into Alverno's campus was a sight to behold, according to Edward S. Kerstein, an Alverno neighbor since 1941. Hundreds of construction workers of various trades—bricklayers, electricians, plumbers, carpenters, and steelworkers—descended on the site.

> Their united skills produced amazingly beautiful stone and brick structures of learning and residential facilities that have proven to be an invaluable asset in a residential setting on Milwaukee's south side.

The first resident building was named Corona Hall.

> When the construction workers completed their task, landscape experts spread tons of black ground over which they had scattered grass seed with massive planters to provide a beautiful lawn around the new buildings. The landscape men also planted scores of new trees and a wide variety of bushes.

Construction of the new building was barely completed in time for the opening of classes in 1953. The E-shaped, buff building was filled with dust and dirt—certainly not ready for occupancy. The young sisters were the most affordable labor to complete this work. Down on their hands and knees, they scrubbed the classrooms, swished mops to and fro down the lengthy terrazzo corridors, climbed ladders to vanquish the dust, and made the windows sparkle in the sunlight. All of this was done wearing long habits! These same sisters soon found themselves sitting in the classrooms as students. Once moved into a clean building, the faculty returned to their foremost concerns: their teaching and their students.

The exciting day arrived—April 21, 1954—the dedication of Alverno College. Excerpts from a featured article, "Cardinal Stritch Dedicates New Alverno College," in the *Catholic Herald Citizen,* May 1, 1954, were as follows:

> The setback experienced by the Church in Germany during the nineteenth century was to the advantage of the Church in this country, stated Samuel Cardinal Stritch in his dedicatory address Wednesday, April 21, at Alverno College. For the political and intellectual war on the Church, resulting in the expulsion of Religious Orders from that country, resulted in the establishment of the School Sisters of St. Francis in Wisconsin.
>
> In speaking of the work of Alverno, he stressed the value to the Church of its nursing and teacher training program. He saw in the latter a particular significance because of 'the new vocation being born,' the lay teacher in our Catholic schools, and stressed that this was the highest form of Catholic Action.
>
> Earlier in the day, the Cardinal blessed the stained-glass windowed chapel of Mary Immaculate and each of the rooms of the five-million-dollar college and residence halls. He chanted the prayer:
>
>> Fill them who teach herein with the
>> spirit of knowledge, wisdom, and fear
>> of Thee. Support the pupils with
>> heavenly assistance so that they may
>> grasp, retain, and practice all useful
>> and wholesome lessons.

From the oak doors of the chapel that lead to the vestibule, through every step toward the altar, there is beauty in color and design. Slender blue-toned, stained-glass windows, glass mosaic stations of the cross, a coffered ceiling, oak pews and balcony, hammered bronze altar-railing gates and hanging lamps, marbles rich in coloring and design, lend themselves to the patterned beauty of the chapel.

For the entire building, but chiefly for the chapel, marbles were imported from Europe and Africa. [Once again, Mother Corona's passion for marble and beauty was emphasized in the article.]

Also present for the dedication ceremony were 20 monsignori and 140 priests from ten states: Illinois, Indiana, Iowa, Michigan, Minnesota, Mississippi, New York, Ohio, South Dakota, and Wisconsin. Besides diocesan priests, there were members from 11 different Religious Order of men. Sisters were represented by 15 Religious Orders of Women.

Walter Kohler, governor of Wisconsin, opened the afternoon program in the college auditorium with a short address. He commended the college for its dedication to the three arts of womanhood: teaching, nursing, and music. 'Alverno has been and will continue to be a great asset to Milwaukee, even more to Wisconsin, and truly also to the nation.'

Mother Corona informed the sisters of the dedication of Alverno:

> April 27, 1954
>
> My dear Sisters,
>
> In a separate envelope you will receive a copy of the Alverno College Dedication Book. As mentioned in a previous letter, patrons will receive one gratis; if anyone wishes to have

additional copies, they may be had for $2 each. For your convenience, and order blank is provided below.

The dedication of Alverno College was an impressive event. The weather was ideal. It rained all night and early in the morning, but the Sisters prayed the sun out and the rain away. God be praised for His goodness!

It was wonderful to have with us His Eminence, the Cardinal, our own Archbishop, Bishop Atkielski, Archbishop Hoban, five other Bishops, two Abbots, twenty Monsignori, and a large group of Priests. If the dates of the National Catholic Educators Association meeting had not conflicted with the dedication program, more Priests would have been there.

His Excellency, Archbishop Meyer, was prevented from offering the Pontifical Mass on account of a severe cold, but he was present and spoke at the dinner. His Excellency, Bishop Atkielski, offered the Mass. His Eminence, Samuel Cardinal Stritch, gave a most inspiring sermon. During the blessing of the house, the Cardinal was heard to say on one of the floors, 'This is a beautiful building.'

The concert in the afternoon was impressive. The Right Reverend Monsignor Frederick Arnold, pastor of St. Rita Parish, Milwaukee, delivered an eloquent and scholarly address. The Governor of Wisconsin, Walter J. Kohler, and the Mayor of Milwaukee, Frank P. Zeidler, each gave a brief but pithy talk. I shall try to send you all of the speeches as soon as they are ready for distribution. The Madrigal Singers (an Alverno College Group) sang beautifully, and the All-Sister Orchestra (School Sisters of St. Francis) climaxed the program. Judging from their comments, our guests enjoyed the tour of the building. In the evening, many of us felt like singing: 'This is the end of a perfect day.'

Lovingly,

Mother M. Corona, OSF

The Dedication Book contained the following message of gratitude from Mother Corona.

Gratitude needs no advertisement. Its glow penetrates quietly and steadily. Its warmth spreads in ever-widening circles. But there comes a time when gratitude claims a voice to supplement its light and warmth.

Such a time for the School Sisters of St. Francis is this occasion, the dedication of their new Alverno College building. It is with a voice made resonant in the unison of twenty-five hundred strong that we express our sincere and prayerful thanks to all our benefactors. Without them, our work could not have been begun. Without them, it could not be continued.

We are especially indebted to the Reverend Pastors and the Priests of the schools and institutions at which our Sisters are working, for their continued interest in the Congregation as manifested anew by their generous financial assistance in our Alverno building project.

Ours could be extended to a very litany of gratitude: to the parents, relatives, and friends of the Sisters of our Congregation, to the architects of the building, to the contractors and sub-contractors, to our friends in cities, towns, and villages, to our benefactors wherever they may be.

The voice of our gratitude will continue to sound day by day and year by year before the Blessed Sacrament in our chapel of Perpetual Adoration. Day by day and year by year we shall beg God to bless abundantly you, the friends and benefactors of the School Sisters of St. Francis.

Even the Vatican sent a congratulatory message that was published in the Dedication Book.

VATICAN CITY, April 2, 1954

Reverend Mother General,

The Holy Father was much gratified to learn of the forthcoming dedication of Alverno College, and He has graciously directed me to express to you and to your good Sisters His cordial felicitations on this auspicious occasion.

In His paternal solicitude for the spiritual welfare of the flock that God has chosen Him to rule, the Sovereign Pontiff cannot but view with apprehension the dangers which life in the modern world entails. For unless the men and women of today are fortified by a sound Christian education, they run the risk of being swept away by the currents of materialism and by the mad race for pleasure and wealth which are characteristic of our times.

His Holiness, therefore, welcomes the establishment of Alverno College, and He prays that Almighty God may bestow special blessings upon its work and enable it to fulfill the praiseworthy purpose for which it was founded.

As an earnest of that divine favor, the Holy Father cordially imparts to you, to the Sisters and students of Alverno College and to all those assisting at the dedication ceremony, His paternal Apostolic Benediction.

With the renewed expression of my religious devotion, I remain,

Yours faithfully in Christ,

J.B. Montini

At the time of the dedication, newspaper accounts hailed Alverno's present-day campus as a six-million-dollar wonder, a development as notable for its price-tag as for its purpose. None of the newspaper accounts, however, addressed a question that is usually asked by any reporter: Where did the money come from, especially since there was no fund drive?

The story of how Alverno's construction was financed is nearly as interesting as the construction itself. Mother Corona was a great fundraiser during a time when the congregation had no office of mission advancement. School Sisters of St. Francis financed a large part of the building of Alverno College through hundreds of quiet, earnest and oft-repeated appeals to the neighborhoods and parishes the sisters served. Their help was the result of numerous appeals from Mother Corona, which could well be a publication in itself.

At first, Mother Corona's requests for fundraising help were presented almost as after-thoughts. Two letters from 1950 provide examples of this fundraising by gentle suggestion:

March 16, 1950, in a letter to all School Sisters.

> I am wondering if our schools could do something to help our Alverno College Building Fund. Our Community has served the respective parishes for a long time—in many instances over a long period of years. It has educated the Sisters for the benefit of the parish schools, and I feel certain most of the priests will gladly permit you to arrange some activity for the benefit of our college fund or even offer to do something themselves.

May 12, 1950, in a letter to Chicago area School Sisters.

> On Tuesday evening, May 23, Mr. Parichy of St. Bernardine Parish, Forest Park, will sponsor a ball game for the benefit of Alverno College at Parichy Memorial Stadium, 751 S. Harlem Avenue, Forest Park, Illinois. The thought occurred to me that many of our Sisters have relatives living in or near Chicago, who would be willing to purchase or even help dispose of tickets. If you feel inclined to do so, you may contact your relatives and tell them of this ball game for the benefit of Alverno College.

Once construction began, her requests took on more urgency. In an appeal of February 17, 1951, she left no doubt about why the School Sisters of St. Francis ought to do this.

> From far and near we are told by friends and well-wishers that we have undertaken an immense project, and that is true, but we are not doing so alone. We are making an appeal to all of our schools to find ways and means of contributing to our building fund. The Sisters are resourceful and with the permission and cooperation of the pastor, all can help in some way to ease our financial burden—a musical recital, a children's bazaar, or some other activity...
>
> But the college is a real necessity. Even without considering lay students, we need a building for our own Sisters. They must be trained for the schools and for the hospitals. Their training forms a vital part of the progress of every one of our houses and parish schools. Without Sisters, it would be well-nigh impossible to conduct parochial schools. Without Sisters trained for the work, our schools could not compete with other schools. Therefore, in a sense, our college is a vital part of the parishes in which our Sisters teach. A number of our good pastors seem to realize this and have been liberal in coming to our assistance.

I believe I have given you a clear picture of our plans for raising funds for Alverno. Some of these appeals admit of no delay—the donation tickets, the Victrola records, and the articles for the sale. This letter may overwhelm some of you. I have never written one like it before, yet I can almost hear most of you acquiesce in your usual wholehearted, willing manner, ready to roll up your sleeves and get to work. All of you can do something, and I am confident that you will, dear Sisters.

Mother Corona appealed to business leaders by mail, too. An April 9, 1954 letter sent to hundreds of business people and community leaders simultaneously announced the dedication ceremonies and offered readers a chance to be listed in a special dedication day brochure:

We, the School Sisters of St. Francis, announce with pleasure the dedication of the new Alverno College, 3401 South Thirty-ninth Street, Milwaukee, Wisconsin, on April 21, 1954.

Friends and relatives of the Sisters, business people, and others interested in promoting the education of youth, will have an opportunity to manifest their interest and good will by making a contribution for the benefit of Alverno College. The names of those who contribute $10 or more will be listed as patrons in a special brochure.

On a separate sheet you will find the cost of various items such as furniture and equipment. Some of our friends and benefactors may wish to establish for themselves or someone near and dear to them a lasting memorial by defraying the cost of one of these articles.

In that same appeal letter to potential donors, Mother Corona strongly emphasized the purpose of the college.

> Alverno is dedicated to the education of women. Its purpose is to help its students become cultured Christian women prepared to live effective personal and social lives in our modern democratic society and to contribute their share towards the 'maximum of well-being possible here below for this society.' (Pius XI.) Excellent facilities for the preparation of teachers and nurses enable the college to help meet the current critical need for qualified teachers in our private and public schools, and for competent nurses to minister to suffering mankind in hospitals and sanitariums. Business and science laboratories are equipped to promote the education of efficient and responsible women for the industrial and business world. The music and art departments provide rich opportunities to assist students to develop a sensitivity of response to the beautiful and the noble. An attractive home economics department is designed to prepare young women to establish the kind of Christian homes the world is desperately in need of today.

It seems fitting, finally, to conclude with Mother Corona's constant closing to all her letters:

Lovingly,

Mother M. Corona, OSF

An article in the *Catholic Herald Citizen*, May 1, 1954, entitled "Alverno College Dream Comes True for School Sisters of St. Francis," states:

> While the nuns have dreamed and saved for years, Sister Augustine credits Mother Mary Corona, OSF, superior general of the order, and the late Rev. Adolph J. Klink,

spiritual director of the order, with most of the actual planning for the building.

Sister Augustine Scheele, president of the Alverno Teachers College, was named president of Alverno immediately following the merger. Graduating from Marquette University on June 29, 1939, she was the first person in the congregation to receive a Ph.D. Sister Augustine was a leader in the movement for improvements in teacher education and for years was the only woman to serve on the Board of the National Council for the Accreditation of Teachers Colleges. Her first task as president was physically unifying the school, and that she did with great success.

Sister Xaveria Friedrich, director of Alverno College of Music, at the time of the merger, became interested in music therapy, a use of music to aid the mentally ill and handicapped. The field at that time was unorganized. Professional training for music therapists was extremely limited. Sister Xaveria was determined to start a music therapy program at Alverno College, placing the college in the vanguard of a movement which grew rapidly over the succeeding decades.

Sister Josepha Schorsh, a member of the Alverno College music faculty, became a charter member of the National Association for Music Therapy when it was incorporated in 1950. Through her work, the college contributed greatly to the new profession. Sister Josepha served in executive positions of the National Association for Music Therapy, including the presidency for 25 years.

Mother Corona wanted to educate sisters in this profession if they were interested. It was the choice of the individual. Few sisters went into music therapy. Alverno College, however, has had considerable influence in the profession in training lay music therapists; students today are able to pursue a degree in music therapy.

Archbishop Meyer appointed Father Raymond A. Parr as chaplain of the college in 1953, and he remained so until 1977. In addition to chaplaincy, he also taught ethics. From 1977-1980, he taught in religious studies and served the college well for 27 years. He preached and taught Vatican II before it ever came into existence. Father Parr shaped and expanded the thinking of the sisters, so that when Vatican II was promulgated in the 1960s, the School Sisters of St. Francis was among the first congregations to enact the changes. He greatly influenced the sisters in openness to the "new." Who could ever forget his one-liners:

- ❖ Theology is not authenticated by conformity to the past, but by relevance to the present.

- ❖ The search for self and the search for God are the same search.

- ❖ We are to God what we are to each other; nothing more, nothing less.

- ❖ We do not believe in dogmas. We believe in God. We believe in each other.

- ❖ All creation is the speaking presence of God.

After the accreditation of Alverno in 1951 by the North Central Association as a four-year college for women, the new college stood poised for growth. But ahead, the college had to boldly face the 50s and 60s, two of the most tumultuous decades that higher education had ever experienced. The unique way in which Alverno navigated those two decades left the college with an undivided commitment to teaching and a rare expertise in curricular planning, which is still a hallmark of Alverno today.

This history of good teaching and learning was stressed by Mother Corona before the college was ever built. On November 15, 1945, Mother Corona initiated an *Education Bulletin* that was sent to all the missions. The objectives were clearly stated.

A STATEMENT by Reverend Mother M. Corona, Concerning the Objectives of the 'Education Bulletin'

Milwaukee, Wisconsin
November 15, 1945

My dear Sisters,

With this first issue of the Education Bulletin, we are inaugurating an organ of the School Sisters of St. Francis to help our teachers become more efficient and our schools better. The specific objectives of the Bulletin are the following:

1. To promote common understandings among our teachers and a spirit of co-operation and united effort in the community's educational Apostolate

2. To keep the Sisters informed of the objectives, curriculum, methods, and provisions for evaluation advocated by the Motherhouse school in the various areas of teaching

3. To acquaint the Sisters with the proposals of educational experts

4. To present new books and new materials helpful to the teachers and to the children

5. To provide a basis for professional growth through co-operative faculty study and discussion

6. To enable the Sisters to share their experiences with one
another

To derive the greatest benefit from this Bulletin, I suggest
that it be studied and discussed at teachers' meetings held
periodically. At each meeting, one phase of the content of the
Bulletin should be concentrated on and plans drawn up to apply
the proposals in your school. Previous to the meeting, each Sister
should read that phase of the Bulletin to be considered so that
she will come prepared to enter into the discussion and offer
suggestions. The Bulletin will be published in September,
November, January, and March, or at other times when a special
need arises.

May God bless our efforts to accomplish the work we
have set out to do by means of this Bulletin.

Lovingly,

Mother M. Corona, OSF

Over time, superiors from 18 religious orders sent their
sisters to Alverno to be educated. The college continued to
have a large population of sister students until about 1966.
Alverno was a leader in the Sister Formation Movement.

In the fall issue of *Alverno Today*, 1978, Edward Kerstein,
who lived in the neighborhood, wrote the following about the
early days of the college.

Before Alverno became a private Christian college for
women, the students were members of the School Sisters of
St. Francis and of other orders of teaching sisters.

One of the annual highlights at Alverno in those years
was a festive Fourth of July picnic on the campus. The large
number of teaching sisters enrolled in the summer sessions
competed in highly competitive softball games.

It was amazing how many of the sisters proved to be outstanding sluggers, hitting the ball far beyond the grasps of the outfielders for home runs.

Others, on the other hand, were strikeout specialists on the pitcher's mound, fielding artists, and swift runners.

* * * * * * * * * * * * * *

The upheavals of renewal prompted by Vatican II affected Alverno in various ways, among them in a drastic reduction of the number of students from religious orders. The formation of the School Sisters of St. Francis provinces in the United States, begun in 1959, had already decreased the sister enrollment by providing for the education of young religious in the provincial areas. This is probably why Mother Corona held off on establishing provinces as long as possible, so as not to destroy the college in its infancy stage.

The School Sisters saw Alverno no longer as a preparation for the order's ministry, but as a ministry in itself. For the first time in its history, Alverno had to have a new mission.

Two years later, in 1968, Sister Augustine resigned as president of the college, an office she held for 20 years. She was replaced by Sister Joel Read. With the change in president came a change in the structure of the Board of Directors, as well as in policies and philosophy of the college. In 1968, for the first time, a 15-member board composed of lay persons and School Sisters of St. Francis was elected. The sisters were in a minority on the board, although they continued to serve as guarantors.

Frank Miller, who has had multiple positions at Alverno, wrote in his article, "Sharing a Century," 1987, the following:

The challenges ahead of the new board and president were substantial. With dwindling numbers of eighteen-year-olds on the horizon, campus unrest spreading, and the inflation mounting, it was not the best of times to focus a strong teaching tradition on a new set of student needs. But Alverno's board and president did not face these challenges alone. With them stood a proven, talented faculty who understood the business of teaching better than most. Thanks to their experience in the merger of 1951, construction of a new campus, and their continuous work on coordinated teaching, this faculty may also have been more experienced than any in the country in collaborating on common goals. Together, this group confronted the question of how to best tailor their teaching expertise into a curriculum that fulfilled the college's revised mission.

Nothing at the college has gained more international attention than the abilities-based curriculum. This new curriculum was years in the making. It was not introduced until 1973 and continues to this day. There are eight expectations. To graduate, each student needs to prove competency in the following:

1. communicate
2. analyze situations
3. solve problems
4. apply values consistently
5. interact with others effectively
6. act responsibly in the global environment
7. fulfill the obligations of citizenship
8. respond to the aesthetic

The dedicated faculty teaches these abilities through the existing body of liberal arts courses and professional specializations. Content and performance are integrated in every course, and the learning of one reinforces the learning of the other.

To ascertain the student's progress in their mastery of the eight abilities, volunteers of all professions, known as "assessors," a tool is used that measures the progress of each student and points the way to future learning. Thus, Alverno does not issue letter grades, unless they are required on a student's transcript.

In 1977, Alverno made another revision in its curriculum when it created Weekend College. The program offered adult women a convenient time frame in which to pursue studies leading to degrees in business or professional communication. For nurses who held their Registered Nurse certification, the college offered a two-year degree completion program on weekends. Weekend College was an instant success.

Barbara Wyatt Sibley, who enrolled in the program, expressed the following:

> I was a young manager at a telecommunications company (Wisconsin Bell) at the time. I knew that if I wanted to move up in the organization, I was going to need more than my 'work experience.' One of my peers, who was an Alverno graduate, introduced me to the school. I decided to look into it and found out they were offering Business Management as a new program. I applied, was accepted; however, the program was weekday. I decided to pursue it anyway. So, my first management class was during my lunch hour. Shortly after I started, Alverno announced the Weekend College program. Praise God!

I was able to go to school on the weekends to earn my degree. I was married, had a child, and working full time. It was a challenge, but I made it work. The School Sisters, who were my instructors, were my saving grace. They encouraged and challenged me not to give up. As a result, my graduation in 1982 was one of the high points of my life. I had the skills and abilities to pursue my dreams. I am thankful for my college education and it was the catalyst for my daughter to not only have an undergraduate degree, but a master's as well. I am proud of her, but I am most of all 'proud of me.'

Barbara is an active alumna who serves on the Board of Trustees.

From the early years of the college to the present, Alverno has proven to be "a place where all belong," as expressed in its Alma Mater song. *The Milwaukee Journal*, May 17, 1955, published an article entitled, "Alverno Gets Racial Award: Club's Work Lauded." It reads as follows:

The Thomas J. Crowe interracial justice award has been given to Alverno College, 3401 S. 39th Street, in recognition of the program carried on by the Alverno Interracial Club, a campus group.

A citation presented to Sister Augustine, president of the college, cited the group's efforts 'to create a greater student awareness of the profound and unbreakable relationship between all peoples.'

Members of the club hold campus meetings on interracial problems and also have established a scholarship fund for Negro students at Alverno College.

The article continues expressing various ways of student involvement.

Five Negro girls now are students at the college. Two of the students live in Milwaukee. The other three are from out of the city and live with white girls in the college dormitories.

Members of the club also have aided in conducting a Negro housing survey in Milwaukee and contributed aid to needy Negro families.

They have shown movies on race problems, sponsored guest speakers, conducted surveys of student opinion, and held open discussions.

* * * * * * * * * * * * * *

A recent honor awarded to Alverno College was publicly announced in the *Milwaukee Neighborhood News Service* on Friday, June 22, 2018: "Alverno College First in Wisconsin to be Named Hispanic-Serving Institution."

Alverno College met the enrollment criteria to be considered a Hispanic-Serving Institution (HSI) by the U.S. Department of Education, a national designation that provides access to federal grants and scholarships to not-for-profit institutions of higher learning that serve a significant population of Hispanic students. Alverno is the first HSI-designated institution in Wisconsin...25% of an institution's total undergraduate full-time equivalent enrollment must be Hispanic. Alverno's fall 2017 total enrollment of Hispanic students was 27%.

The designation aligns with Alverno's mission of commitment to educating an ethnically-diverse population of women, integral to the college's success of 130 years.

Each president of Alverno College has made significant contributions and was in touch with what was necessary during her term of office.

1. Sister Augustine Scheele, President from 1948-1968, laid the foundation of a strong teaching and learning institution.

2. Sister Joel Read (1968-2004) initiated the abilities-based curriculum, a highly innovative method of education.

3. Dr. Mary Meehan, the first lay president (2004-2016), conducted a successful Capital Campaign that allowed expansive remodeling, additional building, and beautifying the interior and exterior of Alverno College.

4. Sister Andrea Lee, IHM (2016-present), launched a Strategic Plan, 2017-2022, that has already begun to unfold and addresses the "needs of the time" and reinforces Franciscan values.

Ralph Waldo Emerson said, "The earth laughs in flowers." Many colorful flowers adorn the Alverno campus. A walkway under a trellis leading into the Joel Read Center, which opened in 1999, is lavishly garnished with hanging baskets of bright, beautiful flowers. A large silver sculpture of flying birds soaring into the sky with flowing water beneath provides music for those who will listen. This exterior beauty is a manifestation of Alverno's warmth, inspiration, and aspirations within those hallowed halls and classrooms. Vivaldi's "Four Seasons" without music in Wisconsin is vibrant and energizing in the rhythm of life. Mother Corona's commitment to the "true, good, and beautiful" continues to pervade the campus.

A high degree of professionalism and persistent striving for excellence, imbued with the spirit of St. Francis, is the hallmark of Alverno College. The nurturing efforts of the School

Sisters of St. Francis, board members, administrations, faculties and staffs have led the college to laudatory heights through the decades. Mother Corona's passionate sense of mission in the field of education is most realized in Alverno College, her greatest legacy.

ALVERNO COLLEGE – 1954

MARY IMMACULATE CHAPEL
ALVERNO COLLEGE

SISTER LUCINDA HUBING
ALVERNO ART PROFESSOR, 1953–1991

ALVERNO COLLEGE ORCHESTRA
UNDER THE DIRECTION OF
SISTER LAUDESIA (LAURA) LAMPE

ANTHONY WIRFS WITH DAUGHTER
ANNA WIRFS

FATHER AND SISTER OF MOTHER CORONA

1893

KATIE WITH HER TWO YOUNGER
SIBLINGS, ANNA AND JOSEPH

KATIE WIRFS (STANDING)
WITH HER SISTER ANNA
AND AUNT AGATHA WIRFS THOME

HOUSE WHERE THE WIRFS CHILDREN LIVED
WITH AUNT AGATHA AND UNCLE
FREDERICK THOME

11238 EDBROOKE AVENUE
CHICAGO, ILLINOIS

MARGARET RUHLMAN AND KATIE WIRFS

MARGARET WAS A FRIEND OF KATIE FROM ST.
NICHOLAS PARISH IN CHICAGO, ILLINOIS

IN 1906, MARGARET BECAME SISTER JUSTILLA,
SISTER OF SISTER CONFIRMA RUHLMAN

EDWARD DOYLE, HIS WIFE, ANNA WIRFS
WITH AUNT AGATHA AND HER FRIEND

JOSEPH WIRFS, WIFE KATHRYN KENNEDY
WIRFS, DAUGHTER AGATHA WIRFS DURNELL,
AND MOTHER CORONA

MOTHER CORONA
RIDING IN A RICKSHAW IN CHINA
1936

FACULTY AT ST. JOSEPH MIDDLE SCHOOL
GRADES 7–12, CHINA, 1936

SISTERS IN MIDDLE ROW:
EUGENDA KESSLER, HILTRUDIS KAPPES,
CHRYSANTHA KLAAS, JUSTIN WELCH,
DONATILLA LORENZ, CALLISTA MESSMER

SISTERS IN FRONT ROW:
TURIBIA SOEHNLEIN, EUSTELLA BUSH,
MS. CHEN (PRINCIPAL), MOTHER CORONA,
LUCILLA DOFFING, BLANDA JOHNS, FIDES BETHKE

ST. JOSEPH CHAPEL
WHERE MOTHER CORONA ATTENDED DAILY MASS
WITH THE SISTERS

PERPETUAL ADORATION CHAPEL
WHERE SISTERS PRAYED DAY AND NIGHT

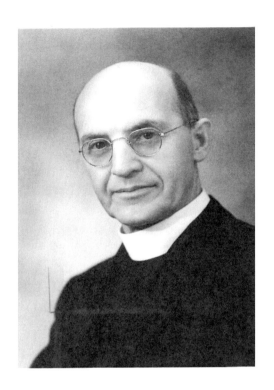

FATHER ADOLPH J. KLINK
SPIRITUAL DIRECTOR
1926–1953

FATHER ADOLPH M. KLINK
SPIRITUAL DIRECTOR
1953–1961

SISTER VIOLA BLISSENBACH, POSTULANT DIRECTOR
MOTHER CORONA VEILING POSTULANTS – 1957

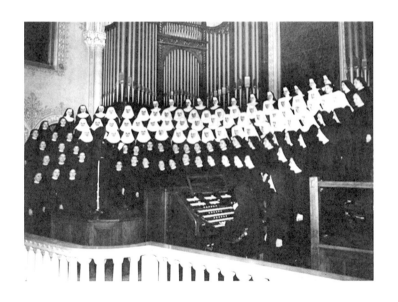

ST. JOSEPH CONVENT CHOIR
SISTER CLARISSIMA NEUMANN – DIRECTOR
SISTER THEOPHANE HYTREK – ORGANIST
POSTULANT CLASS, 1951

RECEPTION CEREMONY

ST. JOSEPH CONVENT CHOIR
NOVICE CLASS ~ 1954

CHAPTER THIRTEEN

COSTA RICA

For 13 years, the School Sisters of St. Francis made serious attempts to integrate Honduran candidates into the sister formation program in Milwaukee and obtained questionable results. Thus, the congregation decided to open a formation program in Central America. Mother Corona chose Costa Rica since Honduras proved unsuitable because of strong military rule and poverty in health care, education, and finances. While the primary purpose of the Costa Rican effort was the formation program for Latin Americans, there was also need of financial support. Therefore, Mother Corona accepted the invitation of the North American Franciscan priests to open an English language secondary school for girls.

In December 1956, Sisters Deodigna Schirra, Joaquin Garcia, Mina Schaub, and Severina Sontag sailed from New Orleans with the aim of opening a novitiate and a secondary school in the San Jose metropolitan area of Costa Rica. In the following letter, Mother Corona informs the community of this new venture.

January 23, 1957

My dear Sisters,

Our temporary novitiate in Central America has been progressing nicely, but it is important that we choose a permanent location. A beautiful site near San Jose in Costa Rica has been selected. Most likely the Sisters will leave here next

---

week. Our good Father [Adolph M.] Klink, who is a missionary at heart, having worked with the Propagation of the Faith for twelve years, will accompany them. Sister M. Deodigna will be in charge and remain until the mission has been well established. She will be accompanied by Sisters M. Mina, Severina, and Joaquin.

Their first activity will be to open a high school for girls on March 1. The Costa Rican educational system differs from ours. High schools begin with the seventh grade and continue for five successive years. Their course of study covers a larger field than ours. High schools in Central America are called colleges—ours will be known as 'Assumption College.' [Later this was changed to St. Clare College.]

Once the high school is well underway, the novitiate will be transferred from Tegucigalpa, Honduras, to Costa Rica. In time, this foundation will become the principal house of our Central American Missions under the beautiful Franciscan title: 'St. Mary of the Angels.' Costa Rica is the best of the five provinces that comprise Central America. There are many good Catholic families in this province, and we have every reason to hope that we will be blessed with many good vocations.

I most earnestly recommend this new venture to your fervent prayers, dear Sisters. Ask God to bless the undertaking and to give the Missionaries the special graces they will need to fulfill their duty according to His holy will. Pray, too, for a safe journey. In union of prayer, I am

Your loving,

Mother M. Corona, OSF

When the sisters first arrived in Costa Rica, they were introduced to André Challe, a wealthy businessman and property owner. He provided them with living and working quarters, which they called the Challe "Casa Grande," until the school and convent could be built in the following year. He became the sisters' constant benefactor, advisor, and general facilitator throughout the 25-year lifetime of the school.

"The Costa Rican Four" wasted no time in getting started, as a portion of this February 28, 1957 letter indicates.

> Someone told us that things would move slowly here! We fail to see it. We have already acquired a school house, had two walls removed from it, registered with the American Embassy, met the medical men of Costa Rica (had our chests X-rayed, throat cultures taken, lost a vial of blood), had our degrees verified, and have drawn up a teaching schedule, dittoed a bulletin for parents, held a parent-teachers' meeting, dealt with the architects and land agents, all in about four days. Slow! – We don't think so.
>
> Sister Joaquin will teach religion, Spanish, crafts, gym, and the history and geography of Costa Rica. I will teach English, math, chemistry, physics, and zoology. Sister Deodigna will teach English to those who know no English; she will be administrator of the school and house; she will also go a distance of about 1500 yards from our mansion to supervise the new building project.
>
> For those of you who are wondering how we sleep and where: Sister Joaquin and Sister Severina have a large bedroom with a private bathroom. (A real bathtub just like yours.) Sister Deodigna has a private bedroom and so do I, with a private bathroom between the two rooms. (The bathroom also has a tub.) We have hot and cold water, even in the morning when we wake up!) Our dining room table is round; the chairs are armchairs, very pretty (not exactly Franciscan though). We never finish marveling at Sister Severina's American cooking. If we do as well with the teaching, as she does with the cooking, all will go well.
>
> Before we close this first letter installment, we should like to thank everyone who made all this possible: those who prayed for us and those who gave us things to make this kind of

life possible. We wish especially to thank all who made our going easy and pleasant. We think of you very often. (Incidentally, we don't think of ourselves as foreigners. The ladies really look like Americans; only their speech betrays them.)

Lovingly yours in Christ,

The Costa Rican Four

Sister M. Deodigna, OSF
Sister M. Joaquin, OSF
Sister M. Severina, OSF
Sister M. Mina, OSF

(Please pardon the typing. Our typewriter is broken and this one is borrowed. Sister Deodigna registered 52 pupils, who must bring their own chairs to sit on.)

Mother Corona, Father Adolph M. Klink, and Sister Viola Blissenbach visited Costa Rica in 1958. Mother Corona, who was always eager to inform her sisters, wrote the following:

Costa Rica, February 15, 1958

My dear Sisters,

Our visit here in Costa Rica with the dear Sisters is coming to a close. Tomorrow morning at 8:40 we shall begin our flight to Honduras and start on our homeward flight February 24, reaching home on February 25.

To live with our own dear Sisters for more than a week has been a delightful experience. They have a comfortable home which is occupied above capacity now. Tomorrow I will give the postulant's veil to Margaret Keith, who has a bachelor's degree. She will be able to assist with the teaching next year. At least six more postulants are expected within the immediate future.

The people have accepted our sisters most graciously. They vie with each other to be of help to them. In the one year that the Sisters have been here, they have accomplished a great deal. At present, they are having vacation. School will begin on March 10. The new building is not completed; some fixtures are still missing, but the Sisters will move in anyway. They have no other place to go with their 110 girls. The new school, which will also serve as a convent for the time being, is a practical, well-planned structure. After the landscaping is taken care of, it will be a beautiful place.

There is a great need here for catechetical instructions. Most people call themselves Catholic, but they are poorly instructed in their religion—in fact, priests tell us many are leading real pagan lives. They lack a knowledge of the fundamental teachings of the Church. It is so necessary that the children be taught their religion. Since we have undertaken to work for these poor native people who know so little about God, we (all of us) should share in the apostolic work of the sisters who are laboring here for souls by praying fervently that God may pour His light and grace upon the people of this country and draw their hearts to Himself. You know St. Theresa by her prayers and good works converted as many souls as did St. Francis Xavier by his active missionary work. You can be a missionary and stay at home and fulfill your duties as assigned by obedience.

We have spent more than a week here, and a full week it was of business and pleasure combined. God blessed the business end of it—thanks to your prayers—and we saw many spots of interest and natural beauty. Flowers, many of which we have never seen and of which we do not know the names, abound here. Those of the same kind as we have at home are usually much larger and sturdier. Here in these temporary quarters of the Sisters, we can enjoy their lovely garden. An Easter lily about four feet tall is about to burst into many blossoms—ten at least. Tall poinsettias add to the picture; giant honeysuckles and daisies; as well as orange and lemon trees, and grapefruit. The Sisters enjoy fruits in many varieties. From the Sisters' porch we see mounds of coffee every day. Many are working hard to shovel the green beans from one hill to another so that all the coffee beans have an opportunity to be exposed to the sun's rays.

We were taken up into the mountains to see the crater of the volcano. It was something worth seeing—the name of the volcano is 'Iraza' and it is 11,000 feet above sea level. A few pleasant hours were spent in 'little Switzerland,' a resort up in the mountains; a very quiet, restful place. There is so much more I would like to tell you, but I cannot do so now. The main thing is that the Sisters are well and happy and are doing good work. Everything here is very promising. Tomorrow we shall fly to Honduras; and hope to be with you again on February 25.

Dear Sister Viola enjoyed the trip very much. Her heart went out to the poor little children we met along the wayside. Reverend Father Klink, having been here before, is well-acquainted with the Franciscan Conventuals, who operate a college for boys nearby; he has made other friends, too, during his visits. He has been most kind and patient and left nothing undone to make our trip pleasant. Father joins in our regards and kind greetings to each and everyone of you. Sister M. Deodigna and the Sisters send loving greetings, and Sister Viola and I extend our best wishes and ask for your continued prayers.

With love and blessings, I am

Your loving,

Mother M. Corona, OSF

February 14, 1958

My dear Sisters (Professed),

Happy Feast Day to you on St. Valentine Day. We offered Holy Mass for you today and prayed that your heart becomes more and more like unto the Sacred Heart.

Heartfelt thanks to you for the 'day' on February 11. My name day is never monotonous because it has been celebrated in a different place each year since I have been with you. But it had the 1501 touch again this year. Even three musical numbers by all the Sisters stationed here.

The quote on the Spiritual Bouquet was most familiar. How I wish each one of us could live it! It reminds me of something a man told me about a Father David who was recalled to the States in December. He said, 'I miss him very much. I always felt better after seeing him.'

You will be happy to hear that Mother Corona and Sister Viola seem to love Costa Rica immensely. The weather is each day like what we would consider a perfect June day. Our first trip was to the Basilica of the Lady of the Angels. Since then all the business has turned out well, too.

Thanks for your prayers. Half of the trip is over. No flaw or difficulty! God is good because you intercede for us. We'll not be with you Ash Wednesday. So, a blessed Lent in the footsteps of the Savior! Blessings!

Father Klink

Sister Deodigna informed the sisters in the office and the community about the move from the Challe "Casa Grande" on March 7, 1958. Her sense of humor is well depicted in the following letter.

Easter - 1958

Dear Everybody,

Alas, it has come to this – I must send you a 'rubber stamp' letter. I fear I won't have any friends left in the States for the simple reason that I haven't the time to write.

Just to keep you up to date on our activities. You probably know that we moved from the Challe 'Casa Grande' on March 7. Despite the many things that were missing, we opened school on March 10. One hundred and ten girls, and what seemed like almost as many parents, were on schedule at 8:00 a.m. on the opening day. Everyone 'Oh'd' and 'Ah'd' at the beauty of our building. We, however, are still frustrated by the lack of many things, such as light fixtures, and an abundance of undesirable things, such as dust, mosquitoes, and noise. Carpenters are still pounding around. We are still hounding workingmen. It is a difficult job to get even a minimum of accuracy out of these people. When we thought a job was finished and looked pretty good, the next workman would come along and ruin what the other had just finished.

It is interesting, and I might add, exasperating, to see how these people operate. They have absolutely no taste for details and no finesse whatsoever. A sander will do a room with a machine, but when it comes to the corners, he will take a chisel and hack out the dirt instead of getting down and doing it by hand with a piece of sandpaper. The architect advised me to take it easy or I would develop a stomach ulcer or two for sure. His comment was, 'We Latins like to have a good time and enjoy parties—we like to live, but all you Americans like to do is work.' I daresay that I wouldn't exactly choose supervision of a building down here as a hobby.

All in all, we do have a nice building even though it is quite empty. The only furniture we have are the desk units in the classroom. Our kitchen is fairly well-equipped with good stoves, sinks, work counters, and a large combination refrigerator and freezer. The chorus room has a good second-hand German piano and plenty of chairs. Sister Verna [Vasen] is doing a fine job with her choral group. The girls just love to sing the simple arrangements of the music to Walt Disney's films: Cinderella, Alice in Wonderland, Lady and the Tramp.

Perhaps I should mention that our school is situated in the midst of a coffee finca. We hear sounds of strange birds all night long. Some screech like what I imagine a laughing hyena sounds like. The three Sisters who came here to sleep the first night did practically no sleeping at all. Picture them in a new building amid all the debris with no light and worse still no water, and millions of mosquitoes. And to top it all, the electric bell which was set for forty-minute class periods went off throughout the night. Now we can laugh about it. How we look back and sigh for the peace and cleanliness of the Casa Grande! One of the Sisters went over to Challe's the other day and was gazing at the Casa Grande with feelings of nostalgia when Mr. Challe chanced along. Sister told him how much we miss the peace and quiet of the grand old house. He said, 'Believe me, we miss you too!' and then with a meaningful twinkle in his eye, he repeated it, adding, 'I never thought I would miss a bunch of nuns.' He said this as though he hated to admit it. When Mother Corona and Father Klink were here, we invited him to dinner on Father Klink's name day. He came and honestly seemed to enjoy being with us.

We had all the Holy Week services in our own little chapel. The Sisters were happy to do all the singing. To think we could have this just for our own little community! What a blessing! In this country, Holy Week services really mean something—particularly to the medium class and poor people. The rich people take advantage of this time to go to their finca or to the beaches and summer resorts. Not even the buses run on Good Friday. And no good Christian even travels in a car. The people have processions commemorating the events of Holy Week. Men are dressed like the twelve apostles; women take the parts of the Virgin, Mary Magdalene, and the weeping women. Little girls in white dresses and fancy wings are carried overhead on litters surrounded with billowy white clouds. The pageantry is reminiscent of the miracle plays of the Middle Ages.

In the States you are looking forward to Spring. That is something we never experience in Costa Rica. This is the land of everlasting Maytime. We are coming to the end of the dry season and the rain will be welcome. It will be wonderful not to have to eat dust from morning until night. March was a warm month, but there wasn't a night that we didn't use blankets. The sun is extremely hot, but there is always a cool breeze in the shade.

Oh, yes, I must add that we have acquired a German Police dog. He's only a puppy, two months old. He is so cute that I have my doubts about our being able to make a watch dog out of him with fifteen women around.

With belated wishes for a joyous Eastertide, I am

Sister M. Deodigna, OSF

The dedication of Saint Clare College is portrayed in the lengthy letter that follows. In typical School Sister manner, all the work behind the scenes done by many hands, made the historical day a memorable occasion for all.

August 18, 1958

Dear Sisters,

It's almost one week since the historical day of the Dedication of Saint Clare College. Truly, for our seven Sisters, two novices, and six postulants, as well as for our 105 students and their parents, the day was significant in many ways. But, before the day itself, there were many preparations, without which the event would not have been so splendid.

For weeks Sister Verna had been practicing the solemn High Mass, both with the students and with us. The girls mastered the ordinary of the Mass and the *Ecce Sacerdos*. Sister had them divided into two choirs for the Gloria; the effect was very beautiful. For weeks we too had to sing the Proper, blending the young voices of the postulants and novices with the Sisters. Then, one fine day not too long before the 12th, Sister Joaquin glanced at the Franciscan calendar, only to find that for the Introit, *Vultum tuum* was used and not the melodic *Dilexisti* which we had almost perfected by that time! But naturally, we mastered the new Introit quickly enough.

Many an hour Sister Deodigna worked the crochet hook for the lace for a new altar cloth. And then, after it was hemmed,

Sister sewed the lace on too. The cloth fitted the new altar which our carpenter, Mr. Zuniga, made for the occasion. He also made two simple but very fitting pedestals from cedar to harmonize with our candle holders. In a way, it's very thrilling to begin a new mission because what is needed has to be made, and that when needed. So we needed a new alb and some suitable drapery for the throne of the Papal Nuncio. And we needed a Papal flag and one of Costa Rica. There's lots of good taffeta in the tiendas of San Jose, so off we went for white, gold, red, and blue. Having the material, we began to question just how to make the flags. Luckily, we've a new set of World Encyclopedias, which contained all the information needed. One Saturday evening, the sewing machine hummed away, the irons were heated, and a few stitches ripped and resewed. Result—the college proudly placed two large flags beside the altar. White rayon taffeta trimmed with gold was also the choice for the throne.

In another house in San Jose, the needles, machines, and irons were kept in use for three packed weeks. The seamstress who makes the uniforms for the students literally worked her fingers to bleeding in a concerted effort to make a school hat for each girl. And she did so! The hats involve a lot of work; they are styled on a stewardess' hat, such as one often sees in a plane or train. Some of the girls looked wonderful with it, but those with long faces are loud in their complaints that the front part of the hat is made too high. Ah well, no two women ever want to appear with the same hat anyway!

We're now up to the vigil of the feast. All the rooms have been scrubbed and waxed, the windows sparkle, the bulletin boards are trimmed, the students are having a holiday— excepting about twenty volunteers who are ready to be of service wherever they may be needed. Everyone is in readiness for the signal to begin transforming our porch-like corridors into dining rooms, and our largest, brightest room into a chapel. Out go the tables, around them are placed the chairs—some of them ours and some of them borrowed from Saint Francis College. New benches, just made for the two-fold purpose of serving as risers and seating space on the playground, are brought to the back of the cafeteria to make a choir with gradations. All prie-dieus are brought from the chapel on the second floor and placed near the front of the cafeteria for the diplomatic corps, the distinguished clergy, the special guests, and the guest Sisters. For the parents and the other guests, chairs are arranged in every available place. And thus, the morning passes swiftly, but one more item was tucked into it; for just today the last of the curtains which we made for the occasion was hemmed. All the curtains really look classy, with lovely designs silk-screened on them. No one would ever guess that so common material as muslin and linen is all we have on our windows.

All of us having been fortified for the afternoon work began with new zest. Now the committee of mothers have come to prepare the food, arranging pretty trays of meats, cookies, brownies, sandwiches. One mother, however, has come here for another important reason. She is an expert in the arrangement of flowers for various purposes. And she really is! Just tell her where you would like to use the flowers, and within minutes she produces a perfect floral arrangement for the setting. Several mothers had brought large, good-formed silver vases for our use; we have some elegant copper waste paper baskets, and then there's a special inexpensive but lovely source of flower vases to be had by splitting bamboo poles, nailing them to a wooden frame, and passing a filling station for some empty oil cans. With all these containers and a large supply of vermiculite which had been saved from the packings of the scientific equipment, Mrs. Aguilar and two of us were ready to attack the twelve-dozen white and six dozen red gladiolas which we had ordered. But that was only a start—more and more glads, white, red, pink ones; giant red dahlias kept coming from our friends. One after another, exquisite floral arrangements of delicate pink roses, dozens of gardenias, rare dahlias, mums, and more glads kept coming from more friends, mothers of the students, the President of the Municipality of Moravia, the Minister of Agriculture, etc., etc. Seems that in a little country, all the 'big shots' make it their business to remember a new college for dedication. Is this rumor too—but Mr. Challe told us that his lawyer wanted to send us some glads as well, but there were no more to be had in the city of San Jose!

Really, our school was a beautiful, fragrant spot for the feast of Saint Clare, and added to all that, the weather was perfect all that day. How very much joy we had in arranging some of the flowers. How much joy all of us surely had in our community efforts to make the day memorable and perfect. Toward late evening, we were very glad the day was not longer; everyone of us was exhausted and needed rest. Several mothers and a few dads were still here making more sandwiches; they urged us to retire because they said that the place was in good keeping. But in a building erected according to tropical architecture, there's no possibility of quiet on the second floor when a group of adults are enjoying themselves in the kitchen below.

Tuesday morning dawned—bright, cool and glorious. There was no doubt in our minds about the abundant blessings of this day. Father Aloysius, the superior of St. Francis College, had our Mass, which the Fathers offered for our intentions. Following the Mass, we recited the magnificent Office in honor of our patron with enthusiasm and festivity. Soon thereafter, Sister Rafael [surname unknown] served a fortifying breakfast in cafeteria style, because our dining room was prepared for the serving line of the people after the dedication. Now we were ready for the crowds who soon began to arrive.

The girls looked lovely, all dressed up in carefully pressed blouses, cleaned and pressed skirts and jackets (we didn't notice a single button missing), white bobby socks, and, for the most part, patent leather slippers. They were eager to don their school gorras (hats) for the first time. It was amusing to have each girl come up to the teacher for the final adjusting of the hat.

Soon after the second-year students were fitted out, they proceeded to the main entrance of the building to form a guard of honor for the Papal Nuncio. There were many other people who walked past that guard of honor while we stood waiting for the Papal Nuncio. So much hand-shaking! So many *Buenos Dias*!!! We were pleased with the conduct of the girls; they remembered to be alert and preceded the clergy to the chapel (cafeteria), singing the *Ecce Sacerdos*. The chapel was packed with people. The officers of the Solemn Mass were joyous in offering the Perfect Gift to the Father; their vestments were a rich gold set. These against the blue-green wall of the cafeteria were exquisite. All who had a part in the singing let the joy and excitement of the day come through in the melodic chants of the Mass. After the Mass and just prior to all the speeches, the President, Mario Echandi, came for the rest of the dedication ceremony. There were other diplomats, representatives of the Education Department, representatives of the American Embassy and Honduras, religious, and the Padres de Familias and friends present.

Following the speeches, the clergy, students, and people proceeded to the outside for the blessing of the edifice by the Papal Nuncio and the hanging of the crucifix ceremony in the lobby of the school. In the lobby, on the wall opposite the one where the crucifix was to be placed, was hanging a beautiful painting of Saint Clare which we proudly point to as the work of Sister Marguerite [surname unknown]. When the Papal Nuncio had finished with the ceremony, he wanted to address the students and people. We weren't expecting this. The Papal Nuncio is not a tall man; he wanted something upon which to stand that he might be seen. Father Aloysius, who was the master of ceremonies, proved very resourceful by running into the parlor, removing the bouquet of gardenias from the coffee table, and placing it before the Papal Nuncio. The students sang our school song, and thus the ceremony was concluded.

Meanwhile, the cafeteria was re-made into a place for dining. Here everyone received all he cared for by way of food and coffee. The students were served in one of the science laboratories. They took their plates out to the lawn, sat on the grass and a few lawn chairs and benches for a delightful picnic. Some of their parents came and sat with them. This was a delightful scene. For the students, the day was almost perfect—

almost. We have a six-month old police dog, Prince. The girls so wanted to dress Prince in a hat too for the occasion, but we had him spending the day with his sister, Belle, at Saint Francis.

Well, that's about the end of the story; only the cleanup and the restoration of regular order. The Madres de Familias overestimated the amount of food, so it had to be taken care of. Some of our very poor neighbors were grateful recipients and some was put in the deep freeze. The following day the girls enjoyed another picnic. Then there was the job of restoring the furniture to the various places. In an amazingly short time, all of us, with the help of two men, had every prie dieu, chair, table in the right spot again. It was mid-afternoon, and we were grateful, happy, and tired. In the evening, we celebrated with a picnic on the lawn, during which the electricity was shut off—but it didn't matter. We said our rosary in the quiet darkness, chatted a bit, and waited until the lights were on before doing the dishes. Rich—abundantly rich—were the blessings of God on our first feast day!

Are you tired now? You've a right to be. Today is August 19. Our two Sisters arrived this morning as scheduled. Now we are nine 'norte americans.' We're eagerly waiting for supper for we know the Sisters will have much to tell us.

Lovingly,

The Sisters of Saint Clare College,
Costa Rica

The first reception in Central America, that of Sisters Flora Campos and Margarita Sandi, took place in Costa Rica in 1958. In the early years, the number of School Sisters of St. Francis grew steadily at the mission, as did the student body and the number of candidates. The apostolate expanded to include various charitable works in the San Lucas Island Penitentiary, San Dismas Boys' Reformatory, poor barrios, rural areas during the school year and coastal towns during vacation periods. The ministry begun in Mother Corona's administration thrived and continued for another two decades after her death.

Sister Jo Ann Euper's book, *1ˢᵗ Century of Service*, offers an explanation for the diversified apostolates that evolved in Costa Rica.

> Initially, the sisters at St. Clare had expected a student body similar to those they usually taught in the United States. Upon finding themselves teaching the wealthy instead, they decided to take the opportunity to educate the upper class in regard to their obligations toward the poor and illiterate. This decision influenced the classroom work and led to projects in the surrounding poor barrios where, during vacation time, the students and teachers organized educational and recreational activities for children and classes in nutrition, domestic arts and health for adults. In turn, these projects further influenced the apostolate in Costa Rica, revealing to the sisters more and more of the local needs.

Some of the sisters also taught in night school offering elementary education for adults. In March 1966, three School Sisters of St. Francis joined with Roma Arrieta in opening the Instituto Tilaranense de Educacion (ITEF) in Tilaran for the formation of young women. Within a year, they were already involved in parish pastoral work and in conducting evening classes for older women. By 1974, the school had evolved into a Diocesan Pastoral Center. No more girls were accepted, but School Sisters of St. Francis continued working at the center. In 1970, School Sisters of St. Francis began teaching at the University of Costa Rica.

At St. Clare, originally a girls' school, various developments brought about a shift to coeducational status in 1970. There was also an effort to integrate gifted but economically poor students into the program via a special program called the Vespertina. A pioneer effort in the democratization of education and modifications, the Vespertina proved highly successful and became one of the most significant contributions of the congregation in Costa Rica.

In the late 1960s, post conciliar renewal began to affect both the apostolate and the formation program in Costa Rica. The School Sisters of St. Francis closed the United States novitiate and embarked on re-evaluation of traditional formation procedures. Simultaneously, sisters in Costa Rica began moving away from the centralized institutional work toward varied pastoral and human promotion works in urban and other areas. As a result, the presence of School Sisters of St. Francis decreased dramatically. Enrollment in the school declined also. For years there had been hints that the school might be taken over by the government, which appeared to be nationalizing the private schools in the country. Financially, the School Sisters of St. Francis found it difficult to support. For several years, only two sisters remained on the faculty.

As early as 1972, the community had been seriously pondering the future of St. Clare College as a School Sister of St. Francis institution. In 1977, concerned that the school might not have a 25th anniversary, the Costa Rican School Sisters of St. Francis' community celebrated its 20th anniversary. Sister Deodigna was invited back to celebrate the occasion. At that time, the Sister Deodigna Scholarship Fund was inaugurated. In 1965, Sister Deodigna had written that she believed the sisters' extracurricular works were perhaps more effective than their principal work at St. Clare.

In 1983, the operation of the school was transferred to an association of parents, alumni, and teachers, while the land and buildings were purchased by the Archdiocese of San Jose. This also marked the end of all but a token School Sisters of St. Francis presence. There are presently five sisters in Costa Rica.

FIRST GROUP SENT TO COSTA RICA – 1957
SISTERS DEODIGNA SCHIRRA (SEATED), JOAQUIN
GARCIA, MINA SCHAUB, SEVERINA SONTAG

CHAPTER FOURTEEN

THIRD TERM IN OFFICE

Elections are a serious matter within religious communities. There are definite procedures to be followed. In preparation for the 1948 election, her second term, Mother Corona sent the following letter to the sisters to be followed in accord with the congregation's constitution which has the approval of the Vatican.

November 21, 1947

My dear sisters,

The General Election will be held on January 6, 1948. According to our Constitutions, two delegates from each Province are to be chosen as members of the General Chapter. The delegates for the American community will be elected at a Special Chapter to be held in the Motherhouse on December 13, 1947. This Special Chapter will be composed of nineteen sisters—a representative for every one-hundred perpetually professed members. The sisters who have perpetual vows will cast their votes for the nineteen representatives on November 29, 1947.

The following procedure is to be observed:

1. At an appointed time, the sisters entitled to vote will assemble in the Chapel or Church and recite the Veni Creator, three Our Fathers, Hail Marys, and Glory be to the Fathers in honor of the Holy Ghost, and the Memorare of the Blessed Virgin.

2. They will then proceed to an assigned room, and in the presence of the sisters, the Superior will break

the seal of the enclosed envelope, which contains a folded list of the perpetually professed sisters, a ballot sheet, and an envelope.

3. Each sister personally writes on the ballot sheet the names of the nineteen sisters for whom she casts her vote and the date of their investiture; she folds her ballot and places it in the envelope, which she seals before handing it to her Superior.

4. The Superior encloses all the ballots in the envelope provided for the purpose, seals it in the presence of the sisters, and mails it to the Motherhouse without delay.

Since this is a secret ballot, no sister should write her name either on the ballot sheet or on the envelope. Furthermore, no sister may ever reveal to anyone for whom she cast her vote; neither may she speak of anything that took place in the Chapter. That is a strict rule of the Church, and every elector is bound to its observance. The lists are to be returned to the Superior before the sisters leave the room, and these lists, together with any unused lists or ballots, are to be burned in presence of the two oldest sisters, counting from the date of reception.

The method described herein has the approval of our Most Reverend Archbishop, who will preside at the General Election.

Offer many fervent prayers and sacrifices for God's blessing upon the coming election, dear sisters. You are praying the Veni Creator, three Our Fathers, Hail Marys, and Glory be to the Fathers, and add the Memorare of the Blessed Virgin. Prayer is most important, for 'Unless the Lord build the house, they labor in vain who build it.'

Lovingly,

Mother M. Corona, OSF

The General Election was to be held on January 6, 1948. Due to the delay of the provincial superior and two delegates from Europe, the election was held on January 26, 1948. The results were as follows:

January 26, 1948

My dear sisters,

The General Elections were held today with the following results:

Mother M. Corona [Wirfs]	Superior General
Sister M. Clemens [Rudolph]	Mother Assistant and First Councilor
Sister M. Alexander [Fiecke]	Second Councilor
Sister M. Loretto [Thill]	Third Councilor
Sister M. Jutta [Hollenbeck]	Fourth Councilor
Sister M. Deodigna [Schirra]	General Secretary
Sister M. Justitia [Brill]	General Procurator

The Most Reverend Archbishop presided at the Election and declared the aforesaid sisters canonically elected to their respective offices. Mother M. Amanda requested the electors to omit her name from the ballot because she desired to be relieved of the office of Mother Assistant and First Councilor.

I am confident, dear sisters, you will pledge your loyalty to the administration about to begin, for in so doing, you are proving your love and devotion to the congregation. If we continue to work together in sisterly love and harmony, we may hope for a continuation of God's blessing. United effort makes us one. There is power and strength in unity. Let us then, dear sisters, as our Holy Rule prescribes, 'be united by a single bond, that of true charity, which does not proceed from natural motives but is founded on the holy will of God.'

With love, greetings, and blessings, I am

Your loving,

Mother M. Corona, OSF

---

* * * * * * * * * * * * * *

In preparation for the election in 1954, Mother Clemens petitioned Archbishop Kiley to approve a third term of office for Mother Corona.

March 6, 1953

The Most Rev. Moses E. Kiley, STD
Archbishop of Milwaukee

Most Reverend and dear Archbishop:

May we humbly submit to Your Excellency the enclosed petition to His Holiness to sanction a third term of office for our loved Mother Mary Corona if she is re-elected at the expiration of her second term in January 1954? In the face of present conditions, a change seems inadvisable, and the kindness of Your Excellency in approving our petition will be deeply appreciated.

The sisters are offering special prayers for our loved Archbishop. May God grant you every benediction!

Your Excellency's humble servants,

Mother M. Clemens [Rudolph], Mother
Assistant & First Councilor
Sister M. Alexander [Fiecke], Second
Councilor
Sister M. Loretto [Thill], Third Councilor
Sister M. Jutta [Hollenbeck], Fourth
Councilor

Simultaneously, Mother Clemens and her Council sent their petition to Pope Pius XII.

March 6, 1953

Most Holy Father:

Prostrate at the feet of Your Holiness, we, the members of the General Council of the School Sisters of St. Francis of

St. Joseph's Convent, Milwaukee, Wisconsin, humbly petition that Mother Mary Corona be permitted to accept a third term of office if re-elected.

Mother Mary Corona, prior to her election as Superior General in 1942, served the Congregation in the capacity of teacher, Superior, Councilor, and Mother Assistant. As Councilor she had the privilege of working under Mother Mary Alfons, one of the saintly foundresses of the Congregation, and as Mother Assistant under the direction of Mother Mary Stanislaus, one of the first members of the Community. Thus, she acquired in an eminent degree the spirit, the aim, and the ideals of our revered foundresses.

But, above all, God has singularly endowed Mother Mary Corona with those qualities of heart and soul which are so needed in one who, while guiding and directing, must at the same time take the hallowed place of mother. This she has done, for none, from the senior member of the Congregation to the youngest aspirant, hesitates to approach her.

The two terms of Mother Mary Corona's office—1942-1954—have been marked by war, rumors of war, and great unrest, so that her plans for the glory of God and the welfare of souls were hampered in their execution. At present, a large college building, dedicated to the education of Sisters and young ladies, is still unfinished owing to building and trade restrictions during these years of crisis. Other plans such as the establishment of novitiates in Switzerland and Honduras, the erection of provinces, the expansion of mission work at home and abroad, have of necessity been deferred.

Because at present, the future is even more uncertain, we humbly petition Your Holiness, our loved Father and Pontifical Protector, to grant the favor we supplicate—namely, permission to have Mother Mary Corona accept a third term of office if she is re-elected in January 1954. Mother Mary Corona is totally unaware of this petition. She would be happy to lay down her office, but we know that if, in obedience to God's holy will, she is asked to accept another term, she would be willing to bear the burden of her office for another six-year period. We feel the granting of this favor would be to the greater honor and glory of God and the best interest of our Congregation, for in the present world crisis, a change seems inadvisable.

Again, prostrate at the feet of Your Holiness, we have the honor to profess ourselves

Your Holiness's humble servants,

Mother M. Clemens [Rudolph], Mother Assistant & First Councilor
Sister M. Alexander [Fiecke], Second Councilor
Sister M. Loretto [Thill], Third Councilor
Sister M. Jutta [Hollenbeck], Fourth Councilor

His Holiness
Pope Pius XII
Vatican City, Italy

One month later, Mother Clemens appealed to Mother Pascalina, who had been the pope's housekeeper for 35 years when the letter was sent. The 62-year old German nun ran the papal's private household with an iron will. The Vatican priests knew little about her and simply referred to her by her initials: M.P. The *Milwaukee Sentinel*, March 2, 1958, had this to say about her on the occasion of her 40th year serving as the pope's housekeeper at age 67.

The future Pope's first meeting with her was in 1912 when, as a young priest from the Vatican office of secretary of state, he visited the Einsiedlen Abbey in the Bernese Alps for a rest. He was a frail man and needed to guard his health well. The young nun spoke with Eugenio Pacelli in the bluntest terms. She told him that if he wanted to continue his ministry—and do it well—he must take the local cure: Swiss milk and cheese.

Pacelli did not like milk at that time; however, he took the 'cure' and it worked. He never forgot the nun who had been so firm, yet so solicitous about his health.

When he was appointed papal nuncio to Munich in 1917 and made a bishop by Pope Benedict XV, he asked whether Sister Pascalina might take charge of his bishopric household. The request was approved, and she later accompanied his household to the Vatican when Pacelli was named secretary of state and a cardinal.

NO ORDINARY PERSON

Sister Pascalina became 'Madre' (mother) when Pacelli was chosen Pope in 1939 because she needed help to run the papal household and sent for three German nuns of her order to assist in this work.

The presence of a nun on the third floor of the Vatican apartments, overlooking St. Peter's mammoth square, was certainly a novelty. However, this nun was no ordinary person.

Requesting a third term in office for Mother Corona was not in accord with the Constitution of the School Sisters of St. Francis. When Mothers Corona and Clemens went to Rome in 1952, they befriended Mother Pascalina. What better person to intercede for Mother Clemens in this extraordinary request than Mother Pascalina, who had direct contact with the Pope.

April 8, 1953

My dear Mother Pascalina,

Our visit to Rome last September is for me a hallowed memory. On that blessed occasion, when I had the privilege of meeting you, dear Mother Pascalina, in company with our dear

Mother Mary Corona, you kindly and generously inquired if in some way you could be of help to her. Mindful of this true sisterly offer, I am taking the liberty of writing today not in behalf of our dear Mother Mary Corona, but of the Congregation which is so dear to her.

Our loved Mother Mary Corona will complete her second six-year term of office as Superior-General in January 1954. On March 6, 1953, the General Council, totally unknown to Mother Mary Corona, in a letter addressed to His Holiness, our loved Pope Pius XII, petitioned that she be permitted to accept a third term of office if re-elected in January 1954. Acting upon the advice of our Auxiliary Bishop, the Most Reverend Roman R. Atkielski, the petition was sent to His Holiness through our revered Archbishop, the Most Reverend Moses E. Kiley, Archbishop of Milwaukee.

The purpose of this letter, dear Mother Pascalina, is humbly to ask that you help us secure this great favor if it is at all within your power to do so. We do not know if our petition has already been presented to His Holiness by the Sacred Congregation, but even so, we are appealing to you to put in a good word for us. God has singularly endowed our loved Mother Mary Corona with those qualities of heart and soul which are so necessary in one who must fill the office of Superior and Mother. Her two terms of office, 1942-1954, have been marked by crises which were world-wide in their effects, so that plans for the glory of God and the welfare of souls in mission fields at home and abroad could not be carried out. A change now would not be to the best interest of the Congregation, for, in taking to further the Kingdom of God by the erection of provinces and by the opening of novitiates in Switzerland and Honduras. Her great devotion to our loved Pontiff is known to you, and foremost among her desires is the carrying out of the wishes of his August Person.

Our dear Mother Mary Corona is unaware of this petition. Children, when they cannot appeal to the mother, approach the father. We are doing the same, assured that the Father of Christendom, whom we are privileged to honor as our

Pontifical Protector, will not refuse the appeal of his children who approach him with confidence and trust.

Hopefully, we will await word as to the decision of His Holiness, and prayerfully we shall ask God to guide and direct him in this matter so dear to the heart of the Sisters.

The illness of His Holiness has been a source of grief to all the Sisters, and God is being petitioned in fervent prayer to speedily restore his health and strength. You, too, dear Mother Pascalina, are being remembered in our prayers. We trust the effects of the accident have worn off so that you can carry on your privileged work with ease.

Sister M. Thomasine, who accompanied Mother Mary Corona and Sister M. Alexander when they were in Rome in January 1952, joins me in my prayer that the Risen Savior may grant you an abundance of Paschal Benediction.

Gratefully and sincerely,

Mother M. Clemens, OSF
Mother Assistant

Time was running out. Mother Clemens was anxious because she had not received a reply to her request.

June 26, 1953

My dear Mother Pascalina,

On April 8 we wrote to you on behalf of the Sisters of our Congregation who have appealed to me to petition His Holiness to grant a third term of office to our loved Mother M. Corona, whose second six-year term as Superior General expires in January 1954.

Our letter to His Holiness was referred to His Excellency, the Most Reverend Moses E. Kiley, the late Archbishop of Milwaukee. Day by day we awaited a reply, but in vain. Finally, noticing that the Sisters are growing anxious, I took the liberty of making inquiry at the Milwaukee Chancery, and learned to my dismay that the appeal to His Holiness had never been forwarded. In all probability, our saintly Archbishop was too sick at the time to give the matter his attention, and the appeal was laid aside and overlooked.

The Chancery has advised us to present the petition through our Cardinal Protector. Since ours is the glorious privilege of having His Holiness as our Pontifical Protector, we are taking the liberty of referring the letter to you, dear Mother Pascalina, with the humble appeal that you present it to the Holy Father in our behalf. If you can put in a good word for us, we would be most grateful.

God has seen fit to call our revered Archbishop to himself, and now our deeply loved and esteemed Spiritual Director, Reverend Adolph J. Klink, who has been a faithful father to the Congregation for more than thirty years, will soon be with God. Consequently, we trust that in his fatherly love for us, his Franciscan daughters, His Holiness will see fit to leave Mother M. Corona with us as our spiritual mother and guide.

With sincere and hearty greetings and a prayer that God may richly bless you for any assistance you may give us in this matter, I am

Sincerely yours in Christ,

Mother M. Clemens, OSF
Mother Assistant

For your convenience, we are enclosing a copy of our letter of April 8.

We know Mother Corona would be deeply grateful if our loved Father Klink were recommended to the prayers of His Holiness, and if you too, dear Mother Pascalina, would remember him in your petitions.

Seven weeks later, Mother Clemens frantically sent another letter to Mother Pascalina.

August 13, 1953

My dear Mother Pascalina,

A thousand thanks for your kind letter! My heart filled with gratitude when I learned that you had personally presented our petition to His Holiness. The members of the Council share my sentiments of gratitude and join me in asking God to reward and bless you for your great charity.

As the date for the General Election draws nearer, we realize more and more how difficult it would be to replace our loved Mother M. Corona. Now we are wondering if there is anything further that we are expected to do, or are we simply to wait word from His Holiness as to whether or not Mother M. Corona may be re-elected Superior General. You will pardon us for again troubling you, dear Mother Pascalina, but we are inexperienced in such matters and are eager to do all we can to help the good cause along. Any suggestions you may make will be accepted gratefully.

With loving greetings and prayerful wishes, I am

Sincerely yours in Christ,

Mother M. Clemens, OSF
Mother Assistant

Up to the present, we have not heard anything.

Ah! What a relief to Mother Clemens! Approval for a third term for Mother Corona was granted.

September 24, 1953

My dear Mother Pascalina,

There is great joy in Milwaukee today over the enthronement of our new Archbishop. God is good, and

Milwaukee is grateful to God and to His Holiness for sending us the Most Reverend Albert G. Meyer as our Shepherd and Guide.

However, in my heart and in the hearts of the other Sister Councilors, there is a deeper joy over the message which came in your kind letter early this week. Words cannot express our gratitude, dear Mother Pascalina, but God can and will repay you for what you have done for us. We now feel at ease and look forward to the coming general election with renewed confidence that God will continue the marvelous care He has always granted to our Congregation.

If at any time I can be of service to you, do not hesitate to call on me. I would deem it a happy privilege to serve you.

With inexpressible gratitude and prayerful wishes for God's choicest benedictions, I am

In the Sacred Heart,

Mother M. Clemens, OSF
Mother Assistant

O Happy Day! Mother Corona was officially re-elected as Mother General.

The Mother House
Epiphany - 1954

My dear Sisters,

Today I send you tidings of great joy.

His Holiness, Pope Pius XII, through the Sacred Congregation of Religious, graciously granted to His Excellency, our Most Reverend Archbishop, Albert G. Meyer, who presided at the General Chapter, the faculty to confirm the election of our loved Mother Mary Corona as Superior-General of our Congregation if she were re-elected. I am pleased to tell you that the results of this morning's election are:

Mother Mary Corona [Wirfs]   Superior-General

Mother Mary Clemens [Rudolph]	Assistant & First Councilor
Sister Mary Alexander [Fiecke]	Second Councilor
Sister Mary Jutta [Hollenbeck]	Third Councilor
Sister Mary Wilhelmina [Brenner]	Fourth Councilor
Sister Mary Deodigna [Schirra]	General Secretary
Sister Mary Justitia [Brill]	General Procurator

Needless to say, there is great jubilation in the Mother House today—a jubilation that, with the arrival of this letter, will echo and re-echo through the length and breadth of the missions staffed by the School Sisters of St. Francis.

We are most grateful to God for the signal blessing He has bestowed upon our Congregation and are confident all of you will join us in a fervent *Te Deum*.

Reverend Mother Corona and all the members of the Generalate wish to express a fervent 'May God reward you!' for your wholehearted loyalty and cooperation in the past. We are counting on a continuance of your devotion and support during the years to come, and in turn promise untiring zeal in promoting the spiritual and temporal welfare of our esteemed Congregation.

In Mary Immaculate,

Mother M. Clemens, OSF
Mother Assistant

With an ever-grateful heart, Mother Clemens expressed her deep gratitude to Mother Pascalina.

January 6, 1954

My dear Mother Pascalina,

Our General Chapter is a happy, blessed memory. Thanks to the goodness of God, our loved Mother Mary Corona will continue her beautiful and outstanding work. She was unanimously re-elected Superior-General of our Congregation.

Our beloved and esteemed Holy Father, Pope Pius XII, has listened to our plea which you, dear Mother Pascalina, so kindly presented to His Holiness. We are deeply grateful to our beloved Holy Father, whom we have the honor to look upon as our Pontifical Protector. To you, dearest Mother, we wish to express our sincere 'May God reward you!' You have been instrumental in making us very happy. Today's feast is truly an 'Epiphany' or a 'manifestation' of God's goodness to more than three thousand School Sisters of St. Francis.

May the happiness which fills our hearts today, dear Mother Pascalina, return to you in richest benediction!

Gratefully in Mary Immaculate,

Mother M. Clemens, OSF
Mother Assistant

MOTHER CLEMENS RUDOLPH
MOTHER ASSISTANT
1948–1960

CHAPTER FIFTEEN

CHALLENGES

The story of the School Sisters of St. Francis was a combination of phenomenal growth during Mother Corona's administration (over 3,500 international members by 1960) and a highly centralized government. Mother Corona was the sole administrator, with one assistant, a council of three people, and no provinces or provincial superiors in America.

Not surprisingly, therefore, there was some unrest among the sisters over "inefficiency" and "lack of contact" with the single major superior. Also, the American sisters in the ranks had only two votes at the Chapter. Sister Mina Schaub, in the publication *Light on the School Sisters of St. Francis* in the spring 1964 issue, stated the following:

> Mother Corona stood as a symbol between the old and the new order of things. Misunderstandings, arising from the inability of some to see the deeper motives of the things she did and the changes she tried to bring about, caused suffering for her.

In the 1950s, hearing of the unrest amongst a few sisters, priests of the Milwaukee Archdiocese requested a visitation of the major houses of the community. The canonical visitator was a Capuchin priest, Father Nerius Semmler, a resident in Milwaukee. His report was submitted to Archbishop Meyer, but remained inactive until 1959, when Archbishop Cousins was installed in the See of Milwaukee.

Five requests were then made to Rome through the Archbishop:

1. A new administration, since the former one had been in for 18 years.

2. A new Rule, to be voted on by a representative chapter and submitted to the Holy See for approval.

3. Increased representation in voting, e.g., one delegate for every 50 members.

4. Those who had been superiors continuously to return to the ranks after their term of office.

5. Establishment of at least four self-sustaining provinces.

Each of these requests was approved by Rome and mandated to be completed within the next major superior's term of office.

Already toward the end of Mother Stanislaus' term of office, the subject of provinces was presented to her in a letter by Reverend A.C. Ellis, S.J., which is cited in Chapter Three of this publication.

Earlier, in a letter addressed to Archbishop Meyer on February 4, 1958, Mother Corona had stated the following:

> We would like to inform Your Excellency that we are taking steps toward organizing a province to comprise the dioceses of Rockford, Joliet, Peoria, and Springfield in Illinois; Fort Wayne and Gary in Indiana; and Jefferson City in Missouri. As matters stand now, between 275 and 300 Sisters would be members of this province.

> The Most Reverend Loras T. Lane, D.D., has communicated with the Apostolic Delegate, who advised that we take the steps necessary to organize a province while the sanction of the Holy See is pending. The Bishop of Rockford is planning to have the officials and any other Sisters of the province reside with our Sisters, who will staff the Cathedral schools until such time as the province is financially able to build a provincial house.

Archbishop Meyer replied on February 6, 1958.

> I am pleased to learn from you that definite steps are being taken to organize another province of your community. I will be interested, of course, to be kept informed about the same.

Mount St. Francis Province was established at the end of Mother Corona's third term. The following letter was sent to all the sisters regarding this new province and the appointment of Mother Calestine Schwener.

> October 2, 1959
>
> My dear Sisters,
>
> The General Council met on September 29, 1959, for the purpose of electing a Provincial Superior for our new Province. Sister M. Calestine was elected and will assume the duties of her office immediately. She will have the title 'Mother.' Her address until next summer will be that of the Mother House—1501 South Layton Boulevard, Milwaukee 15, Wisconsin. At the invitation of His Excellency, Bishop Lane, the Provincialate will take up residence in the new convent now under construction for the Sisters who are to staff our new high school in the Rockford diocese. The space will be adequate since the high school will open only one year at a time.

The Sisters of the Province will address their letters to Mother M. Calestine. Surplus money should be sent to her. Continue to send the money for St. Joseph Fund drive to me as heretofore. The pastors of the Diocese of Rockford were not requested to take part in this St. Joseph Fund collection, since we presume they will be asked to contribute toward the Rockford Province.

Mother M. Calestine will start to visit the missions of the Province sometime in October. Her assistants or councilors have been appointed, but their names are being withheld, since they will have no official duties until the opening of the Provincialate in Rockford next summer.

All the Sisters are interested in the new Province. In fact, they are enthusiastic and are praying for God's special blessing on this important undertaking. I am confident that you who have been assigned to the new Province will always prove yourselves faithful and true members of our beloved Congregation by accepting your superiors as a manifestation of God's holy will for you. Assist your Mother Provincial in every way so that by your ready obedience and by your spirit of cooperation, you will help to lighten her burden. 'Where there is unity, there is strength,' and as I know you, you will give your superior wholehearted support. Her post is difficult, but your willingness to cooperate and your sincerity will go far toward easing her burden. In putting forth your best efforts for the benefit of the Province, you will continue your work for the Congregation as you have been doing heretofore. We are all one, but there must be organization so that everything will continue to progress smoothly.

'May the Lord bless you and keep you. May he show his face to you and have mercy on you. May he turn his countenance toward you and give you peace.' This is my prayer for you on the feast of our holy Father and Patron Saint Francis. May his spirit abide with you always.

Sincerely and lovingly,

Mother M. Corona, OSF

The following letter indicates broader representation in the 1960 election.

December 19, 1959

PLEASE READ THIS LETTER TO THE SISTERS WITHOUT
UNNECESSARY DELAY

My dear Sisters,

Accompanying this letter is the list of Sisters eligible as delegates to the forthcoming chapters. The manner of procedure (pending approval of the Holy See) will be found at the top of the list. Our Most Reverend Archbishop is confident that the answer will be here on time, but, in order to forestall unnecessary delay, we think it best to have you go ahead with the voting for delegates. The number can always be changed if necessary. In the meantime, if word comes from Rome through our Archbishop, we shall inform you at once.

In order to have a broader representation at the General Chapter, the Sisters with Perpetual Vows in each Province will vote for additional delegates to participate in the respective Preliminary Chapters on the basis of one delegate for every fifty Sisters. These extra delegates in their Preliminary Chapters will elect one-third of their number to participate in the General Chapter—

Mother House   2,024 Sisters   40 Delegates   13 Electors
Rockford Province   232 Sisters   5 Delegates   2 Electors
German Province   1,050 Sisters   21 Delegates   7 Electors

making the total number of additional delegates to the General Chapter twenty-two.

The two delegates from each province prescribed by our Constitutions will not be counted as extra; the two Sisters who receive the highest number of votes will be considered the delegates prescribed by the Constitutions; the others will rank according to the number of votes they receive. It is doubtful if the German Province will be in a position to send additional electors.

I shall take this opportunity to thank you for your loyal and faithful cooperation. To deal with sincere, trustworthy Sisters was always an encouragement. Crosses and trials must be borne if we want to reach heaven, but the consciousness of your fidelity and your interest in the welfare of our Congregation was always a consolation. I step out of office with a feeling of gratitude to God and to you. I beg pardon and am sorry for any bad example I have given you and assure you of my prayers for your spiritual and temporal welfare. I beg you to give the same help and loyal support to my successor, who will count on your good will and assistance. Continue to work with heart and soul for the welfare and progress of our Congregation, for it must prosper and thrive. In unity and uniformity there is strength.

May our Heavenly Mother with her Holy Child bless you!

Sincerely yours in Jesu Bambina,

Mother M. Corona, OSF

In a letter dated January 2, 1960, Mother Corona informed Archbishop Meyer, who was now Cardinal Meyer, of the Archdiocese of Chicago of the good news.

Our new province has been established. It comprises our schools in the dioceses of Rockford, Joliet, Peoria, and Springfield, Illinois; Fort Wayne and Gary, Indiana; and one small school in the diocese of Jefferson City, Missouri. The Sisters as a whole seem satisfied to belong to the new province, realizing it is for the welfare of the Congregation. Adjustments will be necessary next summer, but they will be minor.

The Provincial Superior with her staff will reside in the convent connected with the Rockford Pro-Cathedral High School, now under construction. Our Sisters will staff the school, one year at a time; when the school has reached the beginning of its fourth year, the new provincial convent should be completed. The Rockford Province is comprised of thirty-four parochial elementary schools and two high schools. About 300 Sisters

> constitute the Province. We have every reason to hope that it is
> an undertaking pleasing to God, and that He will bless it.

However, the unrest in the late 50s continued to brew while the formation of a new province was in process. Sister Leonette Tabat, later known as Sister Joan, led a small band of followers in her crusade to prevent Mother Corona from a fourth term of office and to have more delegates at the General Chapter. Rome had already stipulated that she may not run for a fourth term.

The process of communicating was vastly different a half-century ago. While nearly all homes had landlines with a rotary-dial telephone, the Sisters did not have unrestricted access to phone-calling. Long-distance calls were billed by the minute; therefore, letter-writing was the primary source of communication. But by custom, Sisters did not write to each other, and by rule their letters were read by the superior before being mailed. That adds significance to this letter sent to 35 sisters by Sister Leonette just days before Mother Corona communicated the accurate information to the sisters.

> ALVERNO COLLEGE
> 3401 SOUTH 39TH STREET
> MILWAUKEE 15, WISCONSIN
>
> December 12, 1959
>
> Dear Sister Primosa,
>
> I am sticking out my neck and I trust that you will have the charity not to cut it! What I have to say I say with all sincerity and with the best of motives. I have been on-the-road almost constantly this year, and I am literally ill from what I hear. Sisters are insecure; they are scared; they distrust the administration; they want things different but fear to discuss it even with a friend

much less out in the open. Generally, they feel that what is ahead on January 6th is 'fixed' and that no matter what they are told about increased representation, there's no use—it will only remain the same. The Rockford appointment and the fact that the Sisters were given the impression that they had a voice and then that voice was not counted, has fearfully deepened distrust. I have thought and thought, and this is what I thought:

The community received a letter from Mother stating that there will be increased delegates. How many—who knows?—perhaps 5, perhaps 100. 100 would seem like a dream but what prevents us from dreaming or hoping? It seems to me that if all the Sisters would throw the topic out for community discussion, it would put an end to this negative chatter about dishonesty in the administration. I feel this way: Mother could not say that there will be increased delegates without first petitioning Rome. This must be a very special privilege since our Rule, as it stands, does not so provide. Therefore, the Rule would have to be changed before anything could be done. So, this must be a big permission and we should be grateful to the Church for it. If the Sisters refuse to vote (as I have heard many say) because they feel that this would show the administration that they think they are dishonest, that is utterly stupid. If we are given the right, then we have the corresponding duty to use that right intelligently. If a new administration goes in in the 70-year old bracket, we will have no one to blame but ourselves. It seems to me that we need to pray seriously, think seriously, and openly discuss this matter so that voting will be intelligent. If we begin to talk about what will be for the GOOD of the community, then all this talk about how something will be 'pulled on us despite Rome' will end. We cannot know what to do, if increased delegates are given, unless we begin to consider who and what. As members of this community, we have a responsibility toward it and to so consider this responsibility is the most loyal thing that we can do. We all appreciate what has been done for us in the past, and we are mighty proud of our community and all the good religious in it; therefore, we are much concerned at this moment. It hurts me deeply to hear Sisters (all over) say that this is a 'planned affair' and that we may as well face reality about it. I still trust the Church as well as the Holy Spirit, but intelligent conversation on the part of grown-up, mature religious women also seems essential.

Please do your bit as far as your voice can carry in your own mission, as well as to all you know in your area. Urge the Sisters to open discussion in their circles. Encourage them to open discussions, to lead them objectively so that the Sisters will think along lines of their responsibility and the welfare of the community and so select their delegates on these grounds. I will do my part here; others are doing it in other areas. This is not meant to be disloyal—as things are tagged—but a real sincere effort to think correctly and to save us from the 'revolution' that many predict if 'this doesn't go right.' The fact is: if the Church gives us the chance to vote, what will we do about it? If your mission or your local area would be allowed one delegate, what would you do? It is also a fact that the local superior is not necessarily the delegate; every Sister is a potential delegate. Perhaps this is a dream, perhaps not. If it is sprung the last minute, whose mind will be prepared to think right? Isn't preparedness stressed in every field?

Please destroy this. I trust your confidence that you will not 'turn me in.' Let this be your idea—other concerned Sisters are doing the same: casual conversation, sincere, out-in-the-open discussion should educate the mind. And, I am sure, God will protect us. You may like to consider such names as Sisters Joan and Celine and others in that age bracket (40-50). Meanwhile, God bless you. Pray for us all. Do not answer this letter.

Lovingly,

Sister M. Leonette, OSF

One might ask, "who was this Sister Leonette Tabat?" She was a highly, self-driven, talented musician, intelligent, and always ready to fight for what she deemed a worthy cause. "Upbeat" seems to be the word that best described Sister

Leonette, who often used the term in her life and passion—choral music. Educated at DePaul University, where she earned a master's degree in music, a master's degree in theology, with a major in liturgical studies from the University of Notre Dame, she excelled in all her studies. She had a wide and varied experience as a teacher, music director, choir director, liturgist, and clinician—a "Joan of all trades," so to speak. For many years, in the 70s and 80s, she was the associate director of the Office of Divine Worship for the Joliet Catholic Diocese, director of music and director of the Joliet Diocesan Chorale—80 to 100-voice choir made up of volunteers from many parishes of the diocese. She also taught at the diocesan minor seminary, St. Charles Borromeo, from 1970 to 1989. In her own words, she often said, "I eat, drink, and breathe liturgy no matter where I am in my life. I expect to go to heaven with a baton in my hand."

Sister Leonette was supervisor of music in the Milwaukee and Chicago Catholic schools in 1958 to 1960 when she was targeted by Archbishop Cousins' advisors to initiate discussion with the sisters regarding more representation in the General Chapter and the formation of provinces. What better person to choose than Sister Leonette, who had easy access to the sisters and church authorities.

On January 4, 1960, Sister Primosa Thelen went to Mother Corona with the letter she had received from Sister Leonette pertaining to the upcoming General Chapter. Mother Corona then asked Sister Jutta Hollenbeck, dean of Alverno College, to bring Sister Leonette to the motherhouse. Sister Leonette requested an opportunity to speak to the assembled council and Father A.M. Klink. The request was granted. At 12:30 p.m., January 5, 1960, the special meeting was held with

Mother Corona, Mother Clemens, Sisters Alexander, Jutta, Thomasine, Leonette, and Father A.M. Klink. Excerpts of the meeting are as follows:

Sister M. Leonette:

>I am not a rebel.
>
>I am not an instigator.
>
>What I have done, I have done because I love the Community; for the good of the Church, religion, and our own progress.
>
>You read the letter. You think it is too critical. I wrote the letter to stop chatter and to divert what is evil to what is good. I would have come to you on December 8 (1959), but was advised not to do so, I resorted to the letter.
>
>Everything I have done the Archbishop knows.
>
>On December 5, I saw the Archbishop and told him that if they find out, I will no longer be visiting schools or giving workshops. I was told by the Chancery I must have advice. I have been there. The Archbishop knows every move.
>
>I proceeded, first of all, to think through the problem and decide what to do. I talked to Father Sergius (Wroblewski), OFM. Last May, I went to Father Nerius (Semmler, OFM Cap). He told me this was the most loyal thing I could do. I returned home and felt like a criminal. It is very difficult to do this.

One can only imagine the composure, calmness, and soft voice of Mother Corona as she questioned and listened to Sister Leonette.

Mother M. Corona:

>Why do Sisters think this administration has been dishonest?

Sister M. Leonette:

>I do not know. Everything is vague. There are all sorts of stories. Every place I go they would say, 'Would you like to walk with me in the yard? Sometimes they would come to my room.'

Mother M. Corona:

>Why did you listen if you were not an instigator?

Sister M. Leonette:

>I was bothered by it. I asked four of these people not to speak to me and was told in charity that I had to listen. At this moment I still feel I have not done wrong simply because I have not done one single thing without advice.

>If I had done this on my own, I would feel guilty. I could not take it. This is hard. Because of that (not doing anything without advice), I feel secure. The Archbishop said, 'I am the Local Superior of the Church.'

>The Archbishop said, 'You are the first Sister to come to me. We have been waiting for a Sister to come.'

Mother M. Corona:

>Don't you think you should have come here and laid it bare?

Sister M. Leonette:

>I do not know. I proceeded not through an ordinary priest, but the authority of the Church.

Mother M. Corona:

>You must give one or two points where we acted dishonestly.

Sister M. Leonette:
> I could not do that. I did not say you were dishonest. I said, 'Let us stop talking.'
>
> As I have said, I would have liked Mother Corona to write that letter.

Mother M. Corona:
> You went right ahead to the highest Church authorities.

Sister M. Leonette:
> I believe I have that right.

Here, Mother M. Corona quoted from Sister M. Leonette's letter wherein she stated that "Mother could not say that there will be increased delegates without first petitioning Rome. This must be a very special privilege since our Rule, as it stands, does not so provide. Therefore, the Rule would have to be changed before anything could be done."

Sister M. Leonette:
> This is not easy on me. I lived with this for a year and a half.

Mother M. Corona:
> You did not tell it at the right place.

Sister M. Leonette:
> I thought I did.

Mother M. Corona:
> You worked on your own.

Sister M. Leonette:
> I did not work on my own.

Father Klink:
> I was happy that you (Mother Corona) wrote to Rome for an increased delegation. I was happy to hear that the election was postponed until an

increased number of delegates would be permitted.

Mother M. Corona:

Years ago, even under Mother M. Stanislaus, there was talk of Provinces, but until now the time did not seem opportune. This time we were determined to have more voters.

Father Klink:

I did go to the Bishop a month ago and asked him to postpone the election until an answer would come from Rome. He said he did not have the faculty. I told him for the peace of the Community, we needed increased representation. I inquired if the Apostolic Delegate could grant permission to defer the election, but the Bishop said he did not know. This will turn out good. Something good will result.

Here Father Klink left. Mother M. Corona asked Sister M. Leonette if there was anything further to say.

Sister M. Leonette:

No. I would like to unwind the story from the beginning, but I cannot. I cannot do it at this moment. Perhaps tomorrow.

It is not a matter of trying to expose the administration. All we asked was guidance, direction, and protection. It was not for the purpose of 'digging up dirt.'

Of course, this so-called "subversive movement" rippled through the community. Mother Corona did send a letter to the sisters relating what was happening. Some sisters totally ignored it, others were confused, many to this day wonder what really happened. Others did the "blame game."

Sister Ellinda Leichtfeld, who loved Mother Corona, gave this rendition.

> At the time this happened, I was principal at Our Lady of Sorrows in Milwaukee. Sister Philomena Stutzke, principal at Holy Redeemer in Milwaukee, Sister Anthelma Goeke, principal at St. Monica in Whitefish Bay, and I decided to visit Mother Corona to offer our support. I will never forget this visit. Mother Corona cried. This was the first time we had seen this strong, invincible leader break down. She was deeply hurt. At the same time, she was most gracious in expressing her appreciation and gratitude to us for offering our comfort and loyal support.

The shortest verse in the Bible just might be the most profound, "Jesus wept." God cried. Only the truly strong can allow themselves to be vulnerable.

Mother Corona received many beautiful handwritten letters from the sisters throughout the United States offering their love and support for all that she had done for the community. Sister Leonette had little, if any, support from the sisters. She was often ostracized and made to feel she was a "professional community disturber." A few younger sisters offered their support to her and agreed: "The community needs a new dynasty and young blood." Imagine the stress Sister Leonette endured during this time.

There is another reason why Sister Leonette's letter must have caused great pain to Mother Corona. From 1953 to 1956, Sister Leonette taught music at Alvernia High School. It was there she experienced stress and insomnia and was sent to Sacred Heart Sanitarium and treated for mental illness. In the social context of the mid-20th century, "such things" were not talked about.

Mother Corona's respect for Sister Leonette was undaunted by her symptoms of illness. The best available care was provided, although in retrospect, several sisters wonder why she was not treated at the congregation's psychiatric hospital, St. Mary Hill Hospital. Perhaps Sister Leonette refused to go. Dismissal from the community was an option. Mother Corona considered every angle. Sister Leonette did not choose to leave the community. In 1957, after her second treatment, Mother Corona sent her to Johnsburg, Wisconsin, a small rural town where the pressures were not as great. She was the musician at St. John Baptist School for one year. Only a few years later, she wrote the infamous letter.

H.H. Blanchard, MD at Sacred Heart Sanitarium, gave the following reports:

> Sister M. Leonette Tabat, OSF, was a patient at Sacred Heart Sanitarium under my care and treatment, admitted first on July 11, 1956 and discharged on August 8, 1956. She was in a highly nervous state, exhibiting many neurotic and erotic symptoms. She seemed to have grandiose ideas relative to her ability as an organizer in musical circles and schools.

On October 23, 1956, Sister Leonette was admitted the second time and discharged on June 15, 1957.

> Patient returns to the Sanitarium for further treatment. She has the same difficulties she had when here before, and recently has been taking sedatives to excess. When patient left the Sanitarium, this examiner had doubts about her ability to make an adjustment, but her Superior decided to give the patient another chance. However, as

stated above, patient has again resorted to the taking of sedatives.

Clinical Impression: Psychoneurosis

Mother Corona, in consultation with her Councilors, had a meeting on October 21, 1956.

The purpose of this meeting was to discuss the dismissal of Sister M. Leonette Tabat.

For more than two years, Sister Leonette has been taking a habit-forming drug which she claims was prescribed by Doctor White for insomnia. Sister has been given every opportunity—spiritual as well as physical—to rehabilitate herself. Last summer, Sister was hospitalized at the Sacred Heart Sanitarium and placed under Doctor Blanchard. After her dismissal from the Sanitarium, Sister returned to Alvernia 'on trial.' Sister promised everything, but of late has again succumbed. Sister Finbarr [James], her Superior, says that Sister's condition is known to the Alvernia Sisters, but what she fears more is a scandal among the students. Mother Corona said she will recall Sister Leonette tomorrow.

After considering the case at length, the members of the Council agreed that Sister Leonette should be dismissed; however, it was deemed advisable to try to get her to leave of her own accord.

Mother Corona sent this letter to all the sisters regarding the "subversive movement" with Sister Leonette.

March 23, 1960

Dear Sisters,

It would be wise, dear Sisters, to stop talking about the trial we went through. 'Silence is Golden.' Rather, meditate on the words: 'And Jesus was silent!'

> At the time of his visit, our Most Reverend Archbishop told us not to worry about what had taken place—to forget it and not to think of it even for a minute, which he repeated. God sees the heart. He knows the intentions and does not bless underhandedness toward superiors. Continue to be the good, faithful Sisters of our beloved Congregation as you have always been. Work openly and sincerely. Help your superiors in every way possible to build, and avoid every semblance of intrigue.
>
> Your loving,
>
> Mother M. Corona, OSF

Sister Leonette was removed from her job as supervisor of music and for one year did not receive an assignment from Mother Corona. She was sent to Omaha, Nebraska, "in exile," as Sister Leonette herself described it. There, Sister Maria Augustine and Jesuit Alban Dachauer from Creighton University, journeyed with her during this time in the lonely desert of her life.

The following is taken from the remarks of Archbishop William E. Cousins at St. Joseph Convent, May 10, 1960.

> I am still convinced there is no disunity in the Community.
>
> I think it was a bit of talk, which was natural in many instances because the closer the day of election came, and the less there was known about what was actually happening, the more confused some became. This gave rise to misunderstandings and misconceptions.
>
> One Sister wrote a very ill-advised letter. She had no authority. It was harmful in that the subject presumed to direct the actions of the administration when, as a matter of fact, Rome is the only one who can give direction at such a time. No one acquainted with the Community would have

given such advice. It is unfortunate that the letter was written.

At the same time, I believe always in closing ranks and healing wounds. There is nothing to be gained by continued punishment.

I think Sister was not speaking for a group but for herself. No doubt, she also spoke to other Sisters; in this there would be no disloyalty, disobedience, or criticism. Gossip is the most natural thing in the world when an election is approaching, and there is rumor that a new method is being considered. This is particularly true when a priest, who does not know the background, is consulted and states, 'This is all wrong.'

A combination of circumstances brought the matter to a head at the wrong time. The petition for a change in the matter of electing delegates had been presented months ago but was returned for clarification by the office of the Apostolic Delegate. This was not by way of criticism, but more 'What is this all about? What is going to happen?' Thus, six weeks were lost before the petition actually went to Rome. *(Both Archbishop Cousins and the Apostolic Delegate were comparatively new in their respective offices.)*

There was a good bit of speculation as to what Rome would decide, and in this case, a particular Sister presumed to do what should have been left undone. Continued punishment could make a martyr out of Sister. The Community does not want it, and she does not want it.

It would be better if the whole matter were buried. Forgiveness is to follow graciously; there is to be no recrimination.

No one was unfairly treated. I am convinced there is no disunity. The whole Community went along according to custom. You have a marvelous Community to work with—it has inbred loyalty. There is cohesion.

Excerpts from the following letter speak for themselves regarding the General Chapter.

April 19, 1960

My dear Sisters,

The election of the officers for the Generalate will take place at the Mother House on Saturday morning, April 23, as you already know. His Excellency, our Most Reverend Archbishop William E. Cousins, will preside in Cappa Magna at a Solemn High Mass beginning at 9:00 a.m.

Following the Mass, the Archbishop, with members of the General Chapter, will go to St. Joseph's Hall for the election. Immediately after, His Excellency will return to the Chapel to announce the results of the election to the assembled community. You, too, will be notified without delay.

The number of electors will be thirty. One delegate was lost because the German Province had about seventy Sisters in each group for the election of the Provincial Chapter members. The letter from Rome states that the groups may comprise from fifty to seventy, and Mother M. Archangela took the largest number so as to save one delegate; thus, there will be one elector less from the German Province. Our Most Reverend Archbishop sanctions thirty.

Friday evening, His Excellency will come here to address the members of the General Chapter.

Again, I say, 'God reward you, dear Sisters!' for your cooperation and good will. May your faithfulness and devotion to our Congregation ever increase.

May our Heavenly Mother with her Holy Child bless you now and always!

Lovingly yours,

Mother M. Corona, OSF

The results of the 1960 election were as follows:

April 23, 1960

Mother M. Clemens [Rudolph]	Mother General
Sister M. Hyacinth [Kirch]	Mother Assistant/First Councilor
Mother M. Corona [Wirfs]	Second Councilor
Sister Wilhelmina [Brenner]	Third Councilor
Sister M. Ursula [Vogel]	Fourth Councilor
Sister M. Thomasine [Nels]	General Secretary
Sister Samuel [Nalefski]	General Procurator

March 6, 1964

Sister M. Alphonsa Puls	Elected to replace Mother M. Corona Wirfs, deceased

* * * * * * * * * * * * * *

When Mother Clemens retired and lived in Marian Hall, she wrote a handwritten letter that follows. Sisters who were interviewed about this letter have no recollection that it was actually mailed to the sisters. The letter was found in her personal file in St. Joseph Convent Archives.

MARIAN HALL

June 18, 1972

Dear Sisters,

In the name of the Father and of the Son and of the Holy Spirit, and for the love of our Community, I am writing this letter to you.

I feel it my holy duty, already too long delayed, to clear the reputation of a Sister who has worked very hard for our Congregation. I feel in conscience, bound to tell you what and how it happened.

The Community, prior to 1960, had a highly centralized form of government: The United States Generalate and one German Province, with a superior general who already had been

---

in office three terms and was seeking a fourth term. The Milwaukee Chancery and the Canonical Visitator, Father Nerius Semmler, OFM Cap, were convinced that five governmental reforms were necessary: a new administration, increased representation in voting, a division of the Community into several independent provinces, an end of permanent superiorship, and a Constitution revised to make these governmental changes possible.

At this time, Sister Joan Tabat (Leonette) was, by reason of her work, one of the few Sisters in a position to make the necessary contacts between Church authorities and members of the Community. At the request of the Archbishop's advisors, she accepted this high-risk task reluctantly because it looked like, and would be interpreted as, a personal attack on Mother Corona with whom she had a satisfactory relationship. As it turned out, Mother Corona discovered that Sister Joan (Leonette) had been drawn into the move for a new administration from which Mother Corona would be excluded. Sister Joan (Leonette) was immediately labeled 'disloyal' and 'subversive' by the Community. No one came to her defense. Even the Chancery was silent about explaining her role in the action, which, not she, but the Milwaukee diocesan officials had initiated.

A new administration went into office, and the other recommendations of the Canonical Visitator were accomplished during this administration. At the time, the reform was set in motion and monitored by the Chancery officials.

This set a precedent for the Chancery's continued involvement in the administration of the Community despite the fact that we are a Pontifical Institute.

The role Sister Joan played in the preceding events took courage, self-sacrifice, and loyalty to the Church; but then, nothing was done to clear her name.

I hope and pray that once again, all the Sisters will give Sister Joan the love and respect which are her due.

In conclusion, I am asking you to please remember me in your prayers as I do daily for all our dear Sisters.

I am lovingly and gratefully yours,

Mother M. Clemens, OSF
Superior General, 1960-1966

The following clergymen are well-acquainted with the case. You are welcome to speak with any of these priests.

❖ Right Reverend Gerald Benhert, OSB, then Abbot of Marmian Abbey, Aurora, Illinois
❖ Reverend Alban Dachauer, S. Creighton University, Omaha, Nebraska
❖ Reverend Sergius Wroblewski, OFM, Gospel Brothers, Armitage House, Chicago, Illinois
❖ Reverend Irvin Udulutsch, OFM Cap, St. Francis Monastery, Milwaukee, Wisconsin

* * * * * * * * * * * * * *

On September 26, 2000, Sister Joan Tabat was killed in a car accident in Naples, Florida, at age 79, where she served as director of liturgy and music at St. Ann Parish for 11 years. Sister Nancy Hansen, who was working in Florida at that time, attended Sister Joan's funeral. She said, "People came from all over. The lines extended through St. Ann Church, down the street and beyond. She was loved and respected for her outstanding work in liturgy and music."

When Sister Joan left the Joliet Diocese to begin her ministry in Naples, Florida, Bishop Joseph L. Imesch of Joliet said, "Naples will 'sing a new song' after Sister Joan arrives."

SISTER LEONETTE (JOAN) TABAT
CIRCA 1940

CHAPTER SIXTEEN

POTPOURRI

After the preceding chapters on the various eras and accomplishments in Mother Corona's life, it is appropriate to take a closer look at some of the other important interests and concerns that were evident throughout her personal, professional, and religious life.

FINE ARTS

Mother Corona served as the Mother General during the Renaissance of the Order in the mid-1940s and 1950s. The international membership was over 4,000. The School Sisters of St. Francis was recognized as a great teaching order and achieved worldwide recognition for its music. Consequently, numerous renowned performers visited the motherhouse such as:

Fernando Germani, the Vatican organist, who performed in the convent's St. Joseph Chapel. When he heard the sisters' orchestra, he said, "I wish I could put all of you on a plane and have you play for Pope Pius XII, who loves music."

Marcel Dupré from France, considered the world's greatest organist at that time, also performed in the Chapel. When he heard Sister

Theophane Hytrek play the organ, he said, "She is greater than I."

Leonard Pennario, renowned American classical pianist and composer, performed in St. Joseph Hall. After hearing Sisters Mary Hueller and Benedicta Fritz play "The Flight of the Bumblebee," he said, "I see I have lots of competition here."

Under the direction of Sister Marcina Schlenz, a dynamic orchestral conductor, many people had the exhilarating experience of hearing Dvorak's "New World Symphony," Beethoven's "Fifth Symphony," and Brahm's "Symphony in E Minor," and many others. The orchestra gave public concerts to the religious and clergy of the Archdiocese, the Knights of Columbus, and other organizations. For special feasts and festive occasions, the orchestra entertained the sisters and women in formation.

In addition, the convent choir, under the direction of Sister Clarissima Neumann, recorded all the music used for the Sacred Heart Program daily broadcast in St. Louis, Missouri. The choir made other recordings of its singing, which were used as fundraisers for the community. In a letter dated November 27, 1950, Archbishop Kiley expressed his appreciation.

Dear Mother M. Corona:

I am very grateful for the records of St. Joseph's Choir, which you so kindly sent me. They are really excellent, and I think it would be wise if other records were made, to have them in the name of the choir.

Again, thanking you and wishing you and all the members of your Community every grace and blessing desired, I remain,

Sincerely yours in Christ,

Archbishop E. Kiley
Archbishop of Milwaukee

Mother Corona saw the need of sending talented sisters to prestigious universities, such as the Eastman School of Music in Rochester, New York, to enhance their talents and pursue degrees. This was also true of the visual arts. Sister Jo Ann Euper in *1ˢᵗ Century of Service: School Sisters of St. Francis,* states the following:

> By the thirties, the 'second generation' of professional artists had begun to emerge. The outstanding members of this group included Sisters Sancia Weis and Helena Steffensmeier, both of whom had studied art extensively. With this group, the copying came to an end. Professional training, the need for originality in their work as teachers, and a growing sense of personal integrity as artists made it impossible to suppress creativity as before. The developing Alverno College and increasing assignments to teaching positions away from the Motherhouse were instrumental in freeing the artists. Today they are geographically dispersed, working in a variety of art media, and several of them have achieved distinction. Sister Helena Steffensmeier is widely known for her sculpture and stitchery. Sister Lucinda Hubing has gained recognition for her work in cloisonné enamel.

Needless to say, the arts flourished during Mother Corona's administration.

THE SERAPHIC PRESS

The printing department at the motherhouse was really an outgrowth of the art department, which was doing a volume of business in holy cards, greeting cards, stationery, and lettering—all done by hand. The Seraphic Press expanded upon the artwork in 1917. Sister Valencia Van Driel received professional instruction in printing and attended the Marquette University School of Journalism. Other sisters also were trained to join in the work of the press.

The Seraphic Press thrived during the 40s and 50s. The work of the press became known throughout the world. Catechetical materials were considered an important part of the press apostolate. The best known were probably the Father Francis books, originally written by Father Franklyn J. Kennedy and later continued by a number of School Sisters of St. Francis. Eventually, more than three and one-half million copies were sold throughout the world in English and translated into Asian, African, and Western languages.

The press took care of the printing needs of several orders of priests who were too poor to pay. Some of their regularly-published magazines were printed at no charge by the Seraphic Press. Also, individual priests could count on the press for a bargain if they were struggling financially with a worthy cause and could not pay for their printed matter. Much of the outside work, however, was done as a source of income.

SERAPHIC MISSION AUXILIARY

The Seraphic Mission Auxiliary began in 1940 when Mother Stanislaus, Mother Corona, and Sister Valencia met with four lay women who expressed interest in helping with the congregation's foreign missions. They were also concerned about the American Indian missions and how they might serve African Americans in Yazoo City, Mississippi.

Membership in the auxiliary grew over the years. Annual raffles, card parties, benefit concerts, and other special events further involved crowds of people. The laity's enthusiasm spread its influence long after Mother Stanislaus' death. The following letter addressed to the sisters in 1959 gives evidence of the great work of the Seraphim Mission Auxiliary.

May 6, 1959

My dear Sisters,

We are most grateful to all who helped to boost the drive sponsored by the Seraphic Mission Auxiliary, whose members join heartily in our expression of gratitude. A sincere 'May God reward all of you!' dear Sisters, as well as your relatives and friends and the school children. The project together with the card party netted close to ten thousand dollars. This information is just for you. Let us keep it a family secret.

With loving greetings, I am

Your loving,

Mother M. Corona, OSF

COMMUNAL PRAYER

In 1948, the congregation began praying the "Little Office of the Blessed Virgin," and in 1958, Mother Corona again made a change to "Little Hours of the Divine Office." (Lauds in the morning and Vespers and Compline in the afternoon and evening.) The Office was comprised mostly of psalms chanted, unaccompanied by instruments. During her time in administration, Mother Corona was highly sensitive to how the sisters chanted the Office, especially in the early mornings when 400 some voices dropped lower and lower with many pitches resounding in a chapel with the best acoustics in the city of Milwaukee.

To alleviate the problem, she had one of the musicians stand in the choir loft with a pitch pipe to keep the congregation chanting on the same tone. When that was achieved, the chanting sounded angelic. Her love of choric drama and elocution carried over into praying the Office.

> In praying the Office, be particularly careful to pronounce each syllable clearly and distinctly and to make a definite stop at the asterisks. Avoid drawing out the syllables or making unnecessary pauses. Recite the Office with attention and devotion; then it will not sound as though you are hurrying to get finished. There should be a certain alertness and rhythm in the prayer, and a very definite pause (about one beat) at the star or asterisk.

SEVENTY-FIFTH ANNIVERSARY PAGEANT

In preparation for the 75th anniversary of the School Sisters of St. Francis in April, 1949, Mother Corona once again manifested her flair for choric drama. She organized a group of talented sisters in writing, drama, art, music, and history to depict the story of the congregation. In a letter dated September 13, 1948, she wrote the following:

> September 13, 1948
>
> My dear Sisters,
>
> The committee of Sisters who met at the Mother House last Saturday will meet again next Saturday, September 18, at

2:00 p.m. to consider the reorganization of the choric drama depicting the history of our Community.

The small group assigned to study the drama with a view to reorganization suggested that, with the exception of a few revisions and additions, Actions I and III remain unchanged. What were called Actions II, IV, and V, it was thought, must be reorganized and rewritten.

Please give serious consideration to the section labeled Part II in the outline below, discuss Part II with other Sisters on your mission, and come prepared to make constructive suggestions as to the manner in which this section might be developed.

PART I – FOUNDATIONS

Action I – How they started
    Episode 1 – Arrival in America
    Episode 2 – Months of wandering
    Episode 3 – Founding of the Congregation
    Episode 4 – First school
    Episode 5 – First convent

Action II – Testing and Spiritual Growth
    Episode 1 – The Winona Trial
    Episode 2 – Settling in Milwaukee
    Episode 3 – New crosses: Fire, Companioning with Sister Poverty, Polish separations, Calumnies.
    Episode 4 – The new Mother House
    Episode 5 – Spiritual growth: The Chapel, training of members

PART II – EXPANSION AND COMMUNITY ACTIVITIES

Action I – Care of the sick

Action II – Expansion
    Episode 1 – The European Province
    Episode 2 – Foreign Missions

Action III – Educational Activities

GRAND FINALE

Mother Corona selected sisters from certain schools in Milwaukee to participate in the production with their students.

April 6, 1949

Dear Sister,

The Sisters and students of Alverno are busy rehearsing the choric drama which will be given here at the Mother House between April 27 and May 8. As you know, this drama will commemorate the seventy-fifth anniversary of the founding of our Congregation.

We would like the Milwaukee Schools to assist in the performance, and the purpose of this letter is to ask you to select twenty of your pupils to take part in the ensemble—ten for each alternative night (five boys and five girls). By having two groups, ten in each group, the same children need not come each night but can alternate. You will be told exactly on what dates they are to come.

These pupils will sing the final song. Consequently, in making your selection, have in mind good singing voices. Each school will practice the song with the twenty children selected. Copies of the song can be obtained from Sister Xaveria [Friedrich]. The Sister Superior will confer with Sister Jutta as to how the children should be dressed for the performance.

I am confident you will be happy to cooperate in your usual wholehearted way.

Lovingly,

Mother M. Corona, OSF

On March 29, 1949, Mother Corona stated:

I am well pleased that Sister Beatrix [Wolsfelt] undertook to present our drama in Creighton, and I am certain it will make a great impression on all who see it. The two performances at Madonna and Alvernia made a deep impression on the Sisters and lay people as well.

I have heard indirectly that the play is to be given in Randolph too, but I can give you no particulars about this since I have had no definite word.

Each of these schools performed the history in its unique way, which was beautiful, but it was not the elaborate version of the motherhouse.

Excerpts from a letter dated April 26, 1949, Mother Corona wrote the following, as enthusiasm mounted for attending the big production.

Permit me to repeat:

1. Be sure to have a ticket for the date of the performance you will attend.

2. No one, including our own Sisters, will be admitted without a ticket. No tickets will be distributed at the door; therefore, it will be necessary to secure a ticket beforehand.

3. No money for tickets will be accepted at the door.

Some Sisters from Chicago and vicinity and others from more distant places, who have means of transportation, would like to come for the play. All available seats are taken for next Saturday afternoon, April 30, for Sunday afternoon, May 1, and Sunday afternoon, May 8. In order to accommodate a larger group of high school students on April 29 and elementary school children on May 4, 5, and 6, we obtained Reverend Father Aumann's permission to use St. Lawrence Parish Hall. May 5 is sold out. There is room for:

100 on Friday,	April 29,	1:00 p.m.
750 on Wednesday,	May 4,	3:00 p.m.
300 on Friday,	May 6,	3:00p.m.

> You may arrange to come on any of these three days. Children, even a busload, may accompany the Sisters, but let us know beforehand how many will come.
>
> An expert photographer will take moving pictures of the drama, which means that many of the Sisters will be able to see it in part. The speaking and music will be recorded, and in that way, we hope to have the historic drama reach the entire Community.
>
> The historic drama with some modification will be repeated next summer for our Sisters who are prevented from coming to see it now. The choral speakers will then be novices, but even so they will relate the history of the Community just as they are doing it now.

Who could ever forget this Cecil B. DeMille production performed by the School Sisters of St. Francis portraying 75 years of its history. *Praise the Lord*, a choric drama written by Sisters Edewaldo Endres and Vitalis Kolsters, was a manifestation of the combined talents of many sisters and performers. Twenty-two choric speakers from the class of '49, clad in champagne-rose-tinted silk gowns, with light-blue silk stoles, were trained to perfection. The depiction of the fire devouring the first motherhouse in 1890 due to faulty construction was rendered with clashes of music, flashes of fire, as the choric speakers frantically dashed across the stage.

The following extract is taken from the choric drama.

CHORUS	"Fire! Fire!" neighbors screamed.
	"Fire! Fire!" "Fire!" flew from the first floor to the fourth.
CHRONICLER	The whole Franciscan family –
	Blinded

	Numbed
	Deafened by the crackle of the fire
	Watched their two-year-old home being demolished by demon flames.
CHORUS	Suddenly, a scream from the attic window. "It's Sister Blanche," "Sister Blanche," Sister Blanche."
	Firemen rushed over with a ladder, But the firemen's ladder was chaff to the flames. Anguished, Mother Alexia called out –
M. ALEXIA	In the name of God, Sister Blanche, jump!
CHRONICLER	A moment later, Sister Blanche lay crumpled on the ground, a blackened form at Mother's feet.
CHORUS	The Convent which at dawn Stood vibrant in its two-year newness, At sundown leaned crazily A skeleton with ribs of fire.
CHORUS	And through it all Like a ceaseless chant of immolation, Mother Alexia prayed the prayer of Job:
M. ALEXIA	The Lord hath given, and the Lord hath taken away. Blessed be the name of the Lord.
CHORUS	Neither for a moment did Sister Alfons lose her calm resignation.
S. ALFONS	"It is God's will! It is God's will! May His Holy Will be done!"

An effective use of a scrim on the back part of the stage was a feature that added a touch of class to the entire performance. To summarize, the theater arts in full display were lauded and applauded.

Mother Corona knew what she was doing when she proposed a huge 75th celebration. It was public relations and marketing, the likes of which the community had never seen. Certainly, the performances were instrumental in attracting vocations. Even though the cost of the ticket was not mentioned in her letters, the community must have benefited financially.

APPEARANCE/RELIGIOUS DECORUM/DRESS

On one occasion, a second-year novice was called to Mother Corona's office and was surprised to hear her say, "I am concerned about the large, dark birthmark on your cheek. When you begin teaching, this will be distracting to the students. I want to send you to a dermatologist to see if something could be done about this."

Sister went to the dermatologist and was told that the birthmark could not be surgically removed. Mother Corona said to her, "Then you need to wear pancake make-up."

That statement may seem strange coming from Mother Corona, but in reading her many letters, one has to conclude she was most in touch with the "femininity" of the sisters even though the word was never mentioned. Femininity was not a term used in her time. It was cloaked in words like religious decorum, professionalism, refinement, etiquette, courtesy. In one of her letters, she quoted the words of Helaire Belloc.

Of courtesy, it is much less
Than courage of heart or holiness.

> Yet in my walks it seems to me
> That the grace of God is in courtesy.

Many table conversations to this day revolve around the time in the novitiate when each novice had to walk down the long, middle aisle of the study hall and her movements were critiqued by the novice director and other novices, who nervously awaited their turn. To hear the novice director say, "You look like a covered wagon coming down the trail" still resonates with many and evokes much laughter. To Mother Corona, a woman's beauty also was related to her movements. The sisters were not just a portrait on a wall. They were living, breathing, walking persons.

Sister Collette Lloyd wrote a letter of support to Mother Corona in 1960. In a poetic tribute she asks: "Tell us, who tutored you in queenly ways? Who taught you court etiquette? Mother Corona molds us with loving touch into celestial court ladies. Queenly, she wants us versed in courtly manner pleasing to the King!"

Mother Corona's emphasis on etiquette was not only about what fork to use or not to talk with food in the mouth, it was showing respect for oneself and others in a world where rudeness often reigns. All the feminine qualities were rooted in the virtue called charity according to Mother Corona and were to be modeled by women religious. She certainly would have subscribed to Leon Bloy's statements, "The woman who has lost her womanliness has lost her soul. The more of a saint a woman is, the more of a woman she is."

Many directives on how to wear the habit, the veil—even a sketch on how the back of the veil should hang—all point to women being women and especially being a woman religious. She also stressed her desire for uniformity and conformity.

> Dress neatly, dear Sisters, and wear your veil as it should be worn. Have a high regard for your religious garb and wear it becomingly. Make no alterations of your own accord.

VOCATIONS

A favorite topic in most of Mother Corona's letters was "vocations." In fact, she solicited vocations as much as she requested money. At a time in the community when there was no one assigned as vocation director, the responsibility was on each sister. She was quick to encourage and remind the sisters of their part in seeking vocations, as this excerpt from a 1946 letter indicates.

> Do not relax your efforts to work for good postulants. By your prayers, by your example, and by contact with good girls who seem to have a religious vocation, you can help along very much. Girls should not be coaxed to enter the convent—that would be foolish—but it is well to keep in touch with those who seem to have a vocation.

There were times when Mother Corona's letters were devoted entirely to the topic of vocations. After all, the apostolates of teaching, nursing, and the arts would have been greatly affected without apostles. The following letter of March 26, 1947 offers an interesting approach of her thoughts and feelings regarding the subject.

March 26, 1947

My dear Sisters,

We plan to have a Senior Sister, and perhaps a Junior Sister with a postulant or two, visit the Chicago schools during the week following Easter, in order to address the high school and eighth grade girls on the religious life. This time will be most convenient for us because the postulants will be making their pre-reception visit to their parental home, and school in the Motherhouse will be closed. The group will speak to high school and eighth grade girls only. Even though the visits of the vocation group will be more or less limited to the schools of Chicago and vicinity this year, this letter is intended for all of our houses. Let me know, dear Sister, if you would like to have our 'recruitress' visit your school; if so, please state which day seems preferable and whether you would like the address given in the morning or in the afternoon. Naturally, we cannot accommodate all of you with regard to your preferences, but we shall arrange a schedule and consult with you again.

No doubt, you have instructed your class on the sublimity of the higher life and have explained the great privilege of being called to serve God in the religious state. You have prayed with the children of the entire school that God may call some of their number to the Priesthood, the Brotherhood, and the Sisterhood, and now a brief, stimulating talk by a Sister, with whom the girls are not so well acquainted, may have beneficial results. It is not our intention to coax anyone into the convent—that would be neither wise nor prudent—for the individual soul must cooperate with God's grace. However, we know that many splendid vocations are lost because of a lack of encouragement and stimulation on the part of Priests and teachers. Often the longing for God and the things of God is lost when the delicate flower of a religious vocation is exposed to worldly contacts and questionable companionship. Some of your students may possess more piety than you realize, but timidity keeps them from mentioning their desire to become a religious.

Encourage the children to pray three *Aves* daily and to offer one day a week according to the intention given in VOCATION NOTES, so that your school will produce religious vocations. At the same time, be fervent in your prayers, remembering that example attracts. Be sensible when you speak about religious vocations, for imprudence in this respect may do more harm than good; however, timidity may leave much good undone. The right word at the right time will have a good effect. Young people ought to become familiar with such scriptural texts as: 'Mary hath chosen the better part;' 'How beautiful is the chaste generation;' 'Remember thy Creator in the days of thy youth;' 'He that loveth father or mother more than me is not worthy of me;' 'Everyone that hath left house, or brethren, or sisters, or father, or mother...or lands for my name's sake, shall receive an hundredfold, and shall possess life everlasting;' 'What doth it profit a man if he gains the whole world and suffers the loss of his own soul;' 'I thirst.' Such texts should readily come to mind.

Each Sister, from a motive of gratitude to God for her own vocation and a sense of loyalty to her Community, should be zealous in furthering vocations by prayer, example, and, as far as her sphere of work permits, by making known to young souls the advantages of the religious life. Above all, do not forget your own relatives. A lack of contact often makes one lose sight of the fact that little sisters, nieces, and cousins have a way of growing up, and, before one is fully aware of it, they are standing at the crossroad of life. Sometimes a word from a near relative in the convent is all they need to encourage them to heed the call to the religious state, and 'charity begins at home.'

May the Holy Spirit guide and inspire all of us in leading young souls to the feet of the Master!

Lovingly,

Mother M. Corona, OSF

Sister Maureen McCarthy still treasures the response she received from Mother Corona when Maureen asked to enter the community.

July 2, 1959

Miss Maureen Ann McCarthy
891 Clifton Avenue
Glen Ellyn, Illinois

Dear Miss McCarthy,

This is just a note to tell you that the doctor's reports are satisfactory, and you are welcome to enter St. Joseph Convent in fall. Sister Amelberga [Weinandt] and the Sisters at St. Petronilla Convent will be happy to help you with your preparations. If there are any questions, do not hesitate to ask.

Pray every day for perseverance in your holy vocation, for after baptism, it is the greatest gift God can offer you. We too will keep you in our prayers so that God willing, you may have the privilege of serving Him for many happy years as a School Sister of St. Francis.

With cordial greetings, I am

Sincerely yours in Christ,

Mother M. Corona, OSF

Enclosed with the letter was a prayer leaflet "Meditations on the Mass" by St. John Vianney.

Sister Betty Reinders related that she was attending Marquette University as a lay student when she felt the call to religious life. Father Alban Dachauer, SJ, her advisor, suggested that she go to the convent on Layton Boulevard and meet Mother Corona "who has a heart as big as her body." Sister Betty heeded Father Dachauer's advice and chose to enter the

School Sisters of St. Francis after she had first checked out another community.

As a second-year novice, Sister Dorothy Bock went to Mother Corona to complain about the rigidity in the order and that she wanted to leave. Mother Corona's gentle reply was: "You certainly may leave, but you expressed how much you love to teach. Imagine the thousands of students you could influence were you to remain a sister." Sister Dorothy, at age 89, is still teaching art to retirees and proudly stated, "And I have influenced thousands of students."

Probably most sisters who had been aspirants were not aware of the letter sent to parents when their daughter was sent for a home visit. The following letter was sent to all parents.

Christmas, 1952

Dear parents of our aspirants,

You will be happy to hear that your dear daughter will be coming home soon to spend some time with you during the blessed season of Christmas. With you we rejoice, for truly God has favored you in a special way by calling a child of yours to be among His chosen ones. No greater blessing can come to a family, and we hope the days of your rejoicing together will be filled with many graces for you and for your daughter.

We are grateful to you for entrusting your child to us and hope she will one day be a source of even greater joy to you than she is today by coming to her parental home in the garb of a Franciscan Sister. She has been chosen by God for His service. It is our prayer and our plea that you will do all in your power to safeguard the vocation of our future Sister from anything which could prove harmful to her vocation during her Christmas visit. We are confident you will cooperate with us by keeping your daughter close to you during her visit, and not permitting her to

---

attend parties or worldly amusements which may be detrimental to her calling.

And may we suggest that you say a few words of encouragement before she leaves? It will help to banish any anxiety she may have after the visit is over. If you cooperate with us, God will reward you in this life and in eternity, for no sacrifice goes unrewarded.

May the spirit of the Holy Family reign in your home and in your hearts and may the coming joyful season of Christmas be filled with graces for you and yours!

Sincerely yours in Christ,

Mother M. Corona, OSF

Lest aspirants thought Mother Corona did not know them and that they were only a tiny pebble on the beach, Margery Theiss proved otherwise. She entered the aspirancy after being raised in an orphanage for three and one-half years in Freeport, Illinois. Each year while she was an aspirant, Mother Corona called her to her office. In her kind, motherly manner, she asked Margery, "Are you happy here? Do you really want to be here?"

At the end of her term of office, Mother Corona sent the following letter to all the pastors of parishes staffed by School Sisters of St. Francis. She thanks the priests for the vocations they directed to the community.

December, 1959

Reverend and dear Father,

The close of the year, which brings with it the termination of my office, seems a fitting time to express gratitude for the interest you have manifested toward our

Congregation. You have been understanding and kind, and I appreciate your willing assistance and encouragement. It has always been a pleasure to work with you. Our recent appeal for funds under the patronage of St. Joseph was a grand success, and we owe you, as well as your good people, special thanks. I wish to repeat a heartfelt 'May God reward you!' You will ever be remembered in prayer before the Most Holy Sacrament in our Chapel of Perpetual Adoration.

We thank you, too, for the vocations you have directed to our Community. God has blessed us with a number of good girls, but more are needed. And now, most contrary to what I would like to tell you, there will be no additional Sisters available for the next school term. We are obliged to keep the newly-professed Sisters home for two further years of study and spiritual development. Rome has spoken, and we must obey. Father Gambari, a representative of the Sacred Congregation for Religious, was here last summer to spread the Pope's message among the Sisterhoods. He emphasized the fact that the Pope must be obeyed. If the Sisters are not kept home for further education, no one is to blame but the Mother General.

It is important that you have this information in order to have time to plan for the next school term. We hope and pray for an increase of vocations so that soon there will be more Sisters to relieve the present teacher shortage. I regret that my letter must carry this disappointing message, but I am confident you understand, and in your kindness, will assist us during this crisis.

A Happy New Year filled with God's special blessings!

Sincerely yours in Christ,

Mother M. Corona, OSF

RESPECT FOR PARENTS

Sisters often commented on the great love and respect Mother Corona had for the parents of the aspirants and postulants. Sister Rosemary O'Brien stated, "My parents really enjoyed talking to Mother Corona on visiting Sunday and reception day." Sister Margaret Earley said, "It must have been on reception day that my dad drifted away from the family and spoke to Mother Corona for at least an hour. When he returned, he said, "She is the smartest person I have ever encountered."

During her administration, Mother Corona gave permission to several sisters who had aging parents to leave their ministry and return home to assist them. This is especially true of sisters who had no siblings to help care for their parents. Mother Corona was heard to say, "Before I die, I would like to build a home where the sisters' aging parents could receive care." Perhaps this was the vision for Villa Clement, a skilled nursing home in West Allis, Wisconsin, which opened in 1963, one year before Mother Corona's death. The congregation later sold the facility. It was then incorporated as Allis Care Center on September 28, 2004.

Mother Corona's greatest display of love for parents was sending 105 sisters who had come from Europe to enter the community, back to visit their families. Each time the foundresses went back and forth to Germany, they returned with young women who were interested in becoming sisters. The cruel May Laws or Falk Laws of 1873-1887 were legislative bills enacted in the German Kingdom of Prussia during the Kulturkampf conflict with the Catholic Church. These laws limited the powers of the Catholic Church over its members. Consequently, women who wanted to join a religious order had to seek admission in another country. The women who joined the School Sisters of St. Francis had never had the opportunity to visit parents and relatives. Mother Corona made that happen. She was deeply grateful to these sisters for their many years of service and dedication to the community. What better way to reward them than putting them on a plane and flying them back to their homeland. Many of the sisters' families suffered intensely during World War II. German sisters returned home having lost family members. There was great jubilation in the entire community on July 4, 1956, when the first group left for Europe.

The *Milwaukee Sentinel*, 1956, carried the following article entitled, "Nuns Flying to Europe to See Relatives." There was also a large photo of the 21 sisters with their suitcases eagerly awaiting to take flight.

> A group of 21 nuns of the School Sisters of St. Francis will leave Gen. Mitchell field at 9 a.m. Wednesday to visit relatives in Germany and Switzerland.
>
> The group, which will be gone about a month, will fly from here to New York City and then to Amsterdam, Holland. They will then go on their separate ways.
>
> The nuns came here from Germany and Switzerland to join the order, some as long as 30 or 40 years ago.
>
> It will be the first group of nuns of the order to make this sort of trip. Other nuns of the order will make similar trips in groups later.
>
> The order's motherhouse is St. Joseph's Convent, 1501 S. Layton Boulevard.

Groups of sisters traveled on five different days.

July 4, 1956   — 21

July 10, 1956 — 16
July 13, 1956 — 16
August 2, 1956 — 16
August 20, 1956 — 36

The following was recorded in the Day Book on July 4, 1956.

The Mass this morning was for the safe journey of our travelers, and Mother promised the Sisters that the paschal candle would be kept burning before the Blessed Virgin Altar, a silent reminder to all who enter the chapel to breathe a prayer for the safety of our travelers.

At 7:00, the 21 Sisters left promptly for the airport, via the Grey Line Bus. Father Adolph M. Klink took Mother Corona and Mother Clemens there by car, and there was also a representative group of Sisters there to bid them a fond farewell.

It took approximately an hour to check through their baggage at the Northwest Airlines. At nine o'clock, the plane left the airport, due to arrive in New York at 1:55 p.m. EST. They are scheduled to leave New York at 6:00 p.m. and arrive in Amsterdam at 6:00 a.m. Thursday.

We called New York to ask the Sisters to be at the airport in New York on the arrival this evening of our sisters traveling to Europe, and to see them off.

The Day Book recorded the following on July 10, 1956.

Our schedule was somewhat changed today because of the European travelers. Dinner was at 11:15, and the bus which took the Sisters to the Chicago Airport left at 12:30. Sixteen Sisters left for Europe. Mother Clemens, Sisters Wilhelmina, Deodigna, and a representative group from the house accompanied them to Chicago and waved a fond farewell to the Sisters as they boarded the Lufthansa. Father Buser was also there at the airport and took pictures of the departure.

Each group leaving for Europe had a great send-off. There was equal jubilation when the groups returned as stated in the following:

> There was general rejoicing as the bus came into the convent garden. There was even a false alarm. The big bell sounded when the Alverno College bus came into the convent garden, getting a welcome such as it had never had before, only to learn that the group was mistaken for the European travelers.

POPE PIUS XII

Eugenio Cardinal Pacelli was appointed by Pope Pius XI as cardinal protector of the School Sisters of St. Francis, January 2, 1937. The following letter informed the community of the death of Pope Pius XII.

October 8, 1958

My dear Sisters,

Word has just come over the radio that our Holy Father, Pope Pius XII, has been called home to receive the reward of his holy life. We are deeply grieved, and I know you are, too.

Our Rule calls for special prayers and suffrages by the members of the Congregation at the death of the Pope. Every Sister will kindly offer at least a complete week—all prayers, works, joys, and sufferings—for the repose of the soul of our deceased Pontiff, and pray an additional rosary of fifteen decades.

Each one of our houses and missions will kindly have five Holy Masses offered for the repose of the soul of His Holiness. Since it is difficult to have Low Masses offered in parishes, I would be very pleased to have you send these stipends here. By means of them I can help poor priests.

Yours in sorrow,

Mother M. Corona, OSF

The death of Pope Pius XII ended what has become known as the "pre-Vatican" era in the church. His successor, Pope John XXIII, called forth the Second Vatican Council only months later. The work of the Council brought about momentous changes in theology, Catholic worship, service to others, and religious life. The post-Vatican era was in its infancy as Mother Corona's long life of leadership was ebbing.

ADEQUATE COMPENSATION

Salaries for the sisters was grave concern to Mother Corona, especially when the cost of living expenses escalated and there was no comparable increase in payments to the sisters. Cardinal Stritch of Chicago sent a letter to the pastors of the archdiocesan schools and Mother Corona sent a copy of his letter to the sisters on March 4, 1947.

A problem on which we have been working arises from the inadequacy of present conditions of the stipends given to the Religious Communities of Women who teach in our parochial schools. A careful study shows that with present living costs, these communities are not able to support themselves with the stipends presently received. It is necessary that we increase these stipends and it is advisable that we make them equal in all the parishes of the Archdiocese. Therefore, we have discussed this matter with our Archdiocesan Consultors and with their unanimous approval, we hereby publish, declare, and make immediately effective the following Pro-Synodal Decree:

> In the parishes of the Archdiocese of Chicago with parochial schools, we fix and define the stipend to be given to the Religious Communities of Women teaching in these schools to be five hundred dollars for a scholastic year of ten months from September to July for each Sister engaged in teaching or in full-time supervisory work. This stipend of five hundred dollars is to be given from the parish treasury in such partial payments as may be found convenient to the pastor and the Religious Community. It is definitely understood and made a part of this Decree that the stipend is not given to the individual Sister who is under vows but to her Religious Community and accrues to the benefit and use of the Community. In parishes in which the parish does not furnish a convent for the Sisters with light, heat, and fuel, the customary extra allowance to the Community for each Sister engaged in teaching or supervisory work must be continued.
>
> I am sure, Reverend Father, that you will be pleased with this Decree and that you will see to it that it is made effective in your parish at once.

Mother Corona added her own remarks to the letter, which follows.

> You will note that the salary is $500.00 for the scholastic year of ten months for each Sister engaged in teaching or in full-time supervisory work. The latter has reference to the superior if she does not teach. No Sister Superior has authority to make concessions in favor of the parish. All questions regarding salary are to be referred to the Motherhouse.
>
> Besides the regular salary, the organist receives $1.00 for every Requiem and weekday High Mass for which the priest receives a stipend. A flat rate is not considered. By a flat rate, we mean a sum which covers both the salary of the organist and the stipend for the playing of Requiem masses.

Mother Corona sent the following letter to the sisters in the Archdiocese of Omaha on March 16, 1950.

March 16, 1950

My dear Sisters,

Evidently some of you are not aware that the salary of the Sisters in the Archdiocese of Omaha has been increased. Some of the salary slips still show the old rate.

Effective September 1, 1949, His Excellency, Bishop Bergan, increased the salary for the Sisters teaching in the grade schools to $500.00 a year for each teacher and $600.00 a year for each high school teacher, regardless of the number of months you teach. The salary for church work and choir work His Excellency left to our discretion, but we are not increasing it this year.

Please remind Reverend Father in a tactful way of the amount due us, and be sure to have your salary paid up by the end of the year. The aforesaid affects all the schools in the Archdiocese of Omaha. The new rate is not too high considering present-day prices of practically everything we use. Then, too, the railway fare to and from the mission is paid by the Community, and the House Sister's living and general expenses must be taken from the salary paid by the parish. The dental bill for one Sister often takes two or three months of her salary.

Mother Corona informed the sisters in the Archdiocese of Milwaukee of their salary increase which came several years later.

September 12, 1956

My dear Sisters,

Our most Reverend Archbishop has increased the salary of the Sisters teaching in the elementary and high schools of the Archdiocese of Milwaukee to $650.00 a year. One House Sister, too, will receive a salary of $650.00 a year.

We are most grateful to His Excellency for his kind thoughtfulness and understanding. Be loyal, Sisters, and do not oppose this increase by sympathizing unduly with the parish. We realize that the good pastors have many financial obligations and worries, but so have we. It is difficult to make ends meet with the low salary paid by most dioceses.

I shall supplement this letter with a longer one very soon. Happy Name Day to all of you, my dear Sisters. We had a nice celebration here in the Convent today.

Lovingly,

Mother M. Corona, OSF

In addition to the many, many congregational issues Mother Corona dealt with on a daily basis, she also responded to the needs and requests of other religious orders, as is indicated in the following letter.

URSULINE CONVENT OF THE SACRED HEART
TOLEDO, OHIO

SEPTEMBER 4, 1952

Dear Mother Corona

Because of our recent revision of our Constitution, it is necessary for us to change our system of accounting so as to show our Motherhouse accounts as distinct and separate from those of our local houses.

We realize you have had experience in such a separation of accounts, so we are asking you for some suggestions. Do you have any Community Accounting Forms, or any literature on systems which you could send us?

We shall be grateful for any help whatsoever in the matter.

Sincerely yours in the Sacred Heart,

Mother Vincent de Paul
General Superior

CIVIC RESPONSIBILITY

Mother Corona's regard for the United States Constitution, a love of country, and the obligation to vote was evident from a portion of a 1946 letter to the sisters. This communique was sent during the time Harry S. Truman was president.

In a democracy like the United States, it is immediately evident how much the general welfare depends on the election returns. Our government is the only one in the world whose constitution provides that all major officials in both the executive and legislative branches be elected by popular vote. Great power has been placed in the people. The votes of the people decide in large measure solutions to social, industrial, educational, moral, and religious, as well as the political problems which confront the government.

The obligation to vote, where the right is given, arises from the relation of the individual citizen to the state. There is a certain kind of justice, called 'legal,' which requires that every member of society do all that can reasonably be expected to conserve and promote the general welfare. Voting is such an act.

> Over and above the fact that the country would dissolve, and the Constitution would become another fond memory of history if no one exercised the right of voting, there is patriotism, the love of country, and of the human beings who comprise the country, which should prompt the exercise of suffrage. For the Catholic patriot, this love issues from the virtue of piety, a piety based not only on natural motives but also on supernatural ones. Even though the choice of those who exercise may come through the people, ultimately that authority comes from God. We should look upon our country as a precious gift from God; it offers the temporal happiness we need to attain everlasting happiness promised by Christ, in His Church.
>
> Voting is the best means we have of bettering our temporal welfare; we should guard this right most jealously, exercise it at every opportunity, use it discretely. Free exercise of religion is indeed guaranteed all citizens in the Bill of Rights; but this will not prevent unscrupulous leaders from making conditions intolerable for the Church in an indirect way, as has happened in our day in other lands.
>
> Since no Church as a juridical being can influence the state directly, the duty then, falls upon individual members of a Church to use every honest political device to secure the general welfare of all citizens.

As a matter of fact, when it came to local and state elections, she offered suggestions to the sisters regarding the most qualified candidate and why he would be best suited for the position. Honesty was the first requisite.

DEATH ANNOUNCEMENTS/HEALTH CONCERNS

In this age of technology, it is easy to forget that all communication was done through letter-writing during Mother Corona's time. Manual typewriters, carbon paper, ink erasers were the tools in use. Announcing the death of a sister was included in a letter. Sister Siegberta Haensler died September 6, 1946. Mother Corona's announcement was the following:

> Sister M. Siegberta's death was not expected and was caused by a heart spell suffered on the closing day of Forty Hours' Devotion in Campbellsport. I am happy in the thought that I saw her the night before she died. She promised to pray for the Community and for me in heaven, but she had hopes of getting better. Early the next morning, Sister passed away. The day before she died, Sister M. Siegberta made a number of adoration hours. What a glorious meeting when she stood face to face with her Eucharistic Lord.

Sister Mariel Welter's death announcement:

> October 28, 1952
>
> My dear Sisters,
>
> You will be surprised to receive the announcement of the death of our dear Sister M. Mariel (Henrietta Welter).
>
> Sister was stationed at Johnsburg, Wisconsin, since last September. About a week ago, she became ill and was taken to St. Agnes Hospital, Fond du Lac, where her case was diagnosed as encephalitis, which is inflammation of the brain. Sister was in a coma for several days before her death, which occurred at 3:20 p.m. last Sunday. Christ the King called our dear Sister to Himself on the glorious feast of His Kingship.

Often with a death announcement, Mother Corona pleaded with the sisters to take care of their health, as is indicated in the following:

Truly, death comes like a thief in the night. We must always be prepared to meet our Judge, for we know not the day nor the hour when we will be asked to give an account of our stewardship. As you pray for the repose of the soul of Sister M. Mariel, please add a petition that God may grant health to the Sisters. Safeguard your health, dear Sisters, in every way possible. See that you get your full night's rest; eat well so that you will maintain your strength, for your work is strenuous; and remember that fresh air is essential to health. We have no substitute teachers and must trust in Divine Providence to see us through.

Excerpts from a letter dated January 14, 1958, Mother Corona stated:

One of our very important prayer intentions is good health for the Sisters. It seems unbelievable, but scarcely a day goes by without our receiving word that another Sister has taken ill. Many of these cases are serious; several had to undergo major surgery, and many were brought home suffering with an illness requiring weeks of care here or at one of our houses for the sick. Some will never return to the classroom. With the tremendous teacher shortage facing us, you surely realize our handicap. Do take good care of your own health, dear Sisters. Eat a sufficient amount of wholesome, nutritious food to maintain your strength; get enough sleep, and plenty of fresh air.

I shall use this opportunity to make known to you the dying wish of our dear Sister M. Ubaldo [Neumair]. On the night before she died, she asked Sister M. Gervase [Lisner] to let me know that she is sorry for all the wrong she ever did to anyone and begs pardon. She thanked everyone for all the good that was done to her—everything was appreciated. Pray every day, dear Sisters, for those who have gone before us. May God grant them eternal rest!

DEMANDS FOR TEACHERS

The ongoing demand for teachers to staff schools must have been a source of great stress to Mother Corona. For example, a priest from Texas paced frantically back and forth in the art parlor insisting that she send sisters to his parish. In desperation, Mother Corona finally calmly, and yet emphatically, said, "Father, I cannot crochet nuns!"

Father Aloysius Stier at St. Irene Parish in Warrenville, Illinois, built a new school and was promised School Sisters of St. Francis. When the building was completed and ready for occupancy in 1952, Mother Corona had no sisters to send. The pastor said, "The building will remain empty until I get School Sisters of St. Francis." For one year, the pastor patiently waited. Imagine the pressure on Mother Corona to make sure she had sisters for the following year. She did send four sisters in 1953. If there was any fault in Mother Corona, it was over-extending her commitments to send sisters, and at times, she could not fulfill what she had promised. This was bound to have irked some pastors. She probably had to learn how to say no many times for a better yes.

TELEVISION

A letter dated October 8, 1958, was sent to all the sisters.

> Many Superiors are inquiring about the use of television. Following are the rules for the use of television and radio by religious as given out by our Holy Father, Pope Pius XII, through the Sacred Congregation for Religious on August 6, 1957, Prot. N. 01742/53:
>
> From January 1, 1954, the same day on which television broadcasts began in Italy, Our Holy Father let the local ordinaries

know, with an important exhortation on television, his own concern about the influence this new and more powerful means of communication of news, views, spectacles from all parts of the world could have on the moral and spiritual life of souls.

Having seriously thought over all these things, this Congregation lays down the following norms and calls upon all religious superiors to follow them as binding their conscience under pain of serious sin *(graviter onerata eorum conscientia)*.

1. There is nothing that can justify the admittance of television sets in communities of the CONTEMPLATIVE LIFE whether of men or of women. A radio set could be tolerated but only for the sole purpose of listening to the words of the Holy Father when he speaks to the whole world and to receive his blessing, or possibly for some broadcast of some exceptional religious celebration.

2. RELIGIOUS OF THE ACTIVE LIFE

    a) No religious may be permitted to have a private radio set, much less a television set, to be used at his own discretion without the direct control of the superior.

    b) Radio and television sets must be placed exclusively in some kind of community room, in plain sight of everyone, under the direct supervision of the superior or his delegate.

    c) Superiors must be watchful that the time used for television and radio does not interfere with the work of the religious community nor with the individual tasks of the religious, the apostolate, the practices of piety, and exercises of community life, the hours of rest as specified by the individual communities.

    d) Superiors must forbid the watching of television shows or listening to radio programs which are contrary to the religious spirit either because of their moral tone or worldliness. Except for news programs, instructive and religious programs, superiors must or at least can consider all other programs to be contrary to the

> religious spirit, especially if they are watched merely for recreational purposes.

Mother Corona added her own law-abiding comment to this mandate.

> These are the rules set down by the highest Church authority and must be obeyed. Superiors incur a grave responsibility if they are indifferent or light-minded, and they should use every precaution to see that the foregoing regulations are observed.

Mother Corona's paper presented to the National Congress of Religious at Notre Dame University five years prior to the mandate from Rome addressed the problems that confronted religious in a rapidly-changing scientific age. It is interesting to analyze her approach to new technology and this invention called television (page 332 of this book).

At the invitation of Monsignor James W. Nellen of Holy Redeemer Parish in Milwaukee, the sisters were invited to the rectory to watch the coronation of Queen Elizabeth II on June 2, 1953; Mother Corona readily gave her permission.

THE FALL SALE

Many sisters remember the fall sale in the 50s that was held for two weeks, then eventually went to one week, and presently is held for one day. The following excerpt is an earnest appeal to the sisters.

October 22, 1958

My dear Sisters,

This is a letter of appeal. We are in great need of funds, and yet, because so many of you have gone out of your way to help us, I hesitate to call on you again. I am convinced that many of the Reverend Pastors are willing to permit you to help us because they surely realize it is hard to make ends meet on a meager income when everything is so expensive.

Another reason for hesitating to trouble you is the fact that the greater number of you have been most diligent in working for the coming fall sale. It is edifying and encouraging to note the zeal which animates our Sisters in general in making articles when there is something to be done for the good of the Community. I have mentioned before that I would not want the Sisters to work beyond capacity, for instance, to stay up at night or run the risk of injuring their health in their effort to cooperate. By far the greater number feel that making an article for the sale would not harm them. On those missions where the superior is active and works with the Sisters, I am told that they have a great deal of fun while they work; some sing, some listen to good reading—spiritual, professional, or an interesting story—some talk, and so on. For many it is a recreation, and they do accomplish something. At the same time, the younger Sisters learn how to make useful and practical articles. The work can prove to be very fascinating, but it must never interfere with the preparation for class work or study. It is good for you to get your mind away from books and study for a short time each day. I am grateful for what you have done and what you are doing. Everything is appreciated. May God reward you! I am sure you will pray for the success of the sale.

The sisters were highly creative in making many, many items for the sale. The responses were an indication of everyone working together in a spirit of Franciscan joy to benefit the community.

Sister Francella Geiger and the sisters from St. Mark Convent in Kenosha, Wisconsin, were among many other sisters from missions far and near who responded to Mother Corona's appeals. The sisters at St. Mark Convent spent hours and hours during summers making veils for children receiving their First Communion. The veils were boxed and sold in parishes where the sisters taught. Their efforts provided a good source of annual revenue for the motherhouse. In their spare time, under the expert direction of homemaker, Sister Cecilia Zachman, the St. Mark sisters made candy for the fall sales. In the evenings, after teaching all day, they managed to have fun while making hundreds of pounds of fudge and peanut brittle each year.

In that same 1958 letter, Mother Corona explained why she had to seek other means of revenue, but not at the expense of the sisters.

> I am calling on all of you, dear Sisters, to help your Congregation, for, in spite of the outside help we received, the amount is not sufficient to meet the demand unless we hold together—work and pray together. A number of dioceses are still paying $50 a month for a teacher. Where there are two teachers, the $100 salary must cover the maintenance of three Sisters, including transportation charges to and from the mission, medicine, dental work, oculist fees, clothing, etc. It can be easily understood that the salary does not cover expenses.
>
> Please, dear Sisters, do not take this letter amiss; do not think that I want to deprive you of what is necessary. I would feel very bad if the Sisters were deprived of good, wholesome food. Those who need milk should have it, but it is also important that you eat good, nourishing vegetables, meat, and fruit. Unless

you are well nourished, you will take sick, and then the money goes into expensive medicine. Likewise, you must be properly clad, but you can save by taking good care of your clothes.

VISITATION: SICK SISTERS AND MISSIONS

Even though much of her work kept Mother Corona at her desk in the office, she deliberately took time to visit the sick sisters throughout her administration. The Day Book, May 7, 1955, records her going to the hospitals in Waupun and Beaver Dam.

> At the hospital in Waupun, Sister M. Stellana [Sutter] is very low and can hardly speak; apparently Sister is suffering with cancer of the throat. Sister M. Arthur [Menting], who has been very sick, is slowly improving. Sister had been suffering with an obstruction of the common duct for a long time, but the Convent Doctor did not detect it. Dr. Reslock at Waupun did not let up in his efforts until he determined the cause of Sister's sufferings; she could not have lived much longer if her trouble had not been discovered. Sister Arthur said it was the first day she saw the blue sky again. Sister M. Xaveria [Friedrich], the musician, hopes to be dismissed shortly. Sister M. Benvenuta [Kaufmann], who had been operated the day previous, was very wiry for a person who had just undergone major surgery. Both hospital superiors, Sisters M. Fortuna [Baumann] and Edelwina [Fischer], had gone to Campbellsport for retreat.

In addition, Mother Corona visited numerous missions, especially those in rural areas in Wisconsin, Illinois, and Iowa. Because sisters were not permitted to drive, she was chauffeured by Father Adolph J. Klink, and later, Father

Adolph M. Klink. Eugene Skalecki, a life-long employee, was also a chauffeur.

DEATH OF MOTHER STANISLAUS

Just as Mother Stanislaus informed the sisters on a regular basis of Mother Alfons' dying days, so Mother Corona devoted many of her letters giving an update on Sister Stanislaus' condition. Mother Corona still spoke of her as "Mother" even though she no longer held that position.

> December 28, 1943
>
> Our dear Mother M. Stanislaus is a patient at the Sanitarium at present. The heart medicine has upset Mother's stomach, with the result that her appetite is very poor. Within the last few days, symptoms of a kidney condition seem to be developing. I know you will offer fervent prayers for the recovery of our dear Mother M. Stanislaus, to whom we all owe a debt of everlasting gratitude. When I visited Mother yesterday, she asked me to thank all the Sisters for their prayers and good wishes. She was so pleased with your letters and cards. She repeats again and again, 'We have good Sisters. Ours is a beautiful Community.' These thoughts seem to bring her consolation.

> January 5, 1944
>
> Our dear Mother M. Stanislaus seems slightly better than she was at the time of my last letter. She is quiet and comfortable, and usually very cheerful. She is always pleased to hear that you are praying for her and asked me to thank you and to send you her greetings. Her conversation continues to be on heavenly things. She shows no interest in anything else. I know you will continue your prayers for Mother.

January 10, 1944

Our dear Mother M. Stanislaus is still very sick. At times there is a slight improvement, but on the whole, her condition does not seem favorable. She is dear and sweet withal, and the deep spirituality which she practiced all her life is more manifest than ever in her present illness. Mother's devotion at Holy Communion and prayer is most edifying. I know you will continue to pray fervently for the loved patient.

February 19, 1944

Our dear Mother M. Stanislaus has had a few heart spells today that give rise to anxiety. The doctor tells us that such an attack may be fatal. Mother has had such spells before and came out of them all right, so we are hoping that we will be able to send you more encouraging news within the next few days; however, since there is danger, I thought it well to notify you. I know you are continuing your fervent prayers for one to whom we all owe a debt of gratitude.

Mother continues to maintain her same beautiful, edifying spirit. If in time of sickness we prove what we are and what virtue we possess, surely Mother M. Stanislaus has proved her genuine love for God and her true religious spirit.

Time was running out. Sister Stanislaus felt compelled in her illness to give final instructions to assist the sisters in arriving at closer union with God. She told Mother Corona:

Have the Sisters praise God faithfully, fervently, and lovingly in all earnestness. They should spiritualize their lives—every moment, every hour, every day—by giving praise to God.

On another occasion, she said to Mother Corona:

> Tell the Sisters to spiritualize everything they say or do; to praise God in the most beautiful way they know how. I am serious about this and wanted to tell you long ago; now I am so glad that I can tell you. Write it down and let it be read so that every Sister will get to know it, and let it be spread from one to another in our Community. God should be praised. This praise will then continue throughout eternity. That will be the reward of the Sisters.

Sister Stanislaus' condition became critical because of a terrible heat wave occurring during second retreat—June 14 to 21—while many novices prepared for their profession of vows. Her edema could no longer be controlled. Breathing became increasingly difficult when her lungs began to fill with fluid. On June 19, the end seemed near, but she continued to linger. Prayers for the dying had been said a number of times by both Father Adolph J. Klink and Father Leo A. Wedl. Along with her rosary, Sister held the death candle and her indulgenced crucifix. At 6:30 p.m. on June 20, 1944, while the other sisters were at Matins at the close of profession retreat, Sister Stanislaus died.

"For 81 years her life had been interwoven with the growth and development of the community. Her life story was its history."

Stanislaus, Barbaralie Stiefermann, OSF

Mother Corona wrote of her dear friend and mentor:

> Although Mother's death was expected, it came as a shock. Mingled with sadness was a feeling of consolation and even joy at the thought that she was happy; she had gone to receive the reward of her holy life, for hers was truly a selfless

> one. Mother never looked for earthly joys or possessions. She left nothing behind—no trunk, no trinkets—nothing except her clothes and a few books which she regarded as community property...Mother Stanislaus kept nothing for herself.

She never forgot Mother Stanislaus who gave her so much to remember.

SPIRITUAL ENRICHMENT

The letters of Mother Corona were often filled with spiritual enrichment. Through letters, she shared her wisdom, guidance, and reflections which revealed the depth of her own spirituality. The following partial letter is just one example.

> April 28, 1944
>
> My dear Sisters,
>
> We have been considering important and fundamental practices which have a direct bearing on our religious life. During the past month we have been reminded of the necessity of leading a recollected life. The spirit of recollection is indispensable to a Sister who wishes to attain the end of her vocation. There is no substitute for recollection. Without it, much of the time allotted us during the remaining years of our earthly span will be lost. Our life is passing like a shadow, and we know neither the day nor the hour in which God will call us to give Him an account of our thoughts, our motives, our words, and our actions. The future may hold for us one or two score years, more or less, but we know from past experience that ten or twenty years are not even a drop in the ocean of time. We are moving rapidly toward our eternal destiny, and it behooves us to make good use of the fleeting moments. Lost time can never be recovered.

How carefully and precisely the saints used every minute of their time in order to make themselves more pleasing to God! Through constant, persistent practice, they gradually learned how to keep themselves recollected and united to God even in the midst of their daily occupations. The three patrons of youth, St. Stanislaus Kostka, St. Aloysius Gonzaga, and St. John Berchmans, through the practice of recollection attained greater holiness within a few years than many who have grown old in religion. However, in most cases this grace is obtained only after years and decades of faithfulness to duty, courageous self-denial, and patient striving.

True, our daily duties do interfere with uninterrupted thoughts of God, but the spirit of recollection does not require that we think of Him constantly. What does it require? A loving remembrance of God—a looking up to Him—from time to time, and a faithful striving to acquire a consciousness of His divine presence. St. Catherine of Siena erected within herself a little sanctuary wherein she could seek refuge and entertain the Divine Guest of her soul. This she did to counteract the effects of the distracting work which her parents imposed in order to prevent her from thinking of entering the convent.

It is obvious in all her letters, Mother Corona was not only focused on the sisters' professional lives but was deeply concerned about their spiritual development. Another example is the following portion of a letter dated February 24, 1947.

A soul which has made progress in the life of grace does not perhaps realize its own dignity, and, conscious of its many shortcomings, despises itself, but its Father in heaven beholds it with love. Such a soul is a paradise in which God delights to dwell; it has power over the Heart of God. The incarnation, the redemption, the gospel, the church, the sacraments, graces of all kinds, the religious state, the provisions of Providence—all these

He combines with the goodness of a father that souls may have life. God wishes to give our works a supernatural character. The living God becomes our helper in the work of our salvation. His assistance is never wanting to us, and many times every day, whether we are at work or at rest, in moments of sorrow or of joy, whether we speak or keep silence, He is present with us in order that every action of ours may be worthy of a child of God and a means of arriving at eternal life. We never lose our way when we correspond with grace, whereas if we act without its guidance or resist its promptings, we expose ourselves to a merely human activity with no profit for eternal life. Our heavenly Father has His hands filled with graces and wants empty vessels into which He may pour them. It is always within our power to implore His grace.

The sisters who were to make perpetual vows must have been elated to receive this personal letter from Mother Corona.

May 22, 1948

My dear Sister,

You are among the privileged Sisters who hope to make perpetual vows on June 21. You are now preparing for that great day when 'before the Blessed and Immaculate Virgin Mary, before our Father St. Francis, and before all the Saints of heaven' you will make the holy vows of poverty, chastity, and obedience and promise to God Almighty to keep the Rule of your Congregation for your whole life.

You have been selected from among many, dear Sister, and for this wonderful condescension on the part of God, your heart should go out in gratitude. During the years of your preparation, you should have become attached to your Congregation by the strongest ties, and the interests of the School Sisters of St. Francis should always be your interests. Your gratitude should prompt you to be eager and anxious to do something for your Community and to further its interests in return for all it has done for you. In your words and actions, the love and devotion which fill your heart should be noticeable to those with whom you come in contact. People of the world look up to you and respect you as one of our members, but you would fall in their esteem if they noticed that you are not with your Community one hundred percent. Make yourself deserving of the confidence and trust which your superiors have placed in you, and of the respect and esteem with which the good people regard you just because you are a religious and have consecrated your life to God.

You will receive a copy of *The Soul of the Apostolate* by Dom J. Chautard, OCR. Use this book for your private spiritual reading between now and the opening of your retreat and keep it with you for the years which lie ahead. You will want to read this book over and over again, especially those paragraphs which appeal to you. Look upon this book as a dear friend who is always willing to tell you the truth. Read it prayerfully and reflect on its inspiring pages. God grant that it will lead you to sanctity and assist you in drawing many souls to the path of virtue.

May our Heavenly Mother with her Holy Child bless you during this month!

Lovingly,
Mother M. Corona, OSF

HANDWRITING ANALYSIS

Author's error:

When I wrote the book *Stanislaus...with feet in the world,* I had a handwriting analysis (p. 278) done on what I thought was Mother Stanislaus' writing from her diary of her 1930 European trip. I later learned that Mother Corona rewrote the diary for her. Unfortunately, the book *Stanislaus* was already being printed, so I was unable to correct the error.

I am happy I have the opportunity in this publication to rectify the error. I am sorry that I assumed it was Mother Stanislaus' handwriting based on the fact that it was her personal diary. There's a part of me that is happy for the mistake. Were it not for the error, I would not have the description of Mother Corona to include in this publication. Sisters who knew her confirmed with me that it depicts Mother Corona very accurately.

Roman Catholic priest, Anthony J. Becker of blessed memory, was the clinical psychologist and noted graphology expert who did the analysis which follows:

> First and foremost, there is striking evidence of her great inner peace—peace of mind, heart and soul. Her outer self—her physical behavior—was the direct result of her wonderful interior calm.

Father Becker's analysis continues:

> Gifted with excellent self-discipline, she was very secure within herself, both in day-to-day living as well as in the choice of future goals. She knew where she was going in life and she knew how to get where she wanted to go—no doubt about that.
>
> Consistency is one of her outstanding virtues. By nature, she was reliable, predictable, and dependable to a supreme degree. Moodiness and vacillation cannot be found in her behavioral pattern.
>
> Her level of intelligence was very high. In fact, in all areas—academic or abstract, social and emotional, practical, manual and digital—she was far above average. That would give her a large degree of versatility as she plied herself to life.

As for abstract or academic intelligence, she was superior. She possessed a mind that was quick to comprehend abstract truths or concepts. One did not have to tell her something twice for her to grasp the essence of the message. She enjoyed, also, an elephantine memory. Little details were important; she remembered. She was of the mental bent that 'trifles make for perfection, but perfection is no trifle.'

Her powers of concentration, too, were outstanding. That innate potential made it a joy for her to reflect, meditate, pray alone or with others. She derived much intellectual delight quietly engaged in prayer and reflection.

As for her social intelligence, her ability to get along well with others is demonstrated in many graphic traits. Though she was open but on her guard about her personal feelings, she had the ability to communicate maturely with others on a multitude of topics. She was at heart a 'people person.' In conversation, she made a definite effort to have others understand what she was saying. She abhorred the thought of not being understood. Furthermore, she wanted to understand others, for she was a good listener. She had a natural penchant for accuracy and precision in her expressions, so her communications would be clear and frank.

Another social quality she possessed was a real compassion for people. She was not critical but affirming and nurturing.

Her practical intelligence showed up in the ability to make prudential judgments when it came to a question of the suitable use of time, space, money, and energy. She did not waste any of them. It seemed that she wanted to do the right thing at the right time in the right way. Prudence, the first of the four moral virtues, permeated her whole life.

As for manual or digital dexterity or intelligence, her writing shows that she had great potential for working with her fingers and hands. Arts and crafts, sewing, crocheting and knitting, all came natural for her.

Though she was more at home on a one-to-one basis, she could work with groups or classes, if necessary.

She was a natural leader; leadership qualities are sufficiently present in her writing. She not only liked to be in charge of things but was also able to accept responsibility once she was given authority to go ahead.

She had initiative and could do things independently. She was a self-starter. She could go ahead on a project without motivation from others. She was progressive by nature.

In some areas she had fixed ideas; she would not budge at any cost. She would never compromise herself just to win a cause or win over another to her way of thinking. Nor would she be won over by another trying to compromise with her.

GOLDEN JUBILEE CELEBRATION

Mother Corona celebrated her Golden Jubilee on December 6, 1954, the Marian Year. How fitting that her jubilee coincided with the year devoted to Mary, the Mother of God. Having lost her mother as a child, Mother Corona developed a great devotion to and love of the Blessed Mother. She was also probably influenced by her Aunt Agatha who raised her, to pray fervently to the Mother of God. The celebration of her Golden Jubilee established the tradition of celebrating all jubilees of the sisters, which is still an annual, festive occasion.

Archbishop Albert Gregory Meyer was present at the Mass. Father Adolph M. Klink stated in his sermon:

Joining with the Archbishop in this prayer of praise and thanksgiving to Almighty God on this day are the Chaplains of our various institutions and some of our more intimate friends. Your Spiritual Director also takes great joy in singing the praises of God during this Holy Sacrifice of the Mass for the Jubilarians. Rightly do we say, 'I rejoiced because they said to me: We shall go into the house of the Lord.'

Father Adolph M. Klink offered a bit of history in his sermon:

Fifty years ago this very day, Mother M. Alfons had arranged a reception class in memory of the Golden Jubilee of the Proclamation of the dogma of the Immaculate Conception. It was originally intended to take place on the anniversary date, December eighth, but because Archbishop Messmer could not arrange to be here on that day, the Reception day was anticipated to the Feast of good St. Nicholas. Fifty years later, as we bring to a close the Marian Year commemorating the One Hundredth Anniversary of the proclamation of this dogma, you, the Reception Class of 1904, have come to thank the Lord for His tremendous goodness through the years.

When Archbishop Messmer received you on Reception Day, he posed this question: 'What do you ask?' and you answered, 'For the love of God we humbly ask for the habit of this Community, the School Sisters of St. Francis.' Well have you worn that religious garb. After your years of novitiate, having proved yourself faithful, you were admitted to holy vows. The Bishop at that time said, 'If you remain faithful to your holy vows, I promise you in the Name of God, the Almighty, everlasting life.'

Mother Clemens also had a jubilee address:

Reverend Fathers, dear Mother Corona, and all our Golden Jubilarians,

On December 6, 1904, just fifty years ago, in this very hall which was then our 'Domus Dei,' Mother Corona was received into the family of the School Sisters of St. Francis. This special Reception was arranged by Mother Alfons, then Mother General, in order to commemorate the fiftieth anniversary of the proclamation of the dogma of the Immaculate Conception.

It is my privilege, dear Mother, on this your Golden Jubilee, to tell you that we—the Sisters, novices, postulants, and aspirants—congratulate you and wish you every good. My words are feeble, indeed, but behind them are packed all the love, best wishes, and congratulations from your Sisters in thirteen states of our own beloved country, from Germany, Switzerland, Honduras in Central America, and, yes, even from Rome. The Sisters would all love to be here with you, dear Mother, but since that is an impossibility, their hearts are here, and they are celebrating with us and thanking God with us.

In the name of all, I take this occasion to tell you how much we love and revere you. We thank you from the very depths of our hearts for all you have done and are constantly doing for each member individually and for the entire Congregation. We have no way of repaying you but in our customary Franciscan manner we say with one accord, 'May God reward you, Mother' for we cannot. We know He will do so because He will not refuse His Mother anything. And you have truly been Mary's chosen one. You were received in that year when the Church was observing the golden jubilee of the proclamation of the Immaculate Conception, and now, before the close of the Marian Year and the hundredth anniversary of the proclamation of that great dogma, you are celebrating your Golden Jubilee as a Religious. Is it just a coincidence that the name given you in religion fifty years ago should be the title our saintly Pius XII has chosen for his remarkable encyclical on Mary, '*Fulgens Corona*?'

You must be very close to our Blessed Mother. Without doubt, she has watched over you these long and fruitful years and will continue to protect you until she leads you to her Jesus and yours. We all sing a Magnificat and pray that blessed may be the days that are to come, even more blessed, if possible, than the fifty years that lie behind. With you we thank Almighty God for His goodness to you and through you to us.

There are other Golden Jubilarians here—twenty-three. You are also included in our prayers, congratulations, and good wishes. For you, too, and with you we thank God. You have always been an inspiration to us and we all love and respect you. We pray God and His Blessed Mother to protect you and give you many more years to spend in His special service.

Mother Clemens continued to address at length the other jubilarians and ended with the following:

Rededicate yourselves today. As our Blessed Mother gave herself completely, so will you renew your consecration and dedication. Then you will have treasure in heaven, then you will have the fulfillment of the promise which the Bishop made to you: 'You shall have eternal life.' What more do you wish out of this life. Amen.

Archbishop Albert G. Meyer addressed the Golden Jubilarians and the community.

I could not let this occasion pass without expressing my deep sense of satisfaction at being able to participate in this beautiful ceremony of thanksgiving to Almighty God. Surely,

I wish to express to Mother Corona and to all her classmates my own most hearty congratulations on the Golden Jubilee of their religious life which we commemorate today. I want to express to her and to all the Sisters of this Community not only my deep sense of rejoicing with them, but also a most sincere expression of thanks and gratitude for all the wonderful things not only they but all the members of this Community have done for the welfare of Holy Mother Church and the good of souls.

May our Blessed Mother Mary bring down upon you, Mother Corona, and upon your Community the abundant blessings that come whenever we serve God with a spirit of humble thanksgiving, recognizing the good that has been accomplished with His help. I am sure that as we look back over these years, we cannot help being amazed at the good that has been done through cooperation with His grace.

I wish to take this occasion to give public testimony to the great good that has been and is being done by this Community, and to express my most fervent wish with the assurance of my blessing, that this good will continue in the present and in the future. May our Heavenly Mother's 'Fiat'—'Be it done unto me according to Thy word,' continue to dominate and motivate the Sisters of this Community in the future as in the past, that they may continue to serve God for His greater glory and honor and for the salvation of souls.

May God bless you all on this joyful festive day!

1904   1954

GOLDEN JUBILEE
PROGRAM

honoring our beloved

Reverend Mother Mary Corona
and all the other Jubilarians

in the
Marian Year

The School Sisters of St. Francis
Milwaukee

PROGRAM

Jubilee Song....................................*Sister M. Cherubim* [Schaefer]
Community

Blessing of St. Francis..................*Sister M. Cherubim* [Schaefer]
Choir

GREETING.................................*Mother M. Clemens* [Rudolph]

Tribute to Our Lady
To Fatima's Shrine.....................*Sister M. Theophane* [Hytrek]
Verse Speaking Choir - Postulants

Memorare...*Griesbacher*
Choir

Our Father...*Malotte*
The Mocking Bird...*Berger*
Violin Solos

Allegro..*Sister M. Clarissima* [Neumann]
String Quintette

Waltzes...*Brahms*
(from the Liebeslieder, Op. 52)
Duo Pianos

The Crowning of Our Mother
Choric Speakers – Novices

The Visit of the Magi to Herod...................*Sister M. Gilana* [Halac]

Laughter Song.................................*Sister M. Xaveria* [Friedrich]

Cantate Domino...*Nees*
Choir

A list of jubilarians was also printed in the program. Fifty-four women, including Mother Corona, were received in 1904. In 1954, 24 members were still alive. Mother Corona's jubilee classmates were the following:

JUBILARIANS

Reverend Mother Mary Corona [Wirfs]
Sister Mary Alexander [Fiecke]
Sister Mary Adeline [Knoerr]
Sister Mary Amata [Weinberger]
Sister Mary Archangela [Scherer]
Sister Mary Cherubim [Schaefer]
Sister Mary Concepta [Schaut]
Sister Mary Consolata [Schaniel]
Sister Mary Constantine [Antlsperger]
Sister Mary Cortilia [Seidl]
Sister Mary Damiana [Weitzer]
Sister Mary Florina [Woerner]
Sister Mary Hilary [Eggers]
Sister Mary Holda [Ferring]
Sister Mary Immaculate [Geller]
Sister Mary Irma [Keuler]
Sister Mary Kostka [Waskowski]
Sister Mary Mansueta [Krings]
Sister Mary Mellina [Dergans]
Sister Mary Mildred [Maul]
Sister Mary Mira [Studer]
Sister Mary Nepomuca [Skluzacek]
Sister Mary Seraphine [Bichlmeier]
Sister Mary Vita [Marciniak]

Another musical program was given during the Marian Year, specifically to honor Mother Corona.

PROGRAM

Exsultavit Cor Meum .... *Griesbacher*
GREETING .... Sister M. Augustine [Scheele]
Guide Thou Her Steps .... *Cherubini*
Praise the Lord .... *Schehl*
Choir

From "The Carnival of the Animals" .... *Saint-Saens*
Royal March of the Lion
The Aquarium
The Cuckoo
The Swan
The Wild Horses
Duo Pianos
Legend .... *Docker-Milner*

Ave Maria	*Schubert-Saar*
Three Dances	*arr. By Roberts*
Country Dance	*French-Canadian*
Danza Calabrese	*Morelli*
Slavonic Dance	*Balikov*
Tone Poem	*Dethier*
Orchestra	
The Heavens Resound	*Beethoven*
Orchestra and Community	

Beethoven's *"The Heavens Resound"* was a fitting close to Mother Corona's Golden Jubilee celebration. This concert was not merely for amusement and entertainment, but an expression of appreciation and gratitude. Now, over 50 years after her death, celebration gives attention to the transcendent meaning of her life, leadership, service, and commitment to the School Sisters of St. Francis.

ST. JOSEPH CONVENT ORCHESTRA
UNDER THE DIRECTION OF
SISTER MARCINA SCHLENZ

THE SERAPHIC PRESS BINDERY
SISTERS ALVERNA MARIE WESTHAUSER AND
WALDISLAUS (MARTHA MARY) GROHALL

SISTER PATRICIA MICHAELIN WOECKNER
SPECIALTY: PORTRAITURE AND WATERCOLOR

CHAPTER SEVENTEEN

DEATH AND CELEBRATION

Once life has opened its gates, the day will surely come when they will also close. This thought may fill one with melancholy and sadness. People rejoice when a child is born and grieve when a person dies. The opposite, according to a Talmudic sage, would be more appropriate.

The entrance of Catherine Wirfs into life was like a ship setting out on a journey for an unknown destiny. There was no assurance her voyage would be calm or that the ship would reach its destiny and safely return to harbor. Why rejoice in the face of such uncertain prospect, not knowing whether her journey would be safe; whether she would remain unharmed by the hazards of the journey? When, on the other hand, Mother Corona reached the fullness of her years, when the ship reached port in safety, then is occasion for rejoicing and celebrating.

In haste, Mother Clemens sent the following letter to all sisters.

January 4, 1964

My dear Sisters,

This is going to be just a short, hurried note tonight to beg your prayers for our dear Mother Corona.

While I was away at the hospital, Mother developed a heavy cold. Even though it seemed to clear up, Mother's condition did not improve, and she steadily became weaker.

At the time I returned, on Saturday, December 21, Mother asked me not to come into her room because of her heavy cold; she feared that I might catch it. All during this past week, while we were on retreat, Mother was growing weaker and weaker. Finally, on Thursday we took Mother to the Sacred Heart Sanitarium, for when Doctor Larson visited her, he believed this most advisable, considering her condition. And we do feel relieved, for now someone can be with her day and night—just to know she was alone at night in her room had become a considerable worry, as you can understand.

Just now, Mother Hyacinth [Kirch] and I returned from visiting Mother, where we had gone after supper. Truly, our dear Mother Corona does not seem good! She is suffering from a heart condition, as well as a kidney infection. Her whole appearance is not good, so I am writing this letter before I go to bed tonight. I would never forgive myself if I had failed to keep you informed and something were to happen to our dear Mother.

Since we are all so indebted to our dear Mother Corona— who has always sacrificed herself for and considered only the good of the Community—I knew each one of you would want to be notified without delay, so that you can keep our dear Mother in your prayers especially now when, because of her condition, she needs our help.

Since tomorrow is the Feast of the Holy Name of Jesus, let us all call frequently upon that powerful Name, so that Jesus, together with Mary and Joseph, may be with our dear Mother always!

God bless you and keep you holy in this New Year!

Your loving,

Mother M. Clemens, OSF

Two days later on the Feast of the Epiphany, January 6, 1964, at age 77, Mother Corona died. How fitting that she followed the star and was led to her Eternal Bethlehem. The Christian festival commemorating the manifestation of Christ to the Gentiles in the persons of the Magi is a greater feast in many countries than Christmas. Mother Corona left the earth on a day of celebration around the world. Her death also must have been a personal epiphany—an illuminating discovery, a realization and disclosure of life after death.

The sisters on the missions were immediately informed of Mother Corona's death by a telephone relay. After the funeral and burial of the congregation's saintly Corona, Mother Clemens sent a letter to the sisters dated January 21, 1964.

> It all happened so fast, sisters. She was taken to Sacred Heart Sanitarium on January 2nd to room 317.
>
> On Sunday, dear Sister Wilhelmina [Brenner] arranged with Father Lochowitz to have Mother anointed yet that very evening. This took place between 7:30 and 8:00 p.m. Mother was very sweet all during the anointing, and each time Father made the sign of the cross over her, she tried to bless herself.
>
> The sister nurses said that Mother had a very restless night, but that about 3:45 Monday morning, she became very quiet. Father Lochowitz commented that never before had he gone over so early to the Sanitarium as he did on this particular morning. He really does not know why he did so, but as a consequence, Father was in Mother Corona's room when quietly and peacefully she slept away at 5:30 a.m.
>
> Mother's sister, Anna, the only survivor of the immediate family, was present for the anointing on Sunday. Although she had overnight accommodations at the Sanitarium, Mother passed away so unexpectedly that Anna was not there when Mother breathed her last, but she came shortly after. Even had

> she been present, she might not have noticed that the end had come, for Sister Ebana [Hein] said Mother slipped away so quietly that she herself did not even notice it, and she sat right next to the bed watching her!
>
> Our dear Sisters in the Sanitarium did everything possible for Mother. Sister Eventia [Hartman] took care of her during the day, and Sister Ebana at night. They could not have been more kind and loving than they were.

The *Milwaukee Sentinel*, *The New World*, Chicago, Illinois, *The True Voice* of Omaha, *The Milwaukee Journal*, the *Catholic Herald Citizen*, and the *Alverno Campus News* gave impressive accounts of Mother Corona's life and death. Most of the newspapers attributed the cause of her death to a lung ailment. The cause of death in her personal file is listed as "cerebro-vascular accident."

In *US*, February, 1988, "Women of Influence," Sister Michaela Crowley wrote the following about Mother Corona.

> Her presence to us as very young religious was awesome. Her place in the Chapel, in the refectory, her presence at special celebrations in St. Joseph's Hall—all were held in reverence.
>
> But as I look back now and recall *the person* of Mother Corona, I remember a strong, but in many ways, a very calm woman. When she was present, she had the wonderful quality of being *totally* present to the person or persons, or to the event that was taking place.
>
> Mother Corona's ability to deal with many and varied activities and problems was amazing. Looking back at all that happened during the years of her leadership, most especially as those were years of much growth and expansion, one is struck by her organizational powers as well as her courage in risking and moving the community in clear

and definite directions. One is struck by the strength of her faith.

The same article had the following cutline under Mother Corona's photo.

> Mother Corona Wirfs, who led the Congregation for 18 years, was a strong force in educational and health care fields. She opened St. Clare College in Costa Rica, staffed the middle school in Tsingtao, China, and had to recall sisters during the Communist revolution. She merged the Alverno College of Music, Alverno Teachers' College, and the Sacred Heart School of Nursing to form Alverno College of Liberal Arts. The Congregation reached nearly 4,000 vowed members during her leadership. In 1959, Mt. St. Francis was erected as the first American Province House in Rockford, Illinois, to initiate the decentralization of the U.S. Congregation.

Mother Clemens' letter gave the most detailed account of the funeral.

> On Tuesday at one o'clock, our dear Mother Corona was laid in state in St. Joseph's Hall. All the Sisters who saw her will agree that our Mother looked beautiful and peaceful.
>
> It was most impressive during these days to see the visitors and all the Sisters filing past the coffin to offer their final tribute to the Mother who had done so much, in fact, who had spent her life in sacrifice and suffering for the Community she loved. The Community's welfare was Mother's sole object in anything she ever did. There were numberless priests, monsignori, and even bishops, who paid her tribute.
>
> Preceding the Requiem, we had what was like two processions. Although the Funeral Mass was scheduled for ten o'clock on Thursday, at ten minutes to ten Father Schlaffer with

the Officers of the Mass went out in procession and then brought in the casket, followed by the relatives, friends, and Sisters.

When all were in their places, once more the priests went out. Then there was the solemn entry of the many, many priests (one newspaper cited 150); after them, the many monsignori in their beautiful, colorful robes; then came Bishop Hillinger, followed by Bishop Atkielski, and finally, our loved Archbishop.

At the Solemn Requiem Mass that followed, Father [James] Schlaffer was Celebrant; Father [Donald] Weber, Deacon; and Father [George] Lochowitz, Subdeacon; Father Donald Reiff of St. Mary's Hill was Master of Ceremonies. Presiding was Archbishop [William E.] Cousins, with Bishop [Roman R.] Atkielski and Bishop [Raymond P.] Hillinger in the sanctuary. Just to know that our own beloved Archbishop shared our sorrow was a real comfort to all of us. As His Excellency gave the final absolution, I could not help thinking how this would have pleased Mother had she known—and I'm sure she did.

According to the *Catholic Herald Citizen*, January 11, 1964, the following priests were also involved.

Archbishop William E. Cousins presided at the funeral Mass and gave the final absolution. He was assisted by Msgr. Alex Zuern, presbyter assistant; and Frs. Raymond Parr and Hugh Wish as chaplains.

Mother Clemens' letter continued giving more details of the impressive funeral.

As Mr. Altstadt himself, the funeral director, commented, this was one of the largest funerals—I wish I could tell you how many cars were in the cortege! I can only say that when we turned the corner, and looked back, we could not see the end of the line. Even our two buses were there: one with the novices and the other with the postulants. (Just now a Sister mentioned their car was in about the middle of the procession. Looking back and counting, they concluded there must have been more than a hundred cars in the procession.) Last but not least, an escort of motorcycle police added to the dignity, and, of course, provided for the safety.

Let me tell you about another very impressive incident that took place. Sister Augustine had called, suggesting that if the funeral procession could be routed by way of Alverno College on 39th Street, then their students, as well as the Sisters, could pay respects as the funeral procession passed by. When we asked Mr. Altstadt to arrange accordingly, he very readily agreed. Sisters, it was a most beautiful and touching sight to see, lining the walk as we slowly passed by, the elementary school children, then the college students—lay and Sisters—as well as the faculty members, all outdoors as the cortege passed. Later, many of the Sisters remarked about this, and commented how deeply impressed they had been. This certainly was a beautiful and kind gesture on the part of Alverno College, one for which we are most grateful.

[Mother Corona was buried in Mount Olivet cemetery, which is located on Morgan Avenue, across from Alverno College.]

Although our dear Mother Corona is no longer in our midst, the memory of her life, dedicated to the good of the community, will ever be a constant reminder for us also:

> TO DO ALWAYS MORE for our loved Community;
> TO DO IT ALWAYS BETTER for the Community; and
> TO DO ALWAYS—whatever we do—<u>with great love</u>, for the Community!

Sisters, this is what Mother Corona did—she sacrificed herself, and she suffered for the community. In all that she did, her only thought was ever for the community's welfare. I have worked closely with Mother for more than twenty-five years, so I can vouch that the welfare of the community was Mother's only concern—her first and last thought was always for its good.

> Before the throne of God, I am positive, that we now have a powerful intercessor; our loved Mother Corona will be able to help us now even more than when she was with us.
>
> As you can well understand, we tried our utmost to have a nice funeral for our dear Mother Corona. Our Provinces contributed their share too, thus aiding us in accomplishing our purpose. They provided the two beautiful bouquets on standards on either side in the main lobby. Each bouquet bore two streamers: the bouquet to the left had 'Rockford' written on one, and 'Omaha' on the other; the bouquet to the right bore the names: 'Wisconsin' and 'Chicago' on the two streamers. At either side of the casket in St. Joseph Hall were two more white bouquets: On one streamer was marked, 'Generalate;' the other streamer read: 'OUR MOTHER.'

Written as an afterthought, Mother Clemens stated:

> Perhaps some of you noticed Mother's casket was grey instead of black. Sometime previously in our Council Meeting it was decided that it would be nice to have the Sisters buried in grey instead of black caskets, and it so happened that our dear Mother Corona was the first, but from now on all the Sisters will be buried in grey caskets.

The Right Reverend Monsignor Louis E. Riedel gave the sermon after the funeral Mass of Mother Corona, Thursday, January 9, 1964. His opening remarks were the following:

> While it is not the custom in this Community to speak at the funeral of a religious, in this case a few words seem to be justifiable. As we see it, Mother Mary Corona not only symbolized much of the spirit of sacrifice, so characteristic of this Community, but expressed—as you well know and we

can attest—a great love for Christ's Priesthood, in words as well as in deeds.

In paying a simple tribute to Mother Corona today, therefore, in her hour of homecoming, we recognize and encourage this zealous apostolate of this Franciscan Community, to which Mother Corona and others of this pioneering age have dedicated their life's efforts. It is only fitting and right, therefore, that we, like the Christian family of old—bishops, priests, religious and lay—gather around this Altar of Sacrifice to speed the day of homecoming for Mother Mary Corona, whom to know was to love and respect.

Mother Corona lived her life with nobility of purpose. She knew what she believed and followed those beliefs with laser-sharp focus. She carried the spirit of the foundresses, Mothers Alexia, Alfons, and Sister Clara with solemn responsibility. Nothing in her time was what it used to be. To be creative, therefore, required knowledge and appreciation of the past, but also Mother Corona's vision, intelligence, wisdom, and faith to build a new future and advance the mission of the church and the School Sisters of St. Francis. "The path is made in the walking."

The skill of her influential leadership, at a time in the church when she was surrounded with guardrails, was the ultimate force within for giving, risking, creating, sharing, and contributing more to the common good, especially in education and healthcare. Dedication, consistency, and purpose were tattooed on her heart. Her decision-making started from the heart and brain and spiraled into compassion. She was truly a servant leader in the church and her beloved School Sisters of St. Francis.

Even the closing of the gates at the time of the setting sun was not to be feared because it was a triumphant homecoming. It was a grateful celebration that the ship had returned safely and peacefully to the port from which it had set sail 77 years prior.

*   *   *   *   *   *   *   *   *   *   *   *   *   *

Mother Corona's life and legacy, her CROWNing glory, can never be fully expressed, but can only be addressed in awe and thanksgiving.

MISSIONS BEGUN DURING MOTHER CORONA'S ADMINISTRATION

As Mother Assistant

1938	St Joseph Hospital	Beaver Dam	WI

As Mother General

1943	St John Evangelist School	Beacon	NY
1943	St Frederick School	Cudahy	WI
1944	St Monica School	New York City	NY
1946	Holy Angels School	Chicago	IL
1946	St Mary Assumption School	Staten Island	NY
1947	Sacred Heart School	Walls	MS
1948	Holy Ghost School	Wood Dale	IL
1949	St Alexis School	Bensenville	IL
1949	St Teresa School	Kankakee	IL
1949	St Mary School	Holly Springs	NY
1950	St Patrick School	Beaver Dam	WI
1950	St Alphonsus School	Greendale	WI
1951	St Benedict High School	Chicago	IL
1951	St Beatrice School	Schiller Park	IL
1951	Waupun Memorial Hospital	Waupun	WI
1952	St Walter School	Roselle	IL
1952	St Joseph School	Holly Springs	MS
1952	St Joseph School	Waupun	WI
1953	St Irene School	Warrenville	IL
1953	St Mary School	Stockbridge	WI
1953	Alverno College	Milwaukee	WI
1953	Japanese Martyrs School	Leavenworth	MN
1954	Christ the King School	Jackson	MS
1954	Immaculate Heart of Mary School	Monona	WI
1954	St Mary School	Hales Corners	WI
1955	Our Lady Queen of Peace School	Milwaukee	WI
1955	St Albert School	Milwaukee	WI
1955	Sacred Heart Schl Practical Nursing	Milwaukee	WI
1955	St Joseph School	Big Bend	WI
1955	St Joan of Arc School	Okauchee	WI
1956	St Joseph School	Richmond	IL
1957	St Clare College	San Jose	Costa Rica
1958	Our Lady of Sorrows School	Milwaukee	WI
1958	St Joseph High School	Kenosha	WI
1959	St James School	Rockford	IL
1959	St Gerald School	Ralston	NE
1960	St Luke School	Carol Stream	IL
1960	Santa Maria Addolorata School	Chicago	IL

Missions Begun During Mother Corona's Administration

- ❖ Additionally, in the United States, Mother Corona continued to staff 147 schools.

- ❖ Four schools were discontinued.

- ❖ St. Joseph Academy High School at the Motherhouse continued to flourish.

- ❖ Because of communism, the school in Tsingtao, China was closed in 1949.

- ❖ The Conservatory of Music in Chicago closed in 1955.

- ❖ Sacred Heart Sanitarium and St. Mary's Hill Hospital in Milwaukee also continued to thrive.

- ❖ During these years the European Province, in nine countries, opened 24 missions, continued operating 170 missions, and closed 37 missions. Most missions were schools.

National Congress of Religious
of the United States
August 9, 10, 11, 12, and 13, 1952
The University of Notre Dame
Notre Dame, Indiana

Paper Presented by:
Mother Mary Corona, OSF
Mother General, School Sisters of St. Francis
Milwaukee, Wisconsin
Monday, August 11 – 2:30 p.m.

Modern Comfort and Convenience
In their Relation to the Religious Spirit

MODERN COMFORT AND CONVENIENCE
IN THEIR RELATION TO THE RELIGIOUS SPIRIT

Mother Mary Corona, OSF
School Sisters of St. Francis
Milwaukee, Wisconsin

An age like ours, which is "in process of being born of discovery and the machine," as Cardinal Suhard reminds the Christian world in his great pastoral letter, GROWTH OR DECLINE?, cannot but give rise to new and challenging problems for Religious everywhere. Science and the machine have changed the face of the earth so radically that our founders, were they suddenly confronted with the kind of world in which our Religious must make their way to God, would be momentarily startled and confused.

But, of this we may be certain. Were they living today, our founders would be the first to recognize the need for adaptation to our times—adaptation, not surrender or connivance; the kind of adaptation which, as Reverend J. Creusens, S.J. pointed out, "involves change, not from a mere desire for change in itself, or from fickleness, but from a desire to be able to live or to act more profitably;" the kind of adaptation that does not touch the essential spirit of religious life. Religious of the mid-twentieth century, no less than their brethren of the formative days of their Congregations, Father Creusens continues, "must renounce the world—its ease, its dissipation, its spirit of independence, and of criticism."

Pope Pius X, in his encyclical FERMO PROPOSITO, shows how the Church leads the way in intelligent adaptation, reminding his contemporaries that the Church "is pliable and accommodates herself easily to the new demands of society." But this adaptability, the holy Pope insists, must be accomplished without "attacking the integrity or the changeless nature of faith and morals."

It is this sort of adaptation Pope Pius XII in his SUMMI PONTIFICATUS offers as a directive to modern Catholic Action: "To accomplish this task of regeneration by adapting her methods to the changing conditions of the times and to the new needs of the human race is the essential office of our Holy Mother the Church."

In his counsel to teaching Sisters on September 15, 1951, Our Holy Father applied this principle of adaptation directly to education in our times. His Holiness requested that Sisters be given an adequate education and be provided with what they need to meet modern education demands.

It is all too easy for us to canonize the old because it is old, if we are ultra-conservative, or to reject the old because it is not new, if we are ultra-progressive. Cardinal Suhard wisely warns: "To make yesterday's forms the ideals of the present is a serious mistake of which Catholics should be doubly careful," for "tradition is by no means simply the mechanical transmission of an inert 'thing.' Rather, it is the living communication and the progressive manifestation . . . of a global truth to which each age discovers a new aspect."

Either of two extremes threatens the balanced outlook our Religious need to maintain stability in a fast-changing world. The over-conservative hinder God's work by an unintelligent opposition to everything modern; the ultra-modern fail as Religious by easy surrender to soft living and modern comforts. God-centered living (the only kind worthy of a Religious) in a mechanical civilization demands perspective. The Religious needs to think through the problems with which modern living confronts him to arrive at the convictions which should control his actions. He needs to understand the place of modern conveniences in life; he needs a firm grasp on the meaning of religious life; and he needs practical directives in the correct use of the material universe.

First, he needs to understand that what is true of the machine is true of all modern conveniences. In itself the machine is good. It operates by laws that God established and man discovered by the proper use of his powers. When the machine is a tool for man—that is, when it increases the quantity or quality of his work, and at the same time helps him achieve his final purpose—the glory of God by the maturing of his own powers—it is good. When it is an instrument of social injustice, when it dominates man, takes his work away from him, makes him a flabby automaton, it is bad—not in itself, but for him.

When a Religious uses modern conveniences as means to help him achieve his end—the complete maturity of all his powers through the service of God and his fellow men—these conveniences are not only good in themselves; they are good for the Religious who uses them. But if he uses them as ends to mere comfortability, to pleasure seeking, to indulgence in the things of the senses, they are bad; not in themselves, but for the Religious who misuses them.

Modern conveniences are a part of the material universe, the right use of which is basic to the practice of Christian poverty. Those who reduce poverty to a negative precept, a mere doing without, miss its full meaning and have no share in St. Francis' joy in holy poverty. The poor man of Assisi saw

God's plan for human life whole, and would never say, "Man is made for God and the world is made for man," without adding, "and man is made for the world." God's free creature, man, alone can enable creation to sing its "Benedicite."

To Saint Francis all creatures were holy in themselves and they glorified God in a twofold manner when man made proper use of them. And man, using creatures holily, became holy by their use. Here is our yardstick, made to order, for the right use of modern conveniences.

Saint Francis went without what he did not need. To him excessive use of creatures was abuse of them. He used, as Christ showed him the way, as much as he needed. No more. To him poverty was the living of the OUR FATHER.

In the light provided by a right understanding of Christian poverty, the meaning of adaptation as we have been using the term becomes clear. It is the abuse, the misuse, the excess in the use of creatures that is bad, not the use. Modern conveniences of travel, up-to-date equipment in the classroom, life-saving instruments in the hospital, and labor-saving devices in the home are not only good, but holy, when they are used to spread the kingdom of God on earth.

A safeguard for the Religious in regard to the use of modern comforts and convenience is adherence to the "common life" as it is explained in Canon Law.

When we turn from modern conveniences to a consideration of modern comforts, justification by motive becomes even more imperative. But the same rule holds. If the Religious uses modern comforts reverently, in harmony with the will of God, he is acting holily. The _if_ is the difficult word to justify, for the word _comfort_, by definition, is associated with ease, and carries overtones that disturb the harmony of lives dedicated to the things of the spirit. We should be very unwilling to admit that ease has an authentic place in the life of an integrated Christian, let alone a Religious.

Modern soft garments that flatter the senses, easy access to the radio, television, the motion picture used to gratify curiosity and to participate in worldly amusements to the neglect of duty, easy chairs and couches that invite to undisciplined relaxation, habitual use of cooling devices that cause one to bypass completely the opportunities for self-denial that warm weather provides, unrestricted and unlimited use of the automobile—the list could be extended to alarming proportions. This is not intended as a sweeping condemnation of comforts, but of their intemperate and immoderate use. All such modern comforts indulged in habitually are both the result and the cause of mediocrity. The Religious who is a comfort-seeker is missing completely the meaning of the religious life, for modern comforts are utterly incompatible with the Cross. And what is a Religious if not a Cross-bearer?

To me it seems that the crux of the problem of the Religious and modern conveniences, as well as the Religious and modern comforts, is the right use of the material universe, or the practice of Christian poverty. And this problem, in turn, rests on the understandings that arise from a firm grasp of the distinction between _doing_ and _being_. If what we _do_ emerges from what we _are_, our doing increases our being, contributes to the maturing of all our powers, helps us achieve the end of our existence—sanctity. But, if our _doing_ is an end in itself, the longest life filled with the most frantic _doing_ is a futile one.

Father Gerald Vann points out: "It is of little avail to train the will to choose the right and resist the wrong unless at the same time you are training the whole personality to see and to love. The pursuit of right can be as sterile as remorse: what is creative and life-giving is the vision and therefore the love of truth and goodness and beauty."

Summary of a Paper on Modern Comfort and Convenience
in their Relation to the Religious Spirit

This paper is limited to a brief presentation of some of the aspects of the problems that confront Religious in our rapidly-changing scientific age. Living in a world which is intrinsically involved, not only in the conveniences science produces, but in the comforts these conveniences provide, the Religious needs to be firmly anchored in principles that emerge from the kind of realism Pope Pius XII urged in his address to the delegates to the First Congress of Religious held in Rome in the fall of 1950. His Holiness exhorted Religious as trustworthy and faithful models to let their lives be in conformity with their profession; to be in their hearts what their habit professes.

The basic problem is one of values. In these disjointed times, even the Religious finds it difficult to avoid confusing means and ends unless he keeps his values straight. The problem here is in the correct use of the material world. Both modern comforts and modern conveniences are considered in the light of this fundamental concept. The right use of the material universe serves God's purpose and promotes the perfection of the user; the wrong use is abuse, frustrates God's plan, and is disintegrating to the user.

Noisy Mannerisms

Noisy Mannerisms

The gentle religious has an inward charm that never offends. Outward charm is a necessary quality—especially is it necessary for the individual who wishes to play the game of life successfully. Outward charm consists in the happiest way of communicating with one's fellow creatures. It makes life run smoothly, agreeable and pleasant in the home circle, in the business world, and in social gatherings. We do not live entirely to ourselves: regardless of the walk of life in which we function; we must conform to the rules that govern interactions with our associates. Outward charm can be easily attained by reading the rules of any good book on etiquette of which there are many on the market. These rules constitute the little trifles of deportment recognized as proper by the social group in which we move. All we need do is find out what they are and put them into practice.

Inward charm, however, is not so easily acquired. Inward charm is the outward manifestation of one's inward character and attitude toward life. It is shown in the kindly, gracious, and sympathetic feeling that people have for each other in their inter-social relationships. The absence of inward charm is revealed in noisy, cross-grained mannerisms.

Inward charm is the soul of personal charm; outward charm comprises the delicate sprouts that issue from the soul of the inner. Without the inner, the external would die for want of nourishment. An inward charm is essentially the characteristic of every good religious. Her field of labor takes her into teaching and nursing, where it is absolutely necessary that gentleness should be paramount. The religious has such close contact with those who are dependent upon her, that an inward grace of mind, and an outward winning smile, must be the counterpart of all her actions. The religious who has a deep gentle sympathetic feeling at all times toward all with whom she comes in contact is never guilty of the coarse, repulsive mannerisms that are so painful to her associates.

Noisy Behavior

A person of gracious interior is not likely to race through the corridor, bump into her associates, push and nudge them, nor is she inclined to offend against the proprieties of behavior in any way. Her heart is gentle and kind towards others, and consequently all her movements are gentle and kind. Whether she is a nurse or classroom teacher, or holds any other position, she will not grab the doorknob in a noisy manner, invade the privacy of another's room without a gentle rap; nor will she slam the door behind her, or disturb the occupants by loud heavy footsteps. If she is a nurse, she knows that jarring the bed, slamming the furniture about, tearing off the bed clothes, dropping articles on the floor, are not manifestations of an inward charm.

If she is a classroom teacher, she is aware of the fact that every movement of hers is observed by the children, and that they look up to their teacher as a model for imitation. She is careful that her conduct before her class is exemplary. She is especially tactful, courteous and respectful toward her fellow sisters in the presence of the children. If some little difficulty or friction does arise between them in the home circle, she is very careful not to let a trace of her feelings show itself in any way in the presence of her worldly associates. Her conduct and bearing will inspire the confidence and respect, and the love of her children, and edify their parents. Why is it that a weak, delicate Sister so often gains control and perfect order in a classroom, where a strong and healthy, but selfish one had previously lost complete control. It is the inward charm in the former, and the absence of that charm in the latter that makes the difference. A gentle disposition wields a powerfully soothing influence over the children. Sisters in active life are always closely observed.

> "So let your light shine, that they may see your good works, and glorify your Father who is in heaven." (Matt. V. 16)

Annoying Mannerisms in Speech

Loud talking, boisterous laughing, and the like, are tabooed by the religious of gracious, engaging manners. A loud bragdoccia form of speech does not suggest a gentle interior. A religious of humble and gentle heart will not flaunt the names of some prominent persons of her past social group before her present group to show them how popular she was. She will not be forever gasconading her accomplishments before the laity of her present mission, nor will she stress the pomp of her education, or the circumstances of her practical acquirements before her new associates. She will never speak of her success at some other place to the pastor of her present mission and tell him how well she was liked there. He, as well as the people of his parish, look for the "still waters that run deep" in the teacher they select for their children. Both laity and religious detest a braggart.

Whispering in company is a form of mannerism of speech which should be avoided. Its effect on the company is the same as boasting. The general group is no place for personal secrets, or hidden bits of gossip. In public it always gives offense. Even if an apology is made for the action, it is tabooed and frowned upon by the bystander. The religious who is amiable, gentle and kind is not guilty of such conduct. Nor is she guilty at any time of imparting a confidential matter to a group, and then asking her listeners not to repeat it. If an individual cannot keep her own secrets, she cannot expect anyone else to keep them for her. We should never expect anyone to keep a secret which we ourselves are itching to tell everybody with whom we come in contact.

Quiet use of the Handkerchief

The handkerchief is the most delicate, and at the same time the most offensive article of clothing that we possess. It should be the daintiest. It should be kept spotlessly clean, and even though perfectly clean, it should be kept out of sight. No one should be allowed to pick up a handkerchief that had been accidently dropped by someone else, unless the owner is an invalid and at a great disadvantage. Nor should that article of clothing ever be used for anything except for the purpose of which it is intended. Coughing, spitting, and hawking should be avoided at all times, and in all places if possible, and then only with the least noise or drawing attention. Clearing of the nostrils and throat is always annoying. Only the weak and infirm may be excused from such conduct. When impossible to check a cough or sneeze, the handkerchief should be held before the mouth, and the head turned away from one's associates, the handkerchief removed as quickly and quietly as possible, without any reference to the act. To apologize is only to draw attention to an inconvenience that had best be forgotten as quickly as possible. Vigorous and excessive blowing of the nose is executed only by vulgarians. In passing from a cold freely-circulating atmosphere into a crowded stuffy room, the change in atmosphere brings about a change in breathing; in sinuses, nostrils and throat. The consequent hacking and coughing becomes quite uncontrollable at times in the warmer air, especially if there is putrid matter in these delicate organs. This embarrassing difficulty can be avoided by syringing the nostrils and throat with warm water before entering the warmer atmosphere. The utmost care should be taken to guard against offending in these delicate matters.

Loud Odors

The ear is not the only carrier of noises; noisy smells are equally as offensive. The offender is usually not aware of odors emanating from her own body, and it is a very delicate thing for anyone else to touch upon. Here is where the religious can exercise the foundation quality of the primary aim of her rule; charity. In all Christian charity, she should tell her fellow sisters of the presence of an offensive odor of which the offending individual is not aware.

Perspiration is the most general offending odor, especially where heavy clothing must be worn. Religious have so many various duties imposed upon them that it is difficult to keep their heavy woolen garbs free from the "honest sweat" of the poet, which others might not find quite so poetic. Nothing is quite so repulsive to a patient lying helpless on the sick-bed than to have a nurse bending over her and administering to her, with clothes reeking from old perspiration. We associate perspiration more directly and more perceptibly with the feet than with any other part of the body. The reason is that there are more perspiration glands in the feet than anywhere else. It is well for anyone who has this trouble to put a little alum in the water, and afterward dust the feet with borate powder. A solution of equal parts of alcohol and witch hazel is also a good lotion for tired sweaty feet. Hot water, however, always is a sovereign specific for all sweaty feet.

Halitosis is another offensive odor that must be guarded against. This condition has various causes. It might be caused by an accumulation of putrid material in the sinuses, faulty denture, or from a coated tongue. Usually, however, it is caused by disorders of the stomach. Where no medical cure is required, the ordinary home remedies will suffice. A teaspoonful of soda in a glass of water sipped at intervals will help. In addition, there are mints and peppermints and lifesavers of many kinds on the market that sweeten the breath. They are, however, palliatives and not cures. Good health of the digestive tract and cleanliness of the oral cavity is the only cure. The gentle-minded religious who is considerate of others will be careful not to offend in this respect.

Noisy Emotional Display

Strong emotion is out of place in public gatherings. Exhibitions of anger, outbursts of temper, emotions of fear, hilarity or embarrassment; are all the height of bad form in public. Expressions such as "She gets my goat" or "She gets on my nerves" or any other similar impatient expressions are not indicative of inner refinement. The action and speech of the careful religious is tempered with a dispassionate calmness and tranquility that gives her the appearance of perfect religious poise. The most striking thing about her is her carefully-disciplined emotion. She never gets excited when her duties pile up in preparing for the closing of the school year, or in putting on a demonstration, a musical recital, or a school play.

She plans carefully, does not hurry or worry, does not throw things about and get herself and her co-workers all upset. She knows that over-fatigue begets irritability, diminishes intelligence and liberty, and unbalances the nerves. She guards against these results. She does not attempt to stage a program that is beyond the children's capacity or her own ability. Her motive is not just to "show off" or to "go one better" than someone else. That would not be a holy motive, and it is not the goal of a good religious. Nor does she work overly hard for the sole purpose of making a show and impressing the people with what she can do, so that when the work is commented upon her co-workers say, "Yes, it is good, but we all worked so hard and are so tired that we just barked at each other." Sidney Smith well puts such excess in the following words:

> "The taste for emotion may become a dangerous taste: We should be very cautious how we attempt to squeeze out of human life more ecstasy and paroxysm than it can well afford."

Exhibitions of excessive hilarity likewise shows an absence of refinement, and also of common sense. Loud screaming at indoor games, or even on the tennis court is out of place. A cry of satisfaction when playing a good stroke is quite another thing. When there is harmony between the expression of the emotion, and the good play, there is an undertone of mellowness to the expression, but a scream just for effect has a metallic sound. It is evident that the guilty individual is aiming at drawing attention to herself. Nature has intended for expression to be in harmony with emotion, and normally it is in harmony with the situation also. It is not wholesome to act one thing and think and feel another. The test is this; you are sincere in your reaction toward your fellow creatures, or is your response to them simply for effect?

> "To thine own self be true, and it must follow as
> the night the day, thou canst not then be false
> to any man."

Conclusion

Let kindness, honor, truth be your motto. Put these virtues in a setting of graceful and gracious manners, and you will have that inner charm that appeals to old and young, rich and poor, learned and ignorant.

It should be the aim of every religious to do the greatest possible good in this chaotic world of ours. To accomplish this, she must live with others, of necessity she must live in harmony with them, and be considerate of their feelings and wishes. Not only does she come in contact with her own group, but she is constantly thrown in with other social groups of the outside world. Society is an association of gentle folk. Good form in speech, gracious manners, a knowledge of the social amenities of life, and above all sincerity toward fellow men, and instinctive selflessness, and a strong consideration for the feelings of others; these are the credentials by which society recognizes its chosen members. It is not enough for a religious in active life to be virtuous, she must also be agreeable and pleasing to all with whom she comes in contact if she wishes to win her subjects and do the greatest amount of good among them.

THE LITERATURE OF THE VICTORIAN AGE

SISTER M. CORONA
1921 NORTH KEDVALE AVENUE
CHICAGO 39, ILLINOIS

THE LITERATURE OF THE VICTORIAN AGE

Literature is the expression of life. The age makes the literature and not the literature the age. This being so, it is important that we look into the spirit of the Victorian Age before we begin to speak of its authors and their works.

The Victorian, or modern age, began practically with the accession of Queen Victoria to the throne of England in 1837. We are told that in no other age was there such a vast amount of pure literature produced. This, however, is questionable, for it is too early to determine the value of the literature of the Victorian Age. A survey of the history of the Victorian Age will show us what was the power that shaped its literature. We find that a great epoch of literature is always a period of unrest, an unsettled state of affairs in the country, the nation. The Victorian Age was such a period. Its literature is the answer to a cry. The age, the people were restless; they were living in expectation. Literature embodies the spirit of the age.

Politically, the Victorian Age was very quiet; socially there was scarcely any disturbance. The men of that age were very active, no dreamers. In this they differ from the people of the other ages of English literature. They began to search into science, philosophy, and religion—they were searching for truth. This search for truth is as old as the human race.

Truth is something very much like its author, God. So often He seems obscure. Truth is the same. The search for truth must be either scientific, philosophic, or religious. The Egyptians were scientific; the Greeks philosophic; and the Israelites religious. The Romans worked for truth in applied philosophy as applied to law and government. Their ability to govern the world through such a long period proves this fact.

During the Victorian Age, men were seeking truth in the name of religion. That movement affected the whole nation, not only Keats, Newmann and Manning, and yet we cannot call the Victorian Age religious; we cannot say this search for truth in the name of religion was heard most in the field of religion. We cannot say it marked the age of truth in the world of philosophy. The dominant note of philosophy was Utilitarianism based on a mixture of religion and materialism. From this we see that the search for truth was not strictly religious, not strictly philosophical. It gradually narrowed down to science.

Science it was that really gave the Victorian Age its shape and color. The scientific search for truth in the wrong direction during this age led to the development of the doctrine of evolution which gained a foothold in England and from there spread quickly throughout the civilized world. This idea was not new. It was believed by many of the old scientists, but in the Victorian Age it became popular through Charles Robert Darwin, who paved the way for the acceptance of this doctrine of Evolution by means of his work, "The Origin of Species by Means of Natural Selection." This book, which appeared in 1859, has attracted great interest. Darwin extended his general theory to include man in another of his works, "The Descent of Man."

Associated with Darwin were Wallace, Lyell, Huxley, Tyndall and many others who wrote essays on the theory of evolution. Naturally, these theories came into fierce conflict with the theological views. The theory of evolution greatly affects society, morality, and religion. If this be true, then it affects human life, for society affects morality, and religion explains morality.

We are very much interested in this theory when applied to society. If the doctrine of evolution affects society, then it must pervade literature, because literature is the expression of human life. Evidently, in the Victorian Age the theory of evolution was applied to human life in social, moral and religious aspects. Literature is the reflection of man's life; by reflection of man's life is meant the reflection of his sentiments, connections, aims and ideals. We learn ideals not in history but in literature.

To show how the spirit of evolution affects the literature of the Victorian Age, you have but to listen to the two greatest of its poets, Tennyson and Browning. Tennyson in his poem *"The Making of Man"* says, "Man as yet is being made." Browning in his *"Paracelsus"* says, "Progress is the law of life, Man is not man as yet." In history we find that under every type of civilization an evil was cured by removing it. Not so in the modern era.

The Victorian Age has a different theory. The lower form developed into a higher, slowly, under the influence of time by causing potentialities to blossom forth into realities. That idea of growth is materialistic. It takes into consideration that the individual creature from his own inherent power will develop into something better, only time is needed, and the rest follows. That is the spirit of the Victorian Age. It believes in the idea of growth. That is the teaching of Darwin, Huxley, Tyndall and the rest. They considered it either from a scientific or philosophic standpoint.

If it affected only scientists and philosophers, we would let them fight it out themselves, but this teaching permeates society, and consequently, it pervades literature. Every man must learn the purpose of his existence and the nature of his destiny. He was told very plainly he had no voice in his origin but had to accept it just as it was. He had it in his power to attain or frustrate the purpose of his existence. He could determine the nature of his destiny.

The principle of existence became for the thinking Christian a most exciting adventure. On the one hand, a higher power was urging him to better and nobler things; on the other hand, there was another power influencing him to lower and baser things. That was a malignant power. Between these two powers with their aids, life became an exciting adventure.

In the Victorian Age, we see evolution playing its part in the problem of life. For a thinking man, evolution is very discouraging. It makes of man an irresponsible creature. You never see an animal acting like a man, but you often see a man acting like an animal. In this age, the worst blow was struck morality since Christianity began.

Evolution is a monster with two faces: one of smiles and promises, the other of frowns and threats. We cannot assume that the Victorian Age was more immoral than any other age, but it was the age in which the hardest blow was struck morality. This was not an age to inspire poetry.

The spirit of the time crept into the writings of the greatest Victorian poets, Tennyson and Browning, even though these men were against the spirit of their age. The better part of the work of Tennyson and Browning is due to the fact that they allowed their Christian ideas to take the lead.

The structure of the prose of this age is equal, if not superior, to the work of Addison and Steele. When it comes to style, Keats is better than Addison. That is for the rhetoric class, but when we consider subject matter, that is a different thing. Many of these men wrote to become popular. Their style is good, and as far as this is concerned, they succeeded, but had they propounded clearly, they would not have become popular.

As far as thought is concerned, they are utter failures. Thomas Carlyle and Thomas Babington Macaulay are considered the greatest prose writers of their time. Macaulay's essay on Milton appeared in the *Edinburgh Review* in 1825. It is typical of Macaulay. A careful study of that essay will help us form a true estimate of Macaulay's character. He compares Dante and Milton, favoring Milton. Dante represents the teaching of the Catholic Church; Milton represents private interpretation of the Bible. In this essay, as in his other writings, Macaulay is very inconsistent. He seems to have no thoughts of his own. His thoughts are borrowed—he remembers, and depending on his memory, he gets facts confused and the result is chaos. He undertook to write the history of England which is a masterpiece of style, but the accuracy of it is challenged. He too often draws biased conclusions from statements too incomplete. Poor Tom, the Babbler!

Carlyle wrote the French Revolution which appeared in 1837 and the despised *Sartor Resartus,* which was published the following year. His influence is now well-nigh spent. Carlyle is sometimes classified with Ruskin and Stevenson as a religious teacher. In a certain sense, they protect against the materialistic spirit of their age and tread in favor of the higher ideals of life.

Robert Louis Stevenson cannot be passed over in silence, for he holds a prominent place in English literature. His novels, *Treasure Island, Kidnapped* and *Catriona*, though written for boys, have won a permanent place in literature by their abiding charm and the beauty of their style. His poems, essays and familiar letters all bear the stamp and glamour of his personality. The impulse given by Stevenson to the new romantic movement is seen in the novels of writers of the present day. The *Child's Garden of Verses* contains poems of lingering sweetness and sincerity yet has not the enduring qualities of his other works.

John Ruskin is considered the great critic of his age. His works may be divided into three classes: criticisms of art, industry and life. He is looked upon as an ethical teacher by those who are not thoroughly familiar with his writings. In truth, he is no ethical teacher but an evil influence at work in many of the classrooms of the present day, poisoning the minds of the young with his unsound principles. He wrote on such a variety of subjects that he could not possibly write understandingly on all of them. His work entitled *"Modern Painters"* is considered by many the most accurate of his writings. He had no dogma, no formula, no communion. In his *"Sesame and Lilies,"* he attacked the pope and the hierarchy of the Catholic Church. And, this man poses as a moral teacher! Every man colors his writings with his religious convictions.

Let us now return to the two famous poets of this age, Alfred Tennyson and Robert Browning. Tennyson's one desire was to excel in epic narrative. His *"Idylls of the King"* are among the best examples of non-dramatic blank verse in our language. These *Idylls* are a most wonderful piece of literature. They can be interpreted rightly only in a Catholic sense. The keynote of the *Idylls* is a tale shadowing sense at war with the soul. It is not simply the mythical story of a fabled king on the lips of popular tradition. To Tennyson, in an age whose literature has become replete with the gross spirit of materialism, we are indebted for a noble poem whose theme is exaltation of the beauty of purity, and this where the age is most blind to it, in man.

The message is luminous in those who desire to see. By the deaf and blind unto holy things, the voice will not be heard, and the light will not be seen, the crime of sense becomes the crime of malice and is equal blame. Against this crime of sense, the spiritual man, despite the sin, the crime, and the treachery about him, stands proof passing from the old order in the flesh to the new order in the spirit.

The main purpose of the *Idylls* is to show forth the kingship of the soul, how only through that kingship the beast in man is subdued. His *"In Memoriam"* which was published in 1850, is a series of short poems woven together by one sentiment. It is a complete expression of the spirit of the age. It took him seventeen years to write it. You can see religious growth in this writing.

Robert Browning, like Tennyson, seemed to speak not for himself but for his age and people. He and Tennyson shared a single purpose. In other respects, there was a striking contrast between them. Tennyson looked like a poet; Browning like a business man. Tennyson loved to be alone; Browning loved the excitement of city life. Tennyson's style is musical; Browning's style is rugged, condensed, involved. All of Browning's works are dramatic in spirit and are commonly dramatic in form. *"Pippa Passes"* is the only one of his longer works which can be read with interest. Many of his other works are famous but reading them is like solving a puzzle. *"The Ring and the Book"* is a remarkable piece of literature, but it would be more remarkable if fifteen thousand of its twenty thousand words had been omitted. On the whole, Browning is hard to understand and comparatively few people appreciate his works.

This age has given us poets of lesser renown, among whom mention might be made of Elizabeth Barrett Browning, the wife of Robert Browning. She was a rather sentimental woman and it were better had she left many of her sonnets and most of her letters unpublished.

Matthew Arnold is another of the lesser lights of the Victorian Age. Then we have Algernan Charles Swinburne whose place in the long history of English poetry is yet to be determined. His fatal fluency of speech tends to bury his thought in a mass of jingling verbiage. His writings bring to mind the Dane's answer in Shakespeare, "Words, words, words!" He lived too much apart from the tide of common life and wrote for the chosen few.

Other poets of this age are William Morris, Dante Gabriel Rossetti, Coventry Patmore, Owen Meredith and J.B.L. Warren. It is difficult to give to each of these a definite place in English literature for their works are judged from different standpoints. Many men, many minds! Only after several generations of men will have passed can time record its verdict on the poets of the Victorian Age.

This essay would not be complete without at least a passing glance at Charles Dickens, William Makepeace Thackeray, and Mary Ann Evans, known by the pen name of George Elliot. Each of these novelists, in his own way, wished to better the conditions of their fellowmen. Dickens made an attempt by posing as a champion of the lower classes. Thackeray made an attempt by writing for higher society; Elliot made an attempt by placing moral lessons on a scientific basis. These three, and their imitators, reflect the materialism of their age even though they did aim at a higher and better life for all classes of men. The reason is this, they attempted a reformation of the morals of men along merely natural lines. Therefore, they failed. We are old-fashioned enough to believe there can be no moral improvement among men without the powerful assistance of Him who said, "Without Me you can do nothing." Only that literature is true which reflects life, which is in conformity with the divinely appointed and man's salvation.

METAPHYSICS

GOD IS THE NECESSARY BEING, THE EFFICIENT CAUSE OF
ALL CONTINGENT BEINGS

SISTER M. CORONA
1921 NORTH KEDVALE AVENUE
CHICAGO 39, ILLINOIS

METAPHYSICS

GOD IS THE NECESSARY BEING, THE EFFICIENT CAUSE OF ALL CONTINGENT BEINGS.

References used in the preparation of this paper: Notes taken from Reverend Father Catapang's lectures, Christian Brothers Philosophy, Scholastic Philosophy by Shallo, Psychology and Natural Philosophy by Hill.

Dissertation: All beings contingently existing have their efficient cause and they exist for some end; therefore, there exists a necessary and very real being which is the efficient cause of all beings and toward which all beings must tend as their final cause.

Being: The first idea formed by the intellect is that of being. The most universal idea is that of being, and the intellect first perceives that which is most universal. Whatever exists and whatever can be thought of comes under the name of being. Being is that which in any way is known in itself (*per se*) and positively, or whatever is in itself intelligible. Being is inherent in all that goes to make up things. Being is predicated of God and of creatures, but of each in a different way. Created being and uncreated being are not univocal; that is, have not the same meaning. God is pure, being infinite and eternal while the creature has only participated being, is finite and has a beginning of existence. Being may also be classified as real and logical. That which exists outside of the intellect is called real being, as plant, house. That which has no objective existence exists only in the intellect, is called logical being; as brightness, phantasy. Being means strictly the existing, or that which actually exists.

Contingent Being: From the consideration of being as such, we naturally arrive at the most important distinction of being; namely, contingent and necessary being. A contingent being is a being which is not self-existing; that is, it has not in itself the reason of its existence. Its non-existence is possible; it can be or not be. It has not given itself existence; it has the reason for its existence in another being. Since it is produced by another, a contingent being is a produced being. It must have had an agent by whom it was produced. This agent may or may not have been a contingent being. The contingent being is also called the being *ab alio*, that is a being which cannot exist by itself. All material things are contingent, changeable, finite. Contingency and actual existence are more potent signs of production by another than blaze and smoke are of fire. A contingent being must have received its existence by the action of another being and this being may or may not have been a contingent being; if a contingent being, then, it had an agent which produced it, and so on until we arrive at a Being which holds its existence from itself. No number of contingent beings added together will make a necessary being. The contingent will not change from contingency to necessity. Everything in the world has had a beginning, therefore it must have received existence from a being distinct from itself.

Necessary Being: The direct opposite of the contingent being is the Necessary and Absolute Being or that Being which exists in virtue of its own essence. If everything in this world is contingent there must be some necessary being which is not contingent, which is the first uncaused cause of all contingent beings. Such a Being must be self-existent, necessarily existing, infinite, eternal. Therefore, outside of the series, however numerous, of produced things, an independent, self-existing Being who is the ultimate and proportionate sufficient reason of all caused perfections, whether of mind or matter, exists. This Being is called the Being *a se*, that is, existing by itself. It had no beginning from all eternity; it will have no end; its non-existence is impossible. The only being whose non-existence is impossible, who is eternal and infinite is God. He is not contingent and not *ab alio*; He is the Being *a se*, the only Necessary Being, the Absolute *Necessarium*.

Efficient cause: This necessary and real Being, God Himself, who created the material and spiritual world, is the efficient cause of all contingent beings. Whatever does not exist by itself necessarily must have its efficient cause. By cause is meant that which makes a thing to be what it is. A cause is a principle which by its positive influence determines the existence of a new being, substantial or accidental, other than itself. This new being is called an effect. Since cause is a beginning, it must be prior to its effect. When there is an effect, there is something effected and there must be one who effected it. Cause will be better understood by explaining the meaning of effect. An effect is that which is produced or that which passes from non-existence; but that which is not yet existing cannot receive existence except by the action of something else and to this agent the name of cause is given. There are two conditions which make up a cause; first, it is distinct from the effect, and second, the effect is dependent on it. The distinct cause, that which is ushered into existence, cannot be the same as that which has given it existence; to be brought by something from non-existence into existence implies a dependence on that thing. The very fact that a being received existence from another as from its cause, makes it a contingent being. Produced beings can come from produced beings as from proximate causes, but not as from ultimate causes. A collection of produced beings is unintelligible without a cause, otherwise we would have an effect without a cause, which is absurd. The cause must be outside the collection which embraces all produced beings and must therefore be a non-produced being. The non-produced Being is evidently God Himself, the efficient cause of all created things. By efficient cause is meant that extrinsic principle from which the production of a thing proceeds. It is called an extrinsic principle to distinguish it from the intrinsic principles, matter and form. The efficient cause is itself the agent that produces the thing. The efficient cause may be a cause in itself or by accident. It is a cause in itself (*per se*) when by virtue of its own power it produces the effect, as fire produces heat. It is a cause by accident (*per accidens*) when by its own nature it neither produces the effect nor is connected with it. The efficient cause may be principle or instrumental. A principle cause acts by its own power; as, a tree is the principle cause of another tree. An instrumental cause acts by the power of its principle; as the painter's brush produces a picture. The efficient cause may be first or second cause. The first cause is the cause which receives neither its power nor the exercise of its power from another; God alone is the first cause. The second cause receives both its power and the use of it from another, that is from the first cause; all creatures are second cause. God is the efficient cause of all contingent beings.

Final cause: The final cause may be defined as that on account of which something is done. The end is a true or real cause. It moves the agent to act; without the end there would be no effect. The final cause is the goal. It is the first in the order of intention and the last in the order of achievement. Unintelligible beings may be said to seek an end, but they do so only insofar as their end is determined by an intelligent being which fits them to attain it and directs them toward it. A steam engine can be said to act for a certain end but only because the end influences the conscious mind which controls it. A thing is strictly a final cause when it is desired and aimed at for its own sake. The end is said to be ultimate and final when it is referred to no other ulterior end and all other ends aimed at by the agent are in one way or another referred to it; for instance, God's glory in our eternal happiness. The objective end, or *finis qui*, is the thing which we desire. The formal end, or *finis quo*, is the act by which we possess the thing desired. Riches is the objective end and the possession of riches is the formal end. The *finis cui* is that subject to whom the good is done. The end of the work, or *finis operis*, is that to which the work naturally tends. The end of the agent, *finis operantis*, is that which he determines according to his liking. The end of almsgiving is the relief of the poor, and the end of him who gives the alms is sometimes God's honor and sometimes vain-glory. The end of the agent and the end of the work may coincide since the agent may intend that to which the work intrinsically tends. The natural end is that end which does not surpass natural powers; health is the natural end of medicine. The super-natural end can be attained by the aid of grace alone. The exemplary cause is a representation of a thing to be produced, existing in the mind of the efficient cause which guides and directs his energies in the execution of the work. Men are exemplary causes in the mind of God.

Conclusion: God is the first, efficient cause of this world. It may be thus proposed: the world is a system of contingent beings; but no contingent being can exist without necessary being which is its efficient cause; all beings must tend toward the efficient cause as toward their final cause. We, God's creatures, must tend toward Him as toward our final cause for we are created by Him and for Him.

†

In memory of our beloved

MOTHER M. CORONA, O.S.F.

BORN JUNE 1, 1886
INVESTED DECEMBER 6, 1904
PERPETUAL VOWS JULY 19, 1913
DIED JANUARY 6, 1964

PRAYER

We beseech Thee, O Lord, by Thy loving kindness to have mercy on the soul of Thy handmaiden MOTHER CORONA, and, now that she is set free from the defilements of this mortal flesh, restore her to her heritage of everlasting salvation. Through Christ our Lord. Amen.

Indulgence of 500 days. R. 600

Sources

Letters: School Sisters of St. Francis archives

Ancestry.com

Newspapers.com

FindAGrave.com

Alverno College archives

Stanislaus: With Feet in the World
    Barbaralie Stiefermann, OSF

1st Century of Service: The School Sisters of St. Francis
    Jo Ann Euper, OSF

Oral histories of the sisters

ACKNOWLEDGMENTS

I am grateful, to the international team: Sisters Mary Diez, Tresa Abraham Kizhakeparambil, Barbara Kraemer, and Lucy Kalapuraekel for their support and enthusiasm for my writing this biography. The United States provincial team: Sisters Carol Rigali, Deborah Fumagalli, and Marilyn Ketteler are deeply appreciated for making this publication a reality. I especially owe a debt of gratitude to Sister Carol Rigali who begged me for three years to write about Mother Corona. For her persistence and patience until I finally said "yes," I say, "thank you."

Jean Love, executive assistant to the provincial team, typed my handwritten manuscript. Her professional skills, patience, kindness, perseverance, and enthusiasm for our history were illimitable.

To Sister Naveena Kulathingal, archivist for the School Sisters of St. Francis, I extend special gratitude for assisting me in obtaining information, as well as her words of encouragement. After completing my research and writing, Sister Naveena returned to India. Sister Jamine Angelina, volunteer archivist, deserves a thank you for the many times I asked her to provide family names of sisters, since surnames were not used at that time. I am also indebted to Sarah Shutkin, Alverno College archivist, who was most helpful in acquiring information on the college.

Annette Scherber recently hired as archivist arrived just in time to search for photos for this publication. I am impressed and exceedingly grateful to Annette for her efficiency and expediency treasure-hunting in an unfamiliar archive.

ACKNOWLEDGEMENTS

How will I ever repay Linda Gesbeck, who read the manuscript closely and offered helpful comments and clarifications. She was also most helpful in acquiring information on Ancestry.com regarding Mother Corona's family history. With Linda's computer skills, as well as numerous phone calls, she was able to track down Mother Corona's 92-year old nephew, Thomas F. Doyle, in Prairie Village, Kansas, and grand-nieces, Nancy Jenkins, Kathleen Doyle Rost, and grand-nephew, James Doyle. Through these phone calls, family members learned that Mother Corona was not merely their cousin, but rather, the sister of their grandmother, Anna Wirfs. I am deeply grateful for family photos that Nancy Jenkins provided to our archival collection.

Unfortunately, Thomas Doyle, who was so looking forward to reading this biography of his aunt, died on September 20, 2018.

Special thanks goes to 94-year-old Sister Ellinda Leichtfeld whose proofreading and critical assessment of the text, her wisdom and inspiration were invaluable.

To the many friends who cheered me along the way, I give thanks. Special thanks to the sisters who shared their stories. The sisters who greeted me on a daily basis with such statements as: "I can't wait to read about Mother Corona; how is the book coming along? I hope the book is published before I die," motivated me to write fast and furious. May God reward you, sisters, for your tremendous support.

I offer publisher Michael W. Nicloy special thanks for his gracious assistance every step of the publication process and for the cover design.

ABOUT THE AUTHOR

Sister Barbaralie Stiefermann is a highly diversified woman who has blended the rational approach of the Western mind with the intuitive wisdom of the East. Having taught yoga, tai chi ch'uan, qigong, and meditation, she has helped many discover how to awaken and manifest their highest potential.

Sister Barbaralie joined the School Sisters of St. Francis in 1950. She earned a B.S.Ed from Alverno College, Milwaukee; an M.A. in English from Loyola University of Chicago; a Ph.D. in English from Western Colorado University, Grand Junction. She has been a teacher, school administrator, organist and choir director, campus minister, director of an art gallery, and an author.

"In the final analysis," she says "the greatest tribute is to love and be loved. All the rest is background music."

Other publications:

Stanislaus...with feet in the world
Obedient to God
Creative Sexuality: Memoir of a Catholic Nun
School Sisters of St. Francis History of Associate Relationship